The Celluloid Weapon

THE **CELLULOID**

Social Comment in the American Film

WEAPON

by David Manning White and Richard Averson

Beacon Press Boston

Beacon Series in Contemporary Communications
David Manning White, General Editor

Explorations in Communication, edited by Edmund Carpenter
and Marshall McLuhan

The Mechanical Bride, by Marshall McLuhan

Sight, Sound, and Society, edited by David Manning White
and Richard Averson

Mass Communications and American Empire, by Herbert I. Schiller

The Opinionmakers, by William L. Rivers

The Adversaries: Politics and the Press, by William L. Rivers

Culture for the Millions? edited by Norman Jacobs

Open to Criticism, by Robert Lewis Shayon

The Permissible Lie, by Samm Sinclair Baker

The Celluloid Weapon: Social Comment in the American Film,
by David Manning White and Richard Averson

Copyright © 1972 by David Manning White and Richard Averson

Library of Congress catalog card number: 72-75548

International Standard Book Number: 0-8070-6170-0

Beacon Press books are published under the auspices
of the Unitarian Universalist Association

Published simultaneously in Canada by Saunders of Toronto, Ltd.

All rights reserved

Printed in the United States of America

for
Catherine W. White
and
Mary Elizabeth Barrett

Contents

Preface

The noted anthropologist Hortense Powdermaker once described Hollywood as "the dream factory." It cannot be denied that Hollywood's studio assembly lines have fabricated escapist eyewash for more than three generations of Americans: lollipop boy-meets-girl dreams; dreams of mystery, adventure, and derring-do; dreams of fortunes effortlessly made and plush Everlasting Success. But not all dreams are merely personally gratifying wish fulfillments; there are some that reveal the collective fears and hopes of a society confronting its problems and striving for solutions. Hollywood has given audiences these dreams, too. How these "social dreams" have been expressed in a long and consistently vigorous tradition of the *message film* is essentially what this book is about.

Whether termed "message films," "problem films," or "films of social consciousness," such films indicate a recognition of the potential of motion pictures for more than diversion. Incorporating but going beyond the pleasure principle of mass entertainment, they utilize the film medium for expressing social commentary with the intention of drawing public attention to various social issues. They are purposely, and in the broadest meaning of the word, propaganda films; and their producers, directors, and writers can indeed be called social persuaders armed with a celluloid weapon.

In the chapters that follow the authors are more concerned with a social history of nearly seventy years of the message film than a critical history. As such, there is perforce greater emphasis on the subjects and themes of message films than on their artistic treatment. And although we now and then cannot resist the temptation, generally we neither agree nor disagree with a film-maker's viewpoint. Doing so would be to flounder on the shoal of giving prime attention to those films whose theses compliment our own social prejudices. We have also tried to ride the rapids of artistic evaluation by discussing both critically acclaimed "good" message films and the so-called bad. While art and propaganda are not necessarily antithetical, there are a great many message films that would probably never be included on anyone's Ten Best list. Because they are so rooted in topicality and timeliness message films are severely vulnerable to the changing winds of aesthetic tastes.

Our purpose in these pages is to present an overview of the origins and development of social comment in the American film by describing the range of problems and issues explored, by identifying those filmmakers whose careers reveal a continuing concern for using film as a celluloid weapon, and by noting any relevant sociological "climate" that may have influenced the content of certain message films. The authors recognize that all films — born as they are of a particular nexus of historical circumstances — contain social commentary. With a few exceptions we have restricted this book to films which in our judgment deal with specifiable social issues. But even with this criterion we have not attempted to encompass every message film produced in the silent and sound eras; the genre is so prolific that nothing short of a catalog could do it full justice.

Further, we have limited our overview to the feature-length, commercial, dramatic film — the "Hollywood film," as we have come to know it — and have omitted attention to short subjects, the expressly made-for-TV film, and the documentary. We are aware of the social commentary and propagandistic thrust of TV features like *MY SWEET CHARLIE* and documentaries like *THE PLOW THAT BROKE THE PLAINS, THE SPANISH EARTH, HIGH SCHOOL,* and *MILLHOUSE,* but we do not consider such films a quantitatively significant aspect of the American cinema. Our chief interest here is in the theatrical *story* film, with its plot, characters, and structured situations, that has combined entertainment with social persuasion.

David Manning White
Boston University

Richard Averson
Brooklyn College, CUNY

Acknowledgments

Several people contributed generously to this book. For their help in research and locating various film-history data we are indebted to Professor John Carden of the New York Institute of Technology; Professor Ronald Marquisee of Syracuse University; William Davids, entertainment editor of *Kingsman;* and Charles Silver of the Museum of Modern Art.

Our deep appreciation is also due Mary Corliss of the Museum of Modern Art/Film Stills Archive; Paula and Jack Kramer of Movie Star News; Ernest Burns of Cinemabilia; and Eric Benson, a "Friend of Old Films," for their kind attention to our needs in obtaining and identifying the photos used in the text.

To Max A. White, who was our indispensable companion during a summer of writing, we owe special thanks. The gourmet lunches he cheerfully prepared for us provided the refreshment of body and spirit to return to our desks — and do battle again with that stubborn, demanding infernal machine known as the electric typewriter.

Introduction by Dore Schary

Every few years a self-righteous voice in the movie colony is raised in biting protest. Having invented no new way to articulate what it wishes to say, it repeats, "If you want to send a message, call Western Union." The new laughers roar with first-time joy — the old ones cackle at the old-shoe comfort of a familiar cliché. Everyone else throws up.

This has been going on for as long as I remember, and that's long — thank God — very long. It was Sam Briskin, a hard-nosed studio executive, who first tossed the bit at me during a session when I was outlining a possible story based on the C.C.C. camp project of FDR's New Deal.

That was in midsummer of 1933.

Since then I have heard or read the same comment repeated and it is always tossed in as if it were a new coin rather than a lead nickel.

This book, dealing with film as a propaganda weapon, is a rich and welcome addition to the growing bibliography of motion pictures which up until a few years ago was rather thin and distinguished mainly by Leo Rosten's *Hollywood* and Hortense Powdermaker's *Hollywood, the Dream Factory.*

There is a group of creators who distinguished themselves as makers of films with "messages," but the softer term was used — not "message," but "content." So, as time flew by, definitions became clear. If you hated the film, it was a "message" picture; if you liked it, it was a "film of content."

Of course, the fact is that you simply can't make a picture without content or, more candidly, without a message.

The message may be disastrous (*THE BIRTH OF A NATION*), ambiguous (*LOST HORIZON*), or empty-headed (*BONNIE AND CLYDE*). Often the morals are simple, "Crime Doesn't Pay," "Honor Thy Father and Mother," "Do Not Kill," and paraphrases of other commandments and sentiments.

Hundreds of films have inveighed against the horror of war, but it was Jean Renoir whom Robert Hughes quotes as saying, "Obviously no one has made an effective antiwar picture because we are still warring." It is a neat summing up. However, hard-headed dreamers (there are such) will continue to try by book, play, and film to drum some sense into their neighbor's brain.

The Celluloid Weapon, written by David Manning White and Richard Averson, does a mighty good job of telling the saga of movies that have been fashioned to be used as weapons of propaganda. I have seen most of those mentioned and I believe that Messrs. White and Averson have drawn a good historical portrait of what has been going on in Hollywood for all the years I've known it.

From my point of view there is an overstatement of the "auteur's" place in the history of the making of the celluloid weapon and a concomitant understatement of the contribution made by the producers and writers of those enterprises.

The names of David Selznick, Samuel Goldwyn, Pandro Berman, Sam

Zimbalist, John Houseman, Darryl Zanuck, and Hal Wallis, all of them initiators of important pictures, are underemphasized; and because of the screen writers' failure in public relations names of scribes such as Robert Riskin, Sidney Buchman, John Lee Mahin, Carl Foreman, George Seaton, Herman Mankiewicz, Dalton Trumbo, Lamar Trotti, and scores of others are given less attention than I think they deserve.

But the pictures are there and many of the stories behind their making.

Right or wrong, good or bad, I have been identified in degrees varying from high praise to sarcastic appreciation to utter contempt as one devoted to making pictures that "say something." It would be ridiculous to name the stinkers I laid my sticky fingers upon (others have done so quite eloquently) and terribly immodest for me to name my successes (ah, but how eager I am to do so), but the fact is that I do know something about the mythology of our society that produces our "message" films and I welcome this opportunity to say a few words on the subject.

Adlai Stevenson (perhaps he wasn't the first to state it) told us that we get the public officials we deserve. It is equally true we get the communications we deserve.

If the medium is the message, the message is somewhat scary — but not necessarily hopeless. The message has been scary before this brutal time.

D. W. Griffith showed the black as the freed slave: ignorant, lustful, and greedy. He would get stoned for that today. But in the swampy, soggy flats of South Florida, there are refreshment stands that still post signs "No Niggers, Mexicans, or Jews Allowed."

The sour melody lingers on, but Governor Askew plays a sweeter tune, and Maddox and Wallace are like symbols of a terrible past, not a brighter future.

"The Song of the Green Berets" was quieted by the chatter of guns at My Lai, but the massive bombing of North Vietnam goes on. And yet Nixon — Richard Nixon — goes to Peking.

The powerful and capable President before our present one gets the "deep six" for failing to see that too few wanted a war that could not be won unless we were willing to destroy the world in which we so precariously live.

Very odd — very extraordinary exit for one who wielded such power.

Some trends do change but the hoodlums remain. Crime looks much the same and isn't it about time we really tried to study why we adore our crooks, cheats, confidence men, and killers?

Our hero images stand husky in gangland. We say crime doesn't pay and yet pay homage to the Public Enemy (who kills to avenge his pal), Little Caesar (who was just too ambitious), Scarface (he honored his sister). The clothes have changed — gone are the wide-snap brims, but the wide lapels are back and so are the gunsels. The great mythic figure of the Godfather and the loyalty he earns brings back the majesty of great tragedy that haunts most of our good gangster tales. (*Macbeth* worked well as a gangster tale when Paul Douglas did it in *JOE MACBETH* a few years before his death.)

Our heroes and their victims do reflect our violent history. Indians and Mexicans were our villains until a short time ago. (Well, *that* seems to be changing.)

John Wayne *remains* an imperishable figure of the Old West: tall in the saddle — sharp-eyed with rifle and gun — he has to win and always does. But if he doesn't — as in *THE ALAMO* or *COWBOYS* — his audience is unhappy; old Duke with his cockeyed grin and cockeyed walk has to be and will remain imperishable.

We once were in the age of the sinner with the heart of gold. Now we are in the time of the anti-hero or non-hero. That's because we seem bereft of real heroes. JFK, Bobby, Martin Luther King, Medgar Evers, Malcolm X — are dead. Gone are Ike and Stevenson, two avatars of different tribes. Truman is old and quiet. FDR is an unknown figure to more than half our people. To the young so much of the world seems old and rotted.

So . . .

. . . It's a bad time and we show it with bloodletting — and rape — and drugs — and corruption — and hate — and degraded sexism — and screw you Jack . . . I got mine.

But faintly, a new view can be seen, a new tune can be heard, a new word is written.

The rock music is less rocky — the screams less strident — the riots diminish. Soon the message will show up again on the screen; and that one voice will pop up again, "Send it by Western Union."

The hell with it.

Just answer that Sophocles, Shakespeare, Sheridan, and Shaw sent their messages (so many different kinds) the way they chose and we still cry, tremble, and laugh at what they had to say about man and his nature.

The Celluloid Weapon

Muckraking and Nickelodeon Audiences

Didactic Melodramas

The Preeminence of Griffith

Increasing Rhetoric of Pre-World War I Message Films

Stereotyped Indians

"The Birth of a Nation" and "Intolerance"

The Historical Metaphor

The Futuristic Metaphor

Pacifism vs. Preparedness

Patriotic War Films

"How are we to depict the right unless we show the wrong? Unless we show the evils of a vicious past, how are we allowed to be the means of guiding the footsteps of the present generation?"

David W. Griffith[1]

Lillian Gish in *Hearts of the World* (Artcraft)

A Corner in Wheat (Biograph)

The year 1906 was germinal in American social history and in the development of the message film. It was the year that President Theodore Roosevelt took cognizance of the accounts of corruption in business and government made by such crusading journalists as Ida Tarbell, Lincoln Steffens, Upton Sinclair, and Mark Sullivan. In an address at the laying of the cornerstone of the House of Representatives office building the President remarked, "Men with the muck-rake are often indispensable to the well-being of society, but only if they know when to stop raking the muck."

While avid readers pored over *McClure's* magazine for the latest muckraking exposé by Steffens or Mrs. Tarbell, the ever-increasing numbers of barely literate immigrants were enthusiastically going to the movies. In nickelodeons and crude storefront theaters these immigrant audiences were seeing films which underscored many of the social ills which the muckrakers, with their trenchant pens, were attacking. Obviously, the level of discourse and argumentation concerning these problems did not begin to approach the investigative daring of an Upton Sinclair, primarily because motion pictures had already found that their greatest success with mass audiences was in fictional and entertaining— rather than journalistic or documentary— forms. To assert a viewpoint or critical opinion on a social problem in their one- or two-reel films — to include a "message"— early American moviemakers had to couch it in plots and situations that were familiar to working-class audiences in their everyday lives, in characters whose experiences they could empathize with, and in "happy endings" that sustained their immigrant dreams.

As Lewis Jacobs points out in his history of the American film, many nickelodeon movies took the side of the poor against unscrupulous bankers and politicians, slumlords and exploitative employers.[2] In Edwin S. Porter's *THE EX-CONVICT* (1905), for example, poverty drives a man to rob a mansion to obtain food money for his sick child and malnourished wife. He is caught red-handed by the owner, but in a happy denouement he is "saved" by the owner's daughter, a young girl whom the destitute man had prevented from being run over earlier in the day. *THE EVICTION* (1907) is the story of a drunkard who, after leaving a saloon on the premonition of a dream, finds the landlord removing his family and their belongings from their tenement home. Only through the goodness of passersby who take pity on the family and contribute the rent are their furniture and dwelling restored. In the sentimental morality typical of the films of this period, the husband repents his erring ways, the wife forgives, and the family begins a new life.

Another such "proletarian" film was *THE MONEY LENDER* (1908). Here a young man is unable to return money he has borrowed from an old miser. As the boy attempts to steal money from his own father to repay the loan, he is discovered by his mother and confesses his plight. After pardoning his son, the father calls on the moneylender, makes good the loan, and thereupon thrashes the conniving skinflint.

Didactic and moralizing as the plots of these films may seem, they expressed critical comments on the economic and social ills of the times. And although the plots are simplistic, they were as much as the traffic would intellectually bear if their messages were to be understood by unsophisticated audiences. Whether Edwin S. Porter, Thomas A. Edison, W. L. Dickson, and their contemporaries devised such didactic melodramas intentionally is, of course, open to question; most likely they worked instinctively, knowing what would attract at the nickelodeon box office. Within a decade, however, the content and visual rhetoric of message films were to reach a level of persuasion which the makers of the one-reel homilies could not envision, primarily through the achievement of David Wark Griffith.

At the beginning of his career at the studios of the American Mutoscope and Biograph Company, Griffith, too, directed the same kind of sentimentalized message films as his fellow moviemakers — indeed, hundreds of them; films whose subjects are obvious from such titles as *A DRUNKARD'S REFORMATION* (1909), *GOLD IS NOT ALL* (1910), and *A CHILD OF THE GHETTO* (1910). Interspersed with some of his lesser works is *A CORNER IN WHEAT* (1909), based on Frank Norris's novel *The Pit*. The film tells of an entrepreneur who unscrupulously corners the wheat market, causing a rise in the cost of

Lillian Gish (left) in *The Musketeers of Pig Alley* (Biograph)

bread and the eventual ruin of the wheat farmers. The tycoon suffers retribution: he slips into one of his grain bins and suffocates in his own wealth. Because Griffith was a man of great artistic sensibility — he was also a poet, actor, and playwright — in *A CORNER IN WHEAT* he went beyond the expressive conventions of his contemporary filmmakers. Griffith opened his film with a scene inspired by Millet's famous painting, "The Sower"; and throughout the story he intercut scenes showing the starving poor and the extravagant banquets of the rich. This juxtaposition of contrasting economic conditions emphasized the social comment he intended.

Another Griffith social-problem film was *THE MUSKETEERS OF PIG ALLEY* (1912), with Lillian Gish and Robert Harron. Photographed in a realistic documentary style in the tenement districts of New York, the film was promoted by Biograph as "a depiction of the gangster evil." In it we see the payoffs between criminals and crooked police — "links in the system," as Griffith described such collusion in his closing title.[3]

Clearly, Griffith was consciously and purposively a maker of message films. He was initially a "reluctant director" — like most of the creative people of his time he disdained the movies; and like many artists before (and after) him, only the need to make a living drove him into a mass entertainment medium. Once involved in motion pictures, however, he was impelled by a desire to provide audiences with something more than amusement. He saw the mission of the film as being "the laboring man's university," and prophesied a day when children in schools would be viewing films as part of their studies in history, science, and current affairs. Aware of the importance of enlightened audiences as a contributing force to the development of film art, he would often paraphrase Walt Whitman, his favorite poet: "To have great motion pictures, we must have good audiences, too."

Despite his preeminence in early message films, Griffith was certainly not alone in confronting urgent social issues. In fact, the rhetoric of the message film in the pre-World War I period became even more polemical and topical.

The labor crises of the times, no doubt intensified by the increasing membership in the American Federation of Labor and the I.W.W., were reflected in CAPITAL VS. LABOR (1910), THE GIRL STRIKE LEADER (1910), THE STRIKE AT THE MINES (1911), THE LONG STRIKE (1911), and HOW THE CAUSE WAS WON (1912). Although the solutions to the clashes between labor and capital in these films were resolved generally by a forgiving millowner (whose "progressive" daughter had made him see the light), or by the interventions of the clergy, dissenting opinions were asserted with candor.

In the procapitalist THE STRIKE (1914), the union organizer in a factory is a ruthless hoodlum. To win his unionist point he dynamites the factory. Management reestablishes the plant in another community — as a warning to workers not to listen to labor agitators. But the voices favoring labor were equally insistent. In CHILDREN WHO LABOR (1912), an argument against the exploitation of children, made by the Edison Company with the assistance of the U.S. National Child Labor Committee, we see the drudgery of children working in a mill. As the plot develops, the millowner's daughter accidentally gets lost on a train. She is found by an immigrant who is forced to send her to work with his own children in her father's sweatshop. The girl is eventually recognized by her father, but only after he agrees to free all of the children from their slavish employment does she return to him.[4] The film was embarrassingly sentimental, but the message that child labor existed and demanded public attention was forcibly there.

Corruption in politics and government also came under the scrutiny of the prewar filmmakers in THE REFORM CANDIDATE (1911), THE GRAFTERS (1913), and THE LAND SWINDLERS (1913). In THE LAND SWINDLERS a young, idealistic congressman is determined to expose a real-estate swindle. His dilemma is that his sweetheart's father, a prominent senator, is involved in the fraud. Even though the senator in this film was fictitious, the portraying of a high governmental official as the "heavy" is indicative of the critical vigor of the period.

Usury was another social ill which early filmmakers attacked. Griffith's appropriately titled THE USURER (1910) had an ending of symbolic retribution similar to the conclusion of A CORNER IN WHEAT. Here the exploiter meets his death in his own vault when a woman he had oppressed faints in his office and stumbles against the door of the vault — entombing the greedy man within it. Also as in A CORNER IN WHEAT, scenes of the oppressor were contrasted with scenes of his victims to strengthen the film's message.

Two other films dealing with usury were motivated by the then current investigations of moneylending initiated by the Russell Sage Foundation. THE USURER'S GRIP (1912) tells of a young man who is victimized by a "loan shark" and goes to the Foundation for help. The result is a citywide cleanup by the District Attorney of all usurers. This film was made in cooperation with the Foundation's Remedial Loan Division. In THE SNARE OF FATE (1913), also inspired by the Russell Sage Foundation's investigations, a usurer learns too late the price of avarice. After his wife deserts him to prevent their child from

The Suffragette (Edison)

following in his father's footsteps, he is stricken with paralysis and finally is evicted from his home.

The message films of the prewar years did not ignore the ever-present social problem of penal inhumanity, as real then as it is in 1972. The principal character in THE GOVERNOR'S DOUBLE (1913) is a governor of New York who contrives his own arrest for burglary in order to experience prison conditions firsthand. THE CONVICT'S PAROLE (1912) was suggested by penal legislation which was then being urged by Governor Oswald West of Oregon. The film reveals how labor contractors attempt to smear the parole system by framing parolees. In a similar plot in THE FIGHT FOR RIGHT (1913) a Southern factory owner exploits prison labor to reduce his production costs. His daughter, a student of the New Sociology, persuades him to desist in this policy. Here again a social agency endorsed a film, in this case the National Committee on Prison Labor. The imprisonment of juveniles was also a film subject. SAVED BY THE JUVENILE COURT (1913), which included an appearance by the noted Judge Ben B. Lindsey, dealt with the rehabilitative process of an enlightened juvenile court.

The strongest prewar protest film against inhumanity in prisons was THE HONOR SYSTEM (1917), directed by Raoul Walsh. Drawing upon the description of penal conditions uncovered by ex-Governor Hunt in the prisons of Arizona and the disclosures of Thomas Matt Osborne regarding prisons in New York State, the film was a censure of the brutal treatment of a wrongfully convicted man by a sadistic warden.

"The administration of criminal law in this country is a disgrace to civilization," said ex-President Taft in 1916 in reference to the Stielow case. This widely reported case involved a man who was convicted of murder on circumstantial evidence and was sentenced to die in the electric chair. A few minutes before the planned electrocution he was reprieved — just after the murderer

The Squaw Man with Red Wing
and Dustin Farnum (Lasky)

had confessed. The Stielow case became the basis for a film urging the abolition of capital punishment. *THE PEOPLE VS. JOHN DOE* (1916).

Women's liberation was treated both humorously and seriously. The issue then was for women to be allowed to vote. Among the films pleading the feminist cause were *THE SENATOR AND THE SUFFRAGETTE* (1910), wherein a group of clever women trick a senator into supporting their suffrage program; *VOTES FOR WOMEN* (1912), with Jane Addams, Dr. Anna Shaw, and other officers of the National American Woman Suffrage Association; and *EIGHTY MILLION WOMEN WANT* — ? (1913), featuring Mrs. Sylvia Pankhurst and members of the Women's Political Union. The latter film had all the expected ingredients: crooked city politics, ward heelers, election frauds, packed ballot boxes, and registering of repeaters, as well as a romance between a young suffragette and her recalcitrant suitor, a lawyer. In the end, of course, the "reconstructed" lawyer agrees that his girl friend knows best and joins her crusade. Clearly, the propaganda value of the new medium was apparent in 1913. *EIGHTY MILLION WOMEN WANT* — ? was widely exhibited as a campaign film for the "Votes for Women" movement.

WOMEN GO ON THE WARPATH (1913), with the redoubtable Clara Kimball Young, was a suffrage comedy with a Lysistrata twist. To win an election, the resourceful suffragettes hide their husbands' trousers, thereby preventing them from going to the polls. The male chauvinists of the period were equally inventive. Among the many antifeminist films that spoofed the Votes for Women movement and its speech-making housewives was *THE SUFFRAGETTE* (1912).

An increasing social problem in the early 1900s was enforced prostitution, which became so alarming that the Federal government eventually passed the Mann Act. It is not surprising that this issue, too, became the subject of a message film, since the mass media mirror social problems when they are most crucial and heated. Based on the Rockefeller White Slavery Report and the vice investigations of District Attorney Whitman of New York, *TRAFFIC IN SOULS* (1913) was a daring exposé of the white slave traffic. Produced in secrecy, it spurred the release of similar films, such as *DAMAGED GOODS* (1915), which stressed the danger of venereal diseases. Richard Bennett re-created his stage-role in *DAMAGED GOODS*, and when it opened in New York City the presentation included a promotional lecture by Dr. Carleton Simon on the effects of syphilis on civilization.[5]

The most famous of all muckraking novels, Upton Sinclair's *The Jungle*, was made into a film in 1914. Although other works by Sinclair were later adapted to the screen, this film was the only one he considered faithful to his intentions. (When Sinclair's *The Moneychangers*, dealing with the elder J. P. Morgan and the panic of 1907, was attemped on the screen the plot was "transmuted" into a story of Chinatown's drug traffic!) *THE JUNGLE* was a candid account of the lives of Chicago's packinghouse employees and the filthy environment in which they worked. The depiction of the vile conditions in packinghouses is considered an important factor in the passage of the first Pure Food Act. Sinclair himself appeared in the last scene of the film.

To be sure, the brief appearances in these early message films of personalities the public had come to identify with various social issues increased the promotional and advertising "selling angles" to attract audiences. Yet the screen appearances of such controversial and contemporary newsmakers as Jane Addams, Judge Lindsey, and Upton Sinclair achieved another purpose: their "visual endorsement" provided a means for combining fiction with a factual, documentary approach — thereby lending verisimilitude and a greater sense of urgency to these films.

Although so many films of the prewar period were socially *engagé* with their bold comments on serious problems, there were equally serious matters that filmmakers did not choose to probe. The entire question of race relations was generally ignored. Indeed, in regard to the American Indian most films perpetuated the public's ignorance that a problem even existed. A staple of the silent screen was the cowboy vs. Indian plot, and when the redman wasn't being portrayed as a rapacious scalper, he was treated in a condescending way. In a number of films, e.g., *STOLEN BY INDIANS* (1910), *THE HEART OF A SIOUX* (1910), *AT OLD FORT DEARBORN* (1912), Cecil B. DeMilles's *THE SQUAW MAN* (1914), the Indian heroine sacrifices herself for her white man lover; or a brave and capable Indian chief turns out to be a white man who was kidnaped by the tribe when he was a child. Occasionally a film would break away from the stereotyped depiction of the Indian, as in *THE INDIAN LAND GRAB* (1910), in which an Indian brave fights back against unethical politicians.

Griffith made numerous films dealing with Indians. Although most of them gave an essentially romantic view of the American frontier, Indians were not denigrated. On the contrary, Griffith generally characterized them as noble and self-sufficient. In several Griffith films the villains are white and the Indians

are heroes. Among the films of Griffith's Indian "cycle" were *THE REDMEN AND THE CHILD* (1908), *THE REDMAN'S VIEW* (1909), *THE MENDED LUTE* (1909), and *COMATA, THE SIOUX* (1909). From Helen Hunt Jackson's famous novel of oppression and prejudice against the Indian, Griffith made the first version of *RAMONA* (1910) with Mary Pickford (Gladys Smith). As Robert M. Henderson observed in his unique study, *D. W. Griffith: The Years at Biograph*, "Griffith's interest in giving a fair and honest presentation of the American Indian was unusual for his time, and it is almost as unusual today."[6]

While Griffith's treatment of the Indian was favorable, his depiction of the Negro in *THE BIRTH OF A NATION* (1915) was definitely negative. The plot of this spectacle of the Civil War and Reconstruction is well-known. The most controversial aspect of the film, based on Thomas Dixon's *The Clansman*, was Griffith's glorification of the Ku Klux Klan as a heroic force that saved the South from dominance by venal blacks under the sway of carpetbaggers. In many scenes Negroes were shown as shiftless, untrustworthy, and barbaric.

Because of its tremendous popularity with audiences, *THE BIRTH OF A NATION* made it unequivocally clear that celluloid could truly be a weapon for social persuasion. Whether, in fact, Griffith's film contributed in a large way to the resurgence of the modern Ku Klux Klan is problematical — as it is prob-

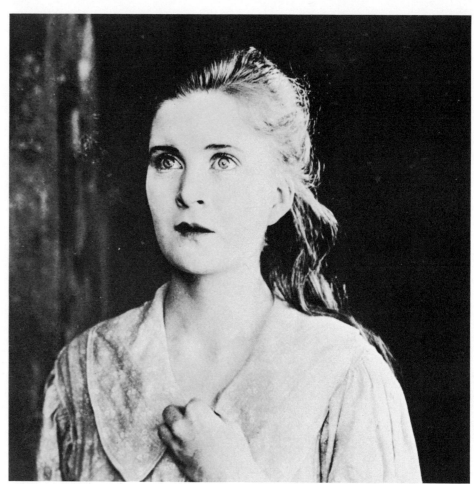

Mae Marsh in *Intolerance* (Wark)

lematical whether any film or book can directly cause social events — but it is reasonable to assume that it reinforced existing racist attitudes throughout the United States.

Edward Wagenknecht in his *The Movies in the Age of Innocence* describes the intense public controversy precipitated by *THE BIRTH OF A NATION*. Its release provoked threats of riot in numerous cities, thus strengthening censors' demands for even greater control of what could be shown on the screen. The Massachusetts legislature actually passed a special censorship bill to halt further exhibition of the film; however, the board created by this legislation voted to allow continued performances. "The State House was stormed," writes Wagenknecht, "the Tremont theater was picketed; there was even crazy talk of dynamite."[7] Injunctions were issued against exhibiting the film in many areas, including Louisville, Kentucky, where the theater owner was arrested under a law prohibiting the incitement of race prejudice.

Among the groups reacting bitterly to *THE BIRTH OF A NATION* was the young N.A.A.C.P. Some of the leaders of the association felt it urgent to make a film to refute the Griffith epic. Booker T. Washington's secretary, E. J. Scott, raised money for the project by selling stock to black businessmen and professionals. Photographed in Florida and Chicago, and taking three years to

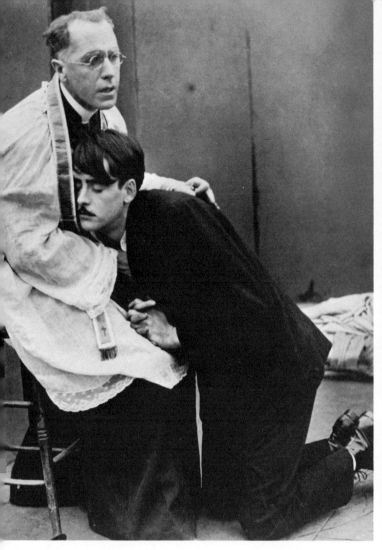

produce, the black-sponsored film was titled *THE BIRTH OF A RACE* (1919). However, if its aim was to serve as an antidote to Griffith's film, it failed to attract substantial audiences.[8]

Robert Harron (right) in *Intolerance* (Wark)

Intolerance (Wark)

Griffith was astonished at the charges of bigotry made against him; he insisted that he had tried to dramatize historical events impartially. Lillian Gish, whose career was so interwoven with Griffith's, recalls his great anguish over these charges and relates that during a conversation with him, shortly before his death, he expressed the wish to make an affirmative film about Negroes.[9]

During the controversy surrounding *THE BIRTH OF A NATION* Griffith was already planning his next film, one he intended to be a convincing statement of his lack of prejudice against any people. Moreover, it would plead for social justice and dedication to the ideal of universal brotherhood by denouncing the roots and consequences of man's inhumanity to man throughout the ages. The extraordinary *INTOLERANCE* was released in 1916. Three hours long, the film told four stories, each of different historical periods and each depicting an incidence of religious, political, or economic oppression: the overthrow of Belshazzar in 639 B.C. Babylon, the Crucifixion of Christ in Judea, the slaughter of the Huguenots in Renaissance France, and a modern tale. Utilizing the technique of "parallel action" in editing the film, Griffith intercut scenes from the four stories as their separate plots simultaneously progressed. Joining all of them into a larger philosophical statement was the repeated image of a woman rocking a cradle — a symbol of the commonality of all mankind. The image was derived from Whitman's *Leaves of Grass*: ". . . endlessly rocks the cradle, Uniter of Here and Hereafter."

Griffith's argument against social injustice culminates in the modern story, which tells of a young man (Robert Harron) falsely imprisoned on a murder charge and sentenced to be hanged. (The basis of the plot was the Stielow case.) Left alone with their baby, his wife (Mae Marsh) is the victim of hypocritical do-gooders who judge her unfit to care for the child. They deprive her of the child and place him in their foundation's clinic. In a last-minute reprieve, after the real murderer had confessed, husband and wife are reunited. *INTOL-ERANCE* ends optimistically with a series of pacifist scenes: after the title, "And perfect love shall bring peace forevermore," soldiers in battle are seen dropping their guns, a prison becomes a field of flowers, and children play happily in the sunshine.[10] "Not only beauty but thought is our goal," said Griffith in 1917, "for the silent drama is peculiarly the birthplace of ideas."

The rhetorical power of *INTOLERANCE* was recognized by other film-makers, both at home and abroad, who used celluloid for social persuasion. The nascent Soviet film school, which included Dziga Vertov, Pudovkin, and later Eisenstein, studied the construction of Griffith's film carefully. Lenin himself arranged for showings in the USSR, where it was exhibited continuously for a decade.

Except for the modern story, *INTOLERANCE* is a vivid example of what might be termed the *historical metaphor* to express a filmmaker's social viewpoint. In the development of the American message film there are numerous instances of historical metaphors. To make his purpose more acceptable to audiences and thereby increase the potential for public persuasion — or, perhaps, to surreptitiously evade censorship — a filmmaker may elucidate a contemporary social problem under the guise of a related historical event. George William Curtis once wrote, "Every great crisis of history is a pass of Thermopylae." Often when circumstances of the present are unpalatable or incomprehensible, a reexamination of the past may give us insight and courage to confront the reality of the present and continue to strive for solutions. Many films that came after *INTOLERANCE* — e.g., *THE LIFE OF EMILE ZOLA*, *JUAREZ*, and *SPARTACUS* — utilized the historical metaphor in a forceful argumentative way.

In 1916 the world was involved in the Great War. News of the war dominated the public mind, and it was only a few months before the sinking of the *Lusitania* and the entry of the United States into the conflict. In the immediate years before America was drawn into the European war the country was divided into two camps of opinion; there were those who urged pacifist noninvolvement as well as those who argued preparedness and armament. Many films served as advocates for these positions.

As early as 1912, two years before the catastrophic assassination at Sarajevo, American films were treating war themes. *THE MONEY KING* of that year used a *futuristic metaphor.* It predicted the impending global conflict. The main character is a steel magnate who, while representing his country at a peace conference to avert the war, betrays his mission by collusive maneuvers to protect his military contracts.

Preparedness was urged in *THE BATTLE CRY OF PEACE* (1915), based on Hudson Maxim's tract *Defenseless America* and produced by J. Stuart

Alla Nazimova (third from right) in *War Brides* (Selznick)

Blackton, the most outspoken proponent of armament within the motion-picture industry. This film also used a future situation — the bombing of New York and Washington by a foreign invader. Making its argument in lurid, sensational terms, it showed the advancing fleet of the enemy, an air raid on Times Square and the Capitol in Washington, and American soldiers being overwhelmed through lack of arms. We see a meeting of pacifists planning to accelerate the peace movement. Just as a wealthy patron of the group is releasing doves over the assemblage, the enemy attacks and a shell rips through the conference hall. To add authority to its message, the film included appearances by the "hawks" of that period, Admiral Dewey, General Wood, and Secretary Garrison. Well-known players such as Norma Talmadge were in the cast. Expectedly, *THE BATTLE CRY OF PEACE* brought sharp and indignant reaction from Henry Ford, who was then a leading figure in the pacifist movement.

A similar film exhorting preparedness was *THE FALL OF A NATION* (1916). Written by Thomas Dixon, the author of the book from which Griffith had derived *THE BIRTH OF A NATION*, the story was still another projection into the future. With the help of disloyal Americans acting as Fifth Columnists, an enemy power invades and conquers America. The country is finally saved and the enemy routed by an Amazon-like army known as The Loyal Legion of American Women who lure the occupying soldiers away from their posts.

Even the popular movie serial became a vehicle for prowar opinion. *PATRIA* (1916-17), in fifteen installments and financed by William Randolph

Hearst, related the adventures of an heiress to a munitions fortune and her sweetheart, a Secret Service man. Each week the heiress (played by Irene Castle) and the agent (Milton Sills) thwarted the dastardly anti-American schemes of Japanese and Mexican spies. The serial went so far as to link these villains with the Black Tom disaster. Both the Mexican and Japanese governments protested. President Wilson himself felt it necessary to rebuke Hearst for his "yellow film journalism." The serial was withdrawn, and altered for subsequent showings.[11]

If there were fervent prowar films in this period, there were equally committed films that opposed the war. Herbert Brenon's WAR BRIDES (1916), with Alla Nazimova in the leading role, takes place in a country suggestive of Germany. A young war widow is forced to become a "war bride" to meet the King's decree that more children must be procreated. Realizing that the child she is carrying may suffer the fate of its father, she rebels and leads other women in a demonstration march to the palace. When the King replies to their antiwar chant with the assertion that there will always be wars, the heroine shouts, "No more children for war!" and shoots herself. To the women who followed her she becomes a symbol of their determination to carry on their pacifist activities, and they hold her body aloft.

Another emphatic antiwar film was CIVILIZATION (1916), produced by Thomas H. Ince. Counteracting the militarism of THE BATTLE CRY OF PEACE, CIVILIZATION was a direct appeal to "the mothers of men." Howard Hickman acted a submarine commander, obviously German, who refuses to torpedo a passenger vessel because of his secret loyalty to the pacifist Mothers of Men Society. His crew mutinies and the submarine is sunk. The spirit of the drowned commander goes to a Dantean Inferno but is redeemed by The Christus. Taking the discarded body of the dead man, Christ reappears before the belligerent King and eventually makes him realize the complete horror of war. The enlightened King heeds the entreaties of the rebellious women and recalls his soldiers back to their homes. An early episode of the film graphically simulated the sinking of the *Lusitania*, a scene made with the cooperation of the U.S. Navy. *CIVILIZATION* was a huge box-office success, so much so that William Cochrane, press representative of the Democratic National Committee, stated that it influenced voters to reelect Woodrow Wilson in 1916 on the key issue, "He kept us out of war."

But before Wilson's second inauguration, Germany resumed unrestricted submarine warfare, and by April 1917 the United States was in the conflict. The motion-picture industry went to war, too, and a spate of anti-German films came in rapid succession: *OUTWITTING THE HUN* (1918), *THE CLAWS OF THE HUN* (1918), *TO HELL WITH THE KAISER* (1918), and *THE PRUSSIAN CUR* (1918). Footage of President Wilson, along with General Pershing and King Albert of Belgium, gave a documentary authenticity to *THE KAISER — BEAST OF BERLIN* (1918). A supposedly "inside look" at the atrocities of Prussian prison camps was *MY FOUR YEARS IN GERMANY* (1918), based on the popular book by James W. Gerard, the former U.S. Ambassador to Germany. *THE LITTLE AMERICAN* (1917), with Mary Pickford, was yet another anti-German wartime film. In it her lover takes on the entire German High Command to prove his devotion to "America's Sweetheart."

Even Griffith, who had made *INTOLERANCE* just two years before, followed Wilson into the war and directed patriotic films. *HEARTS OF THE WORLD* (1918) had Erich von Stroheim as a brutish "Hun." The film was made at the instigation of the British War Office (which also underwrote its production) and was photographed in England and France. Mixing actual newsreels and war footage with restaged events, Griffith depicted the ravishing effects of war on an idyllic French village. When the Germans occupy the town they are characterized as arch-villains, assaulting the women and slaughtering the innocent. Finally the French free the village, and as American troops parade in the closing scene the Stars and Stripes symbolically forecast Allied victory.

Although Griffith directed three other war films, he always had misgivings about his role as a war propagandist. Lillian Gish, in her memoir *The Movies, Mr. Griffith and Me*, recalls his regret for making *HEARTS OF THE WORLD*. "War is the villain," he told her, "not any particular people."

The Little American with Mary
Pickford (Artcraft)

II Problems of Peace

Reds — the New Movie Villains

Drugs and a Hollywood Scandal

"The Vanishing American"

Contraband Messages

The War in Retrospect

Social Comment in Silent Comedies

Von Stroheim's Modern Morality Play

Prohibition Brings the Gangster

Message Films: A Matter of Timing

"I think that we have a responsibility to give out something constructive. That's how I feel my place. I don't know about anyone else, but I don't want to contribute to the downward path of the world, if you can sum it up that way. I don't want to use this great voice continually to push people downward. I'm trying to suggest something progressive."

King Vidor[1]

James Murray in *The Crowd*
(Metro-Goldwyn-Mayer)

As film historian Benjamin Hampton aptly observed, on November 10, 1918, war films were big business; the next day they were failures at the box office. Spurred by wartime patriotism and increasing audiences, the movies in a few years had evolved from one-reel nickelodeon curiosities to photoplays of feature length. *THE BIRTH OF A NATION,* for example, was three hours long; the playing time of *CIVILIZATION* was approximately two hours.

After President Wilson returned from the peace conference at Paris, a fierce political struggle erupted over the ratification of the peace treaty and the proposal to support the League of Nations. To counter the isolationist influence of Senator Henry Cabot Lodge, Wilson took his case directly to the people. A film that espoused Wilson's viewpoint was *UNCLE SAM OF FREEDOM RIDGE* (1920), from a magazine story setting forth the ideal of the League of Nations. Wilson had praised the story, and at the New York premiere of the film a short address was delivered by Secretary of State William Gibbs McAdoo.

The film was an allegory of Wilson's struggle for an international organization to maintain peace. Uncle Sam, an old man of the West Virginia mountains, loses his son in the "War to end war." When the peace treaty is defeated and the old man's neighbors are apathetic toward the problems of peace, he becomes bitter, feeling his sacrifice was for naught. To atone for what he considers the sins of his countrymen, Uncle Sam wraps himself in the flag and dies by his own hand. In an ending symbolic of Wilson's faith that a League of Nations would become viable, we see a glimpse of the future. The spirit of Uncle Sam has inspired the girl his son had loved, and in this futuristic metaphor she is the delegate of the United States at the 1935 convening of the League of Nations.

Recognizing the public's desire to put aside the war, Griffith reedited his *HEARTS OF THE WORLD* for reissue in 1919. This version, with some changes in titles and the addition of several scenes, was advertised as the "peace edition." Yet Griffith was never at ease with his portrayal of the German people and the jingoism of *HEARTS OF THE WORLD.* In 1924 he directed *ISN'T LIFE WONDERFUL,* in effect his apology to the German people. Made on location in a small town in Germany and using the townspeople themselves and a few professional actors, *ISN'T LIFE WONDERFUL* was a sober account of postwar hardship in that defeated country. We see the hunger, riots, and general despair of the people which even at this time were engendering the rise of a frustrated painter named Hitler. There are no stereotyped Germans in this film, for it is poverty that pushes the ordinary workingmen to steal a young couple's potato crop. To the epithet hurled at them by the heroine that they are beasts, they reply, "Yes, beasts we are, beasts they have made us."

The Bolshevik revolution in Russia created genuine anxiety in America. Socialists and more radical political activists were blamed for much of the labor unrest of the immediate postwar period. After the home of Attorney General Palmer was damaged by a bomb, the "Red scare" hysteria mounted. This culminated with the so-called Palmer Raids, wherein 6,000 communists

(real or suspected) were jailed.[2] Whether the Zukors, Laskys, Laemmles, and other leaders of the motion-picture industry purposely supported the Harding administration's Red-baiting or whether they were merely taking advantage again of events in the headlines for the sake of box-office revenues, many anticommunist films were released.

Among them were *BOLSHEVISM ON TRIAL* (1919), based on Thomas Dixon's *Comrades*; *THE UPLIFTERS* (1919), a lampoon of "radical chic" of that era; *THE ACE OF HEARTS* (1921); and *ROSE OF THE TENEMENTS* (1926), presented by Joseph P. Kennedy. These films ranged from satire of all social progressives to violent denunciation. Griffith, too, in his film of the French revolution, *ORPHANS OF THE STORM* (1921), attacked the communists. In a long subtitle, drawing a comparison between the excesses of the Jacobins and the "revolutionists" of the Twenties, Griffith warned audiences not to exchange their good American government for "Bolshevism and license."[3]

Perhaps no film of this period was more vehement in its anti-Red message than *DANGEROUS HOURS* (1920). The hero is an idealistic young man, a university graduate and a believer in the "greater freedom" expounded by Russian revolutionists he has read. In his zeal he supports the workers' strike at a silk mill and is recruited into a Bolsheviki espionage ring intent on sabotaging American industry. "Boris Blotchi," the leader of the conspirators and a Red Army officer, is, as a title in the film tells us, "carried away with a wild dream of planting the scarlet seed of Terrorism in American soil." At the conclusion the hero recognizes that he has been duped and exposes the plotters.[4] The American message film had found a new set of villains to replace the "Huns."

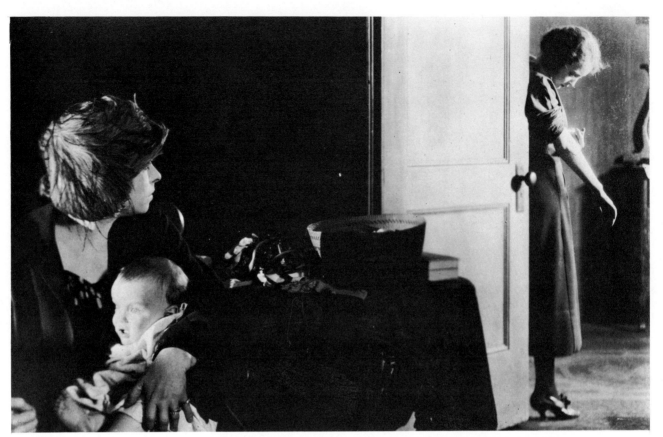

Mrs. Wallace Reid (left) in *Human Wreckage* (Film Booking Offices)

THE ETERNAL CITY (1923) dealt with the political rivalry between communism and fascism in Italy. Set against the background of the war, the story had Lionel Barrymore as the Red "bad guy," Baron Bonelli, who schemes to gain control of the city's food supply. Forcing himself on heroine Barbara La Marr he promises to make her the wife of "the dictator of Italy." Reds and rebellion are routed by the Blackshirt *Fascisti*, and the film is climaxed by a view of Premier Mussolini and King Victor Emmanuel standing triumphantly on a balcony of the palace.

As previously noted, the maker of message films often draws upon major news stories and publicized events of his day. The sensational news story, however, is not unlike an iceberg in that it reveals only the most evident aspect of an underlying social problem. Thus, when a popular movie idol such as Wallace Reid — who personified the clean-cut, young American — died in 1922 of the effects of drug addiction, the public was shocked. Indeed, it was one of several Hollywood scandals which pressured the industry to "clean house" by setting up the Motion Picture Producers and Distributors of America, with Will Hays as president.

An attempt to seriously examine traffic in drugs was HUMAN WRECK-AGE (1923), one of the last productions of Thomas H. Ince. Wallace Reid's widow, along with city, state, and Federal officials in the Los Angeles area, appeared in this forthright disclosure of the pattern of narcotics peddling. In

Richard Dix (right) in *The Vanishing American* (Paramount)

the film a lawyer becomes an addict through friendship with a drug-taking physician. Surrealistic scenes describe the lawyer's dependency on narcotics and his struggle to break the habit; we see the peddler who supplies him symbolized through double-exposure as a hyena, prowling in ghostly form. Only after his wife deceives him into believing that she, too, is addicted to morphine does the lawyer become cured. As the officiating attorney for the narcotics squad he busts the dope ring. At the opening of *HUMAN WRECKAGE* in New York, Mrs. Reid spoke to the audience and expressed the hope that the film's message would prove instructive.

Racial prejudice against Indians, which had been examined only rarely, was the subject of an outstanding message film of the Twenties, George B. Seitz's *THE VANISHING AMERICAN* (1924), based on a Zane Grey novel. Unlike so many of the quasi-racist Westerns that have persisted in the history of the American cinema *THE VANISHING AMERICAN* did not hesitate to show the white man's cruelty toward the Indian. A long prologue in the film unfolds the rise and fall of the American Indian from aboriginal tribes, through the period of the Spanish Conquistadors and their later subjugation by the American government, to the First World War. The culmination of the Indians' oppression comes in the modern episode, which tells of the revolt of the Navajo against the squalid conditions of their reservation. Richard Dix had one of his many unforgettable roles as Nophaie, the returning World War I veteran who dies in the fighting between the Navajo and the whites.

John Gilbert and Reńée Adorée
(lower right) in *The Big Parade*
(Metro-Goldwyn)

The Twenties, in retrospect, had its contradictions as do most periods in a nation's history. Having rejected Wilson's idealism, the decade pursued a hedonistic materialism. The new Golden Cow was enshrined at Wall Street; investors could not envision The Day the Bottom Fell Out, October 24, 1929. Novelists F. Scott Fitzgerald and Sinclair Lewis were both diagnosing the social temper of the times, but in different ways. Lewis's acid pen dissected the Sauk Centers and Zeniths of middle America in which a George Babbitt could support Harding and Coolidge in their quest for "normalcy." Fitzgerald emphasized the America that some typified as the Jazz Age.

Hardly more than a handful of the movies of the Twenties can be termed message films. Indeed, the great majority of the decade's films were closer to the frivolity of Fitzgerald's Jazz Age than to the trenchant social commentary of Sinclair Lewis. The few films that actually attempted to say something pertinent about social ills usually did so in a covert or indirect way. They may be considered *contraband-message* films. Unlike the message film per se, in which the plot and characters are indispensable devices to illustrate and underscore a social problem, the contraband-message film treats the same issue only peripherally. The critical comment in the contraband-message film is incidental; in the message film the social viewpoint is overt and dominant.

Prime examples of the contraband-message films of the Twenties are *THE FOUR HORSEMEN OF THE APOCALYPSE* (1921), *THE BIG PARADE* (1925), *WHAT PRICE GLORY?* (1926), *WINGS* (1927), and *FOUR SONS* (1928), all dealing with World War I. Although each contains some scenes and dialogue that call attention to the brutality of war, none is primarily either pro- or anti-war in its overall theme. The audience leaves such films with a vague, inarticulate feeling that, yes, the war was awesome and overwhelming — they have seen people caught up in its destruction — but for the most part their involvement has been with characters who were concerned more with solving their own personal problems rather than the broader societal problem of war.

Rex Ingram's *THE FOUR HORSEMEN OF THE APOCALYPSE* is basically a romantic treatment of a family divided by allegiances to opposite sides in the war. Sincere as the film was, the Great War and the tragedy it brought to millions cannot be epitomized by a final duel in which Valentino and Rod La Rocque, as the opposing cousins, kill each other. The contraband message is indicated, however, in the symbol of the Four Horsemen — War, Plague, Famine, and Death — racing through the sky at various times throughout the story and in the final shot. The image of the Four Horsemen embodies the pacifist statement in a film which is otherwise socially uncommitted. It is not unlikely that to ensure the box-office popularity of *THE FOUR HORSEMEN* at a time when audiences were weary of World War I movies, its pacifist message had to be camouflaged. When economic pressures dominate creative decisions in filmmaking, any intended message is more often contraband rather than overt.

THE BIG PARADE also expresses its message in a concealed manner. What is remembered from this famous film are not so much the few isolated incidents that point out the futility of war but the John Gilbert-Renée Adorée love story. Perhaps the most effective antiwar comment is a scene in No Man's Land where Gilbert dives into a shell hole and finds a wounded German soldier there. Moved by compassion, Gilbert gives the dying man a cigarette; but before the German can take more than a puff he expires. Gilbert then takes the cigarette from the dead man's lips and stoically smokes it himself.

In this film, too, box-office pressures probably influenced the extent and treatment of the social message. King Vidor, the director of *THE BIG PARADE*, recalls that he had planned it to be a serious film about the war. "I wanted to make an honest war picture," he said in an interview. "Until then they'd all been very phony, glorifying officers and warfare. There hadn't been a single picture showing the war from the viewpoint of ordinary soldiers and privates, not one with some feeling of antiwar, of realistic war."[5] What Vidor intended is very different, however, from the sentimental film that was finally released.

Edmund Lowe (left) and Victor
McLaglen (second from right) in
What Price Glory? (Fox)

Irving Thalberg, then the production head at Metro-Goldwyn, was seeking a script dealing with the war, and having lost out to the Fox company in obtaining the rights to the successful Broadway play *What Price Glory?*, he engaged Laurence Stallings, the coauthor of the play, to develop an outline. Stallings worked on the script under Vidor's supervision, and the first version of the film was subsequently made. After a preview of the film, Thalberg decided that it was "unfinished," that the scope of the story should be broadened by the addition of more battle scenes. Thalberg also decided to reshoot Vidor's epilogue and prologue, showing the rich boy Gilbert in his American home, in order to "heighten the sentimentality for female moviegoers who might find a war story unappealing."[6] The extent to which Thalberg's desire for a financial smash may have diluted the antiwar aspects of THE BIG PARADE can, of course, only be speculated upon.

As in THE BIG PARADE, the isolated antiwar comments of WHAT PRICE GLORY? are peripheral and contraband. Although the Maxwell Anderson-Laurence Stallings stage play on which the film was based expressed caustic viewpoints on the First World War, Raoul Walsh's screen version was primarily a service comedy about the roistering comradeship of Captain Flagg and Sergeant Quirt of the United States Marines. As film historian Eileen Bowser has remarked, WHAT PRICE GLORY? paid only lip service to "war is hell" sentiments. She regards as equally unconvincing Flagg's speech,

"There's something rotten about a world that's got to be wet down every thirty years with the blood of boys like those." One particular scene, however, does take a forceful antiwar position as a dying young soldier at the field dressing station cries out to Flagg to "stop the blood!"[7]

Wings with Richard Arlen and Charles "Buddy" Rogers (Paramount)

While stressing the camaraderie of flying aces and the violence of dogfights, William A. Wellman's WINGS made a muted antiwar comment in its final sequences. In an attempt to escape capture and return to the American lines, Richard Arlen steals a German plane. But he is shot down by another American flyer — his best friend, who has mistaken him for the enemy. As the remorseful Buddy Rogers embraces his dead comrade, a French officer standing nearby says hopelessly, *"C'est la guerre."*

Despite the emphasis of FOUR SONS on the personal rather than the societal implications of war, the contraband message of this John Ford film is not obscured by heroics and "big parades." The terrible ravages of war are unequivocally denounced in the sufferings of Mother Bernle, the Bavarian widow who loses three children in the great conflict. The disintegration of the family under the pressures of war is the thrust of the film. In yet another famous trench scene, one of the Bernle sons, gun at hand, creeps into the trench where another soldier lies dying. Only gradually does he realize that the wounded man is his own younger brother.

After the redounding success of *THE BIG PARADE* Hollywood, as usual, made a number of imitative films. Most of them, such as *MARE NOSTRUM* (1926), *SEVENTH HEAVEN* (1927), and *LILAC TIME* (1928), were primarily love stories set against the events of World War I, and made scant reference to war as a societal cancer.

Although the majority of the war films of the Twenties were romantic reflections of the European conflict, Fred Niblo's *THE ENEMY* went against the standardized Hollywood treatment and presented a virulent antiwar message. The theme of this 1927 film, adapted from a Channing Pollock play, is that war makes money for certain profiteers while the little people suffer great deprivation. In sequences reminiscent of *ISN'T LIFE WONDERFUL* we see the starving villagers of Austria and the meager soldiers' rations at the Austro-Russian front. The preachment of the film is hammered home.

It would be an error to assume that war films constituted a sizable percentage of the several thousand Hollywood productions of the Twenties. It was the decade that glorified Elinor Glyn's "It" and made Clara Bow the symbol of the young people of that day. Before he turned to his historical spectacles, Cecil B. DeMille made a series of socio-sexual films dealing with the "new morality," such as *WHY CHANGE YOUR WIFE* (1920), *FORBIDDEN FRUIT* (1921), *FOOL'S PARADISE* (1922), and *ADAM'S RIB* (1923). There were also the stylized horror films with Lon Chaney, the man of a thousand faces; and the sensuous dramas of *femmes fatales* such as *FLESH AND THE DEVIL* (1927) and *A WOMAN OF AFFAIRS* (1928), both with the great new Swedish star, Greta Garbo.

Some of the silent-screen comedies had bite and actually made incisive comments on American society. Alfred E. Green's *OUR LEADING CITIZEN* (1922) took satiric pokes at small-town life, with its usual *dramatis personae* of vulgar politicians, the landed aristocrats, the cynical newspaper editor, and the typical village ne'er-do-well who "saves the day" for the community and becomes the local hero.

One of the finest silent comedies, Frank Capra's *THE STRONG MAN* (1926), also made fun of the political and moral chicanery of provincial America. Elfish Harry Langdon is a returning war veteran who comes to a small village looking for the girl who was his wartime pen pal. The formerly sleepy, peaceful hamlet has become a nest of vice in which the people are frightened by the toughs the bosses have imported. In his inimitable way Langdon cleans up the town by routing the villains from their saloon headquarters, and, of course, wins little Mary Brown. The Populist philosophy which Capra was to develop so eloquently in his later films was already apparent in *THE STRONG MAN*.

Another comedy employing satire as a method of social criticism was *BEGGAR ON HORSEBACK* (1925), based on the play by George S. Kaufman and Marc Connelly and directed by James Cruze. The characters in this film are an almost Molière-like typology representing the archetypes of the

The Strong Man with Harry Langdon (First National)

Edward Everett Horton in *Beggar on Horseback* (Paramount)

29

money-hungry America of Coolidge's administration. Big business and its handmaiden, advertising, are mercilessly lampooned. Nothing is sacred, not even members of the judiciary.

Novels, such as Sinclair Lewis's blockbusters of the Twenties, *Main Street* and *Babbitt,* by the very nature of the book-buying audience can afford to be less influenced by the demands for popularity. A novel that sells 50,000 copies or more becomes a best seller; millions of ticket buyers are required to make a movie a "best seller." This difference in the mass-media marketplace may account for the dilution of Lewis's pungent message when his novels were transferred to the screen. Where there was potential for acute dissection of small-town bigotry and philistinism, as in *Main Street,* or the bromidic business philosophy of a George Babbitt, the initial attempts to bring his novels to the screen were not at all effective. Unfortunately, *MAIN STREET* (1923) and *BABBITT* (1924) melded with hundreds of other banal films of the decade.

Although the Hollywood versions of Lewis's novels were watered down, Frank Norris's *McTeague* received a surprisingly faithful screen transfer in *GREED* (1924). This Erich von Stroheim classic is not a message film in that it attacked a specific social ill of the Twenties; it is, rather, an indictment of the avarice endemic in the human personality and in all societies, of whatever historical period. In the silent cinema von Stroheim created a modern morality play that exemplified Chaucer's description of human greed in *The Pardoner's Tale:* "*Radix malorum est cupiditas.*"

Equally unusual in a period whose optimism was epitomized by Hoover's campaign slogan, "Two cars in every garage," was *THE CROWD* (1928). Al-

Gibson Gowland and Jean Hersholt
in *Greed* (Metro-Goldwyn)

though King Vidor's film, like *GREED*, didn't focus on a particular social problem, it depicted in stark terms modern man's disillusionment and alienation in the impersonal cityscapes of industrialized society. "The world can't stop because your baby's sick," says a cop to the father whose child has been hit by a speeding truck.

The Twenties were the combination of what Veblen termed a "conspicuous consumption" society and a jazz-age morality. There were, of course, counter-forces from rural, middle America that looked upon the hedonism of the cities with indignation and fear. In their righteousness they mustered enough political influence to pass legislation such as the Volstead Act. This naïve attempt to eliminate the social problem of alcoholism brought about another affliction — gangsterism.

Because the movies reflect the barometric fluctuations of society, the rise of the gangster film paralleled the coming-of-age of organized crime in America. By the middle of the Twenties crime in all its odious byways had become yet another Big Business with its own "corporate heads," boards of directors, and sycophantic finger men. A precursor of the gangster film, which revealed the link between bootlegging barons and the playboys and flappers of the Jazz Age, was *THE GREAT GATSBY* (1926), from F. Scott Fitzgerald's novel. Ostensibly, the character of Meyer Wolfsheim was based on Arnold Rothstein, the flamboyant gambler, racketeer, and bootlegger in New York.

The "authentic" gangster film came only a year later — *UNDERWORLD* (1927), directed by Josef von Sternberg and based on a Ben Hecht story. The main character, "Bull" Weed, acted by George Bancroft, typified many of the

George Bancroft and Evelyn Brent in *Underworld* (Paramount)

hoodlums whose names were making headlines. Another film in this emerging genre was *THE RACKET* (1928), in which two bootleggers shoot it out for supremacy in the "territory."

If even early gangster films tended to glamorize these urban desperadoes, and if there was a moral ambiguity in the description of their illegal activities, clearly audiences seemed to empathize with them. Moviegoers, who probably stopped for a quick drink at their neighborhood "speakeasy" on the way home from the theater and in their own mild way flaunted the law, were fascinated by those who were lawbreakers in a more open and defiant way. What later became *pro forma* for the gangster and crime films of the Thirties — the third-degree methods of obtaining confessions, the fingerprinting by the police, the cellblocks of prisoners' row, and the surveillance of convicts — were new and intriguing to audiences.

Just as World War I became a convenient background for numerous sentimental love stories and adventures during the Twenties, gangsterism became the frame for melodramas and thrillers. Despite their lack of vigorous examination of the roots and causes of criminality, the gangster melodramas often contained contraband anticrime messages, which at least reinforced public anxiety about this social evil.

One film that was an exception to what quickly became the run-of-the-mill gangster shoot-'em-up was Raoul Walsh's *ME, GANGSTER*. Released in 1928, at the very end of the silent era, it did not hesitate to take a moral position. The plot unfolds as the autobiography of a penitent young hoodlum who recalls the events in his life that led him into crime, particularly his relationship to a

weak father who had become a ward heeler. The boy's robbery of a factory payroll and his subsequent apprehension and conviction were shown with restraint and without any attempt to sensationalize lawlessness.

Along with the development of the American cinema from a nickelodeon amusement to a major influence in our popular culture by the end of the Twenties, the message film had evolved from the didactic one-reel homilies of Porter and Edison to the artistry and cogent social criticism of a Griffith, von Stroheim, Vidor, and Walsh. Some of these filmmakers, like Griffith, openly stated their intention to use celluloid for public enlightenment on social ills. Others who were less doctrinaire were not so explicit and treated specific problems only incidentally. Their approach to making audiences aware of America's ills was usually implied rather than overt. Yet whether the message of a film is explicit or contraband there is always another variable that must be reckoned with if the viewpoint expressed is to reach substantial audiences. This variable is the timing of a picture's release, for if any message film is to direct attention to a social ill — and possibly engage the public's interest in ameriliorating it — the film must be exhibited at the germane moment when the problem is most crucial and audiences most malleable.

As the silent period of the American cinema ended, the Great Depression overtook the country. The optimism of the prosperous, roaring Twenties was beclouded with the frightful reality of breadlines, "Brother, can you spare a dime?" and hopelessness. It was as though the grim events of the Thirties were too overwhelming to be evoked by the mute images of the Silent Screen.

Depression Despair

"Our Daily Bread"

Pacifist Messages and "All Quiet on the Western Front"

Glorified Criminals

Prison Reform

Unsavory Politics and Two Unorthodox Presidents

Campus Radicals

Mob Fury

"Black Legion"

Message Biographies

Racial Prejudice and Anti-Semitism

Businessmen as Heroes

Dreiser and Eisenstein

The Sleeper That Became a Classic

"Modern Times"

Screwball Comedies with Bite

Populism and Shangri-La

"I would sing the songs of the working stiffs, of the
short-changed Joes, the born poor, the afflicted.
I would gamble with the long-shot players who
light candles in the wind, and resent with the
pushed around because of race or birth. Above all,
I would fight for their causes on the screens of
the world."

Frank Capra[1]

Our Daily Bread (United Artists)

The infamous stock-market crash of Black Friday in October 1929 ushered in seven very lean years for Americans. The majority of people learned to some degree what Victor Hugo had described as "the degradation of man by poverty." Although the Hoover administration subsidized business, it was unable or unwilling to confront the major crises that the nation faced. Demands for relief cascaded throughout the land; Washington became the arena of "hunger marches." The movie industry, like most other commercial enterprises, suffered; but like the troubled society it mirrored, the American film survived even the deepest hours of the Depression and found new vitality.

Amidst bank failures, mortgage foreclosures, one fourth of the labor force unemployed, and other signs of economic disaster, the Hollywood message film had unexpected social problems to examine. One of the most committed films of the Depression years was Frank Capra's *AMERICAN MADNESS* (1932), which was purposely planned to restore optimism and faith that the country would pull out of its economic morass. As Capra writes in his fascinating autobiography, the film's "theory" was that "money is something you can't eat, wear, or plant, but you can put it to work. And the harder the times, the harder it must work."[2]

In *AMERICAN MADNESS* a bank president convinces his ultraconservative board to make loans to small businessmen on the basis of their character rather than collateral. The idea is successful until the bank is robbed by an indebted cashier. Because of the rumors which exaggerate the amount of the loss from $100,000 to $5,000,000, there is a run on the bank. It is saved only when the businessmen in whom the president had put his trust rush to the mobbed bank and deposit their available cash.

Another film which urged confidence in America's financial resilience and which made a plea to Depression audiences to work shoulder-to-shoulder to solve the nation's dilemma was *THE CONQUERORS* (1932). The film used the historical metaphor, drawing a parallel between the economic crises of the current Depression and those of 1873 and 1892. The story was a saga of a family who start a bank in a small Nebraska community in the 1870s and survive many financial upheavals.

Faith and optimism were also the theme of Clarence Brown's *LOOKING FORWARD* (1933), which took its title from a book by Franklin D. Roosevelt. The story of a clerk's loyalty to a store where he is an accountant, the film was prefaced by a quotation from President Roosevelt's book: "We need enthusiasm, imagination, and ability to face facts — we need the courage of the young."

If films such as these encouraged audiences not to be the victims of their own fears, there were others which took a darker view of the times. In *HEROES FOR SALE* (1933), a veteran of World War I invests in a successful time-saving machine but devotes his share of the profits to feeding the hungry. During the Depression he, too, becomes one of the dispossessed — a homeless wanderer. *WILD BOYS OF THE ROAD* (1933) also was concerned with people whom the Depression had uprooted. Here the wanderers are young people, runaways

Dorothy Coonan and Frankie
Darro in *Wild Boys of the Road*
(Warner Brothers)

from homes struck by unemployment. Frankie Darro was the leader of the young hoboes who hop freight trains to elude the police. Shunted by a society which had dropped *them* out, they survive only by petty thievery and panhandling.

No film of the early Thirties revealed the hopelessness of the unemployed and their degrading existence as did *A MAN'S CASTLE* (1933), directed by Frank Borzage. The setting is "Hoover Flats," a shantytown jungle on the banks of New York's East River. Spencer Tracy and Loretta Young were a desperate couple struggling to keep alive while all around them their neighbors are sinking into alcoholism and violent crime. The film's uncompromising realism caused New York City's censors to protest, with the result that the film was cut and some "tamer" scenes were inserted.

D. W. Griffith's *THE STRUGGLE* was released during the Depression. Based loosely on an Emile Zola novel, this intensely somber film was the story of a beer-drinking family man who turns to whiskey when Prohibition brings in the speakeasies. Because the drunkard is unable to hold a job his family is forced to move to a slum, where he sinks into the oblivion of skid row. Although *THE STRUGGLE* was a sound film, Griffith used titles in which he castigated the moral "uplifters" who were responsible for Prohibition and the social evil of alcoholism which it inadvertently encouraged. But the despairing

A Man's Castle with Spencer
Tracy and Loretta Young
(Columbia)

Depression audiences of 1931 were in no mood to respond at the box office to Griffith's grim tale of an alcoholic, and *THE STRUGGLE* was quickly withdrawn from distribution. It was the last film on which Griffith received official credit.

If the Great Depression of the Thirties had a devastating effect in the urban centers of America, its toll was no less destructive in rural areas. In a film unique to the American cinema, King Vidor's *OUR DAILY BREAD* (1934), the message is loud and clear: hold on to the land, make it thrive, start anew here. The main characters are a young couple, crushed by the city in their attempt to survive, who lease a farm in the Midwest. Because of their inexperience they cannot make the stubborn land workable. But they are soon joined by other remnants of the roaming armies of the unemployed — an itinerant Swede farmer and his family, then a plumber, carpenter, blacksmith, barber, shoemaker, lawyer, violinist, professor, and even an ex-convict. This amalgam of varied professions and crafts becomes a collective farm and the remainder of the film depicts their struggle and eventual victory over many hostile forces, both human and those of nature. The final sequence is pictorially stunning as everyone pitches in to dig a two-mile irrigation ditch to save the corn crop.

OUR DAILY BREAD is one of the most personal of all message films. In his autobiography director Vidor reveals how he was unable to obtain studio financing from Irving Thalberg or bank support for the production. So strong were his convictions about the importance of this film, however, that he mortgaged his house and automobile to raise the necessary funds.[3] Vidor, like many other directors, had learned that to make a picture "for himself" he had to make "three for the box office."

Also proposing cooperatives as a means of economic recovery from the Depression was THE PRESIDENT'S MYSTERY (1936). The title is a misnomer, for the germ of the plot was suggested by President Franklin D. Roosevelt. The idea was developed into a *Liberty* magazine serial by several well-known authors, such as John Erskine, Rupert Hughes, and S. S. Van Dine. Mr. Roosevelt's challenging teaser to the writers was a situation in which a wealthy man, weary of an ineffectual life, converts a $5,000,000 fortune into cash, disappears, and dedicates his new identity to pursuing a humanitarian project.

Screenwriters Lester Cole and Nathanael West took up the President's challenge in their film script with a plot that differed from the *Liberty* serial. The central character is a corporation lawyer and lobbyist for National Can-

*All Quiet on the Western Front
with Lew Ayres and Raymond
Griffith (Universal)*

neries who is able to block passage in the Senate of the Trades Reconstruction Bill, a measure that would provide funds to reopen some of the bankrupt small industries as cooperatives. During a vacation to New England the lawyer chances into Springdale, a town whose only industry, a cannery, is closed, and whose despondent inhabitants had been hoping for passage of the Trades Reconstruction Bill. Realizing the human consequences of his selfish corporate sensibility, he himself sets up a successful cooperative in the community.

As are all periods of stress and social disintegration, the early Thirties was a time of deep introspection. This necessity to seek out the causes of national and even international malaise was also apparent in the war films of the period. There was no longer any audience disposition toward the devil-may-care camaraderie of a *WHAT PRICE GLORY?* or the sentimentalism of *THE BIG PARADE.* On the contrary, the war films of the early Thirties were vehemently critical of the Great War.

Unquestionably, the strongest pacifist statement ever made in the American cinema as well as one of its greatest artistic accomplishments is Lewis

Milestone's *ALL QUIET ON THE WESTERN FRONT* (1930). Adapted by Maxwell Anderson and George Abbott from the best-selling novel by Erich Maria Remarque, the film describes the disenchantment of idealistic young Germans who die futilely in a war already lost. Again and again, in one episode after another, the message is reiterated, underscoring what producer Carl Laemmle announced in his foreword to the film: "To make war against war." No denunciation of war could be more subtle and persuasive than the scene when Paul, the young soldier on furlough, visits the schoolroom of the professor who had initially fired his enthusiasm to enlist. Urged by the professor to proselyte a new group of young adolescents, Paul's words are bitter. He has seen too much of the senseless killing, too much of the brutality of battle, he is too weary of the heroic conception of war held by elderly men. "We live in the trenches and we fight," he says; "we try not to be killed — that's all."

The final, memorable scene epitomizes the poignancy of youth wasted in mankind's folly. As Paul reaches for a butterfly alighting on an empty bean can he is killed by a sniper; ironically, the war had already ended that morning.

Director Lewis Milestone has stated that this was not the ending originally intended for his film; on the contrary, it was added even after the film had been previewed. Several portentous endings had been tried, such as showing all the armies of the world marching toward a common grave. Yet, as Milestone recalls saying about *ALL QUIET*, "This is one piece that you cannot finish with a *crescendo*; you have to have a *diminuendo*. You cannot top the whole piece."[4]

Like many films that do not hesitate to take a firm position, *ALL QUIET ON THE WESTERN FRONT* drew criticism from both American and German sources. Right-wingers in this country labeled it "brazen propaganda which would undermine belief in the Army and in authority"; they succeeded in banning showings of the film at a few Army posts. Nazi propaganda chief Joseph Goebbels denounced it for its pacifism and as "damning the reputation of Germany." Laemmle, on his part, retorted that the film created sympathetic understanding of the German people.[5]

Two other strongly pacifist films also released in 1930 were *JOURNEY'S END*, based on R. C. Sherriff's play, and *THE CASE OF SERGEANT GRISCHA*, from Arnold Zweig's novel, *JOURNEY'S END* also depicted the dehumanizing *angst* and dread that afflict men living in trenches at the edge of No Man's Land. The soldier comrades in this film were British rather than German, but their psychological and spiritual collapse emphasized that there is no partisanship in war's human corrosion.

THE CASE OF SERGEANT GRISCHA was directed by Herbert Brenon, who previously had made *WAR BRIDES* in 1916, also a vigorous antiwar film. This story of a Russian soldier captured by the Germans on the Eastern Front and sentenced to execution castigated the unqualified power vested in high military commanders. Grischa's death is as unnecessary and feckless as Paul Baumer's in *ALL QUIET* and Raleigh's in *JOURNEY'S END*.

Phillips Holmes in *The Man I Killed* (Paramount)

Ernst Lubitsch, who is best remembered for his stylish, witty comedies, directed a pacifist film that ranks with the best, *THE MAN I KILLED* (1932). Set in a German village a year after the war's end, the compelling opening sequence is a celebration of Armistice Day. We first see the parade from behind the stump of a one-legged veteran. Stricken with remorse, a French soldier (Phillips Holmes) visits the German family of the young man he had killed in combat. Because of the family's warm reception and acceptance, he is unable to confess, especially when the dead man's girl falls in love with him. The film is a plea for understanding and compassion as the father of the dead soldier acknowledges the failures of his generation. He admits that he had cheered when his son went off to war and that although he himself had been too old to fight, he had not been too old to hate the French.

The antiwar *THE MAN WHO RECLAIMED HIS HEAD* (1935) and *MEN MUST FIGHT* (1933) stand out by virtue of their unusual approach to their theme. *THE MAN WHO RECLAIMED HIS HEAD* was a censure of war profiteers and munitions makers within the frame of a psychological horror tale. A writer "sells his brain" to an ambitious publisher, who then becomes a hero to the French masses for his brilliant peace editorials. On the eve of the war the publisher betrays his ghost writer and capitulates to the flag-waving mer-

chants of death who will profit from the conflict. The despondent writer goes to the trenches and broods until he becomes quite insane. The "reclamation of his head" by decapitating the publisher was both a personal act of horror and symbolic of the larger horror of war.

MEN MUST FIGHT denounced war within a futuristic metaphor. The projected period of the film is 1940 when there is another global conflict, this time between the United States and a country referred to only as the Eurasian States. The plot concerns a Secretary of State who opposes the pacifist activities of his wife and stepson. Even though the boy joins the Air Force after the bombing of New York in an air raid, there is no glamour or glory in the film's viewpoint toward war.

The problems of the young people who survive war but who can never make the readjustment to their previous lives were examined in a contraband-message film of 1931, THE LAST FLIGHT, directed by William Dieterle. After World War I four injured American aviators remain in Paris because they know they cannot fit in with their families' values. Nursing their pride and holding on to each other's fellowship they become prototypes of what Gertrude Stein so aptly termed "the lost generation."

Richard Barthelmess, Elliott Nugent, Helen Chandler, David Manners, and John Mack Brown in *The Last Flight* (Warner Brothers)

Henrietta Crosman (center) in
Pilgrimage (Fox)

Other films of the early and mid-Thirties dealing with the Great War but in which the pacifist message is also contraband were *DAWN PATROL* (1930) and *THE ROAD TO GLORY* (1936), both directed by Howard Hawks; Stuart Walker's *THE EAGLE AND THE HAWK* (1933); and John Ford's *PILGRIMAGE* (1933) and *THE WORLD MOVES ON* (1934). The Hawks and Walker films stressed war's constant attrition on the sensibilities of officers. The main character in *PILGRIMAGE* is a Gold Star Mother (Henrietta Crosman) who had sent her son to war because of her consuming pride. *THE WORLD MOVES ON* has a family that is split into opposing sides by the conflict (as in *THE FOUR HORSEMEN OF THE APOCALYPSE*).

Although any precise relationship between social trauma and lawlessness can be only speculative, criminality increased during the Depression. Competing for newspaper headlines with the "big time" hoodlums were the freakish rural bandits who robbed cars, banks, and gas stations. Despite the notoriety of these petty thieves, the crime films of the early Thirties were primarily concerned with organized gangsterism and urban lawbreakers. Like their silent-screen predecessors, however, generally none of these films confronted lawlessness as a social problem or tried to elucidate the conditions that give rise to it. To be sure, in such films as *LITTLE CAESAR* (1930), *THE PUBLIC ENEMY* (1931), *QUICK MILLIONS* (1931), and *SCARFACE: SHAME OF A NATION* (1932) a slight reference was made to the evil of gangsterism — e.g., the prefatory statement to *SCARFACE* reads: "This is an indictment against gang rule

in America and the careless indifference of the government. . . . What are you going to do about it?'' — but their emphasis was on mob rivalry and the daring escapades of murderous anti-heroes. If these criminals were not actually idolized they were invariably more interesting characters than the forces of the law. The enormously successful gangster thrillers skirted the strictures of the motion-picture Production Code which the industry had formally adopted in 1930, but they conveniently bowed to it in the last reel by making the toughs meet death as victims of their own greed and violence.

THE SECRET SIX (1931) and I LOVED A WOMAN (1933) expressed more social comment than the plethora of routine gangster melodramas. The "secret six" were a small group of aroused citizens of a city held in the grip of a gang lord and his stooges in City Hall. With the police and district attorney bought off and all legal means stymied, the recourse of the "secret six" vigilante committee is to self-appoint themselves as upholders of the law. This theme of frustrated citizens taking the law into their own hands is found in several other films of the decade.

A ruthless meatpacker (Edward G. Robinson) is the main character in I LOVED A WOMAN. The film drew upon the cause célèbre of selling "embalmed beef" to the Army during the Spanish-American war, and dramatized the attempts to thwart Theodore Roosevelt in his crusade for more responsible government. But when McKinley is assassinated and "Teddy" becomes President the racketeer meatpacker is indicted.

James Cagney (left) in *The Public Enemy* (Warner Brothers)

Edward G. Robinson and E. J. Ratcliffe in *I Loved a Woman* (Warner Brothers)

Wallace Beery and Chester Morris
in *The Big House*
(Metro-Goldwyn-Mayer)

Not all the gangsters ended up like "Little Caesar" Bandello, who dies in a back alley, or James Cagney who at the conclusion of *THE PUBLIC ENEMY* is delivered dead swathed in bandages; some went to prison. Although most of the prison films repeated the clichés encapsulated in George Hill's *THE BIG HOUSE* (1930), a handful of them examined the major American problem of ensuring humane treatment and rehabilitation of inmates. The penal philosophy of Warden Lewis E. Lawes of Sing Sing penitentiary was reflected in *THE LAST MILE* (1932) and *20,000 YEARS IN SING SING* (1933). Warden Lawes himself appeared in a lengthy foreword in *THE LAST MILE* in which he reiterated his well-known opposition to capital punishment. An adaptation of Lawes's best-selling book, *20,000 YEARS IN SING SING* emphasized Lawes's belief that there must not be any brutality on the part of guards and that prison life must be the beginning of social regeneration for convicts. Still another film influenced by Lawes's progressive ideas was *THE CRIMINAL CODE* (1931), in which the protagonist is an enlightened warden.

Inhuman treatment of chain-gang convicts was the subject of Rowland Brown's *HELL'S HIGHWAY* and Mervyn LeRoy's *I AM A FUGITIVE FROM A CHAIN GANG*. Although both were released within weeks of each other in the fall of 1932, the LeRoy film, which provided Paul Muni with one of his many fine performances, had more of a critical and public impact. Based on the autobiographical experiences of Robert E. Burns, *I AM A FUGITIVE* tells of a jobless veteran who couldn't even pawn his Congressional Medal of Honor. He is framed for the robbery of a lunch wagon and finds himself in a Georgia

Paul Muni (second from left) in
*I Am a Fugitive from a Chain
Gang* (Warner Brothers)

chain gang. In a searing condemnation of brutal and sadistic disciplinary measures in the prison camp, the film emphasized the lashings, enforced solitude in sweat boxes, and the ever-binding chains that dehumanize prisoners. The ending also made no concession to the usual clear-cut and easy solution found in so many films. After escaping from the chain gang, the fugitive is asked, "What do you do? How do you live?" and he replies, "I steal. . . ."

Despite being one of the most uncompromising of all social protest films, *I AM A FUGITIVE* was both artistically and commercially successful, indicating the conviction of its producer, Darryl F. Zanuck, that controversy is not necessarily antithetical to box-office grosses. Whether the purposive message of this film was instrumental in the improvement of life among chain-gang convicts in Georgia, as director Mervyn LeRoy contended, is open to question. That it did much to focus public attention on these frightful conditions in a very palpable way cannot be questioned.

Perhaps encouraged by the favorable public response to its *I AM A FUGITIVE*, the Warner Brothers studio produced another striking exposé of penal institutions the following year. *THE MAYOR OF HELL* (1933) uncovered maltreatment of young boys in a reform school. A ward-heeling politician becomes a Deputy Commissioner of Correction in a gesture of the party spoils system. However, he is so repelled by the lash rule by the warden of the reformatory that he gets himself appointed as supervisor of the institution. Gaining rapport with young inmates, he establishes a code of self-government and helps the boys prepare themselves for the outside world.

The Thirties was a period of flamboyant, sensational, so-called yellow journalism, and a number of films had reporters who were not above trading their ethics for a byline. Two of the best were *FIVE STAR FINAL* and *THE FRONT PAGE,* both released in 1931. Amidst the cynical, staccato dialogue of Hecht and MacArthur's script for *THE FRONT PAGE* there was sharp criticism of overzealous elected officials demanding executions and journalists who exploited the feelings and rights of political underdogs to get a "scoop." The "yellow journalism" practices in *FIVE STAR FINAL* cause an attempted murder, two suicides, and the ruin of several young people's lives.

Politics, especially the unethical variety, always makes headlines — and more so during an election year. In 1932 the Depression's millions were hopefully looking for an opportunity to effect some economic and political improvement, perhaps by putting a new face in the White House. Not surprisingly, Hollywood sensed the hum of politics as the nation prepared to go to the polls.

WASHINGTON MASQUERADE (1932) and *WASHINGTON MERRY-GO-ROUND* (1932) gave politics in the nation's capital a rough going-over. Lionel Barrymore portrayed an idealistic Senator from Kansas representing the Forgotten Man in *WASHINGTON MASQUERADE.* The Congress in which this political Lochinvar takes his seat is shown as a corrupt body under the sway of lobbyists of water-power interests. He is subsequently entrapped by a blonde siren hired by the lobbyists and betrays the confidence placed in him by his electors. After leaving the Senate (with a $100,000 bribe) he goes into private law practice. Eventually, however, there is an investigation, and recapturing the dedication of his early political career, he gives testimony which destroys the Interests.

The central character in *WASHINGTON MERRY-GO-ROUND* is also a
naïve political crusader who goes to Congress as "a one-man vigilante committee to destroy the Scribes and Pharisees." Representative Button Gwinnett
Brown (Lee Tracy) perceives Washington as a carousel of tea dances, embassy
receptions, and what he calls a Vassar daisy chain. Again the Congress is depicted as venal and corrupt, and when Brown denounces a $2,000,000 phony
appropriation bill to memorialize a nonentity, he incurs the anger of the
bosses who had sponsored his election campaign. They manipulate a trumped-
up recount election that unseats him. Clearly, in both of these films the "bad
guys" are casuistical politicians who make mincemeat of the starry-eyed
idealists who believe that the highest lawmaking body of the land should be
above moral chicanery.

To make its point, the message film need not always be deadly serious.
For example, Alfred E. Green's *THE DARK HORSE* (1932) was a satiric jab at
the way candidates are chosen, groomed, and "sold" by their campaign managers. In this film, too, a political bumpkin becomes a Trilby to a Svengali-like
manager. Hired by the "Progressives" to find a candidate for governor, the
smooth-talking con man picks Zachary Hicks (played by Guy Kibbee) as a
very dark horse. Typical of the situations the campaign develops is a debate
between Hicks and his rival, the "conservative" candidate. The opponents,
unknowingly, have both been coached to plagiarize a famous address by
Abraham Lincoln, but with the word "state" substituted for "country." Hicks's
rival speaks first — which enables the resourceful campaign manager to leap
on the platform and denounce him as "filching thoughts from a dead man's
grave." In a bit of strategy, which is not uncommon in the politics of the
Seventies, Hicks is advised how to deal with the press: when asked questions

49

by reporters on any issue he is to reply hesitatingly, "Yes — and again — no."

If American politics was often held up to ridicule, there were also films that portrayed honest and dedicated officeholders. One such film was *THE MAN WHO DARED* (1933), written by Lamar Trotti and Dudley Nichols and dramatizing the career of Anton Cermak who had served as mayor of Chicago. After his election "Jan Novak" struggles to rid the city of gangsters and their political henchmen. Like Cermak himself, Novak is killed at a political rally in Miami by a bullet intended for President-elect Franklin D. Roosevelt.

Two of the most controversial political films of the Thirties, *GABRIEL OVER THE WHITE HOUSE* and *THE PRESIDENT VANISHES*, were produced by Walter Wanger, whose career gives evidence of a continuing involvement with message films. *GABRIEL OVER THE WHITE HOUSE* (1933) is a chilling interpretation of the power available to the President of the United States. The premise of the film, that the President should assume dictatorial prerogatives to solve the nation's problems, may seem incredulous. But it should be recalled that 1933 was also the year that Adolf Hitler gained full power with the consent of the German voters.

President Hammond (Walter Huston), who takes office as a typical machine-elected partisan, is injured critically in an automobile accident. While convalescing he is inspired by a vision of the Archangel Gabriel to become a dedicated leader who alone can cut the Gordian knot of problems besetting the land. Hammond dismisses his ineffectual Secretary of State as well as the rest of his cabinet, and just as he is about to be impeached in the Senate he seizes control of the government and assumes the authority of a dictator. But a benevolent one.

After solving thorny domestic problems of unemployment and crime, Hammond turns to the international problems of war debts and the increasing

Arthur Byron and Janet Beecher
in *The President Vanishes*
(Paramount)

rearmament among the world's nations. Radio becomes his major propaganda tool. He also summons the representatives of foreign powers to a conference on his yacht in which he adjures them to stop spending billions on arms and use their funds to repay their previous war debts to the United States. At the moment of his greatest success, the President suffers a heart attack and dies.

This film is particularly fascinating because Hammond's use of radio anticipated FDR's Fireside Chats, one of Roosevelt's most effective methods to reach the people. Under Roosevelt's administration the Executive branch assumed unprecedented influence in national government, and his enemies were never loath to label him a dictator.

When interviewed years later, producer Wanger recalled that Walter Lippmann had proclaimed the picture was ridiculous — to think that a President of the United States would demean his office by speaking into a microphone to communicate with the masses![6]

THE PRESIDENT VANISHES (1934), directed by William Wellman, also depicts a chief executive who uses highly unorthodox methods to save the country. The nation is moving toward involvement in a European conflict, despite President Stanley's efforts for peace. He is opposed by a militant Congress that is preparing to vote on a declaration of war. Suddenly the news media announce that the President has disappeared. The stunned nation suspects the President's enemies, the munitions manufacturers and a neo-Fascist organization called the Gray Shirts, have kidnaped him. With the country in a state of unrest and intense anxiety, a cabal of munitions makers, banking czars, and jingoistic publishers manipulate the Gray Shirts, led by the fanatical Lincoln Lee, to try to seize power. The people who have believed in the President's pacifist policies are beaten up by Lee's bullyboys.

This Day and Age (Paramount)

Robert Young (center) in
Red Salute (United Artists)

Finally, the President reveals himself — his disappearance was a subterfuge he himself had devised to make his enemies show their hand. He arranges
for the Secret Service men to find him, gagged and bound, in the Gray Shirts'
headquarters. By thus framing Lee and the warmongers, he crystallizes public
support for his program. Although the solutions to acute national problems
offered by *GABRIEL OVER THE WHITE HOUSE* and *THE PRESIDENT VAN-
ISHES* are bizarre, these films made daring denunciations of the military-
industrial complex and demagogues who thrive on war.

Clearly, political ideologies, of both the right and left, were much on the
public mind during the Thirties. Aggravating the domestic uncertainties of an
America trying to work its way out of its worst Depression were international
tensions caused by the totalitarian muscle-flexing of Germany and Italy. And
for many, the Soviet Union was the greatest threat of all to American democracy.

Many college students of the Thirties were political activists of the left,
Marxian in philosophy if not deeds. In *RED SALUTE* (1935) Barbara Stanwyck acted the intellectual daughter of an Army general who falls in love with

a campus radical, a member of the Liberty League of International Students (no less!). The general, fearing the embarrassment his freethinking daughter might cause his career, ships her to Mexico to separate her from her revolutionary lover. There she meets a soldier (Robert Young) who is a fugitive from the military police, and after a series of romantic adventures with him she returns defiantly to her radical Romeo. The soldier is picked up by the MP's, but the general prevents his daughter from marrying the budding bomb thrower by arranging the soldier's release. In return, the intrepid soldier — proving once again that one good American can whip ten pinkos any day of the week, with one arm tied behind him — breaks up the radicals' meeting, trounces the girl's Commie boyfriend, and wins her hand. Part burlesque, part serious, this film is one of the freak shows that emerge when Hollywood bludgeons moviegoers with the celluloid weapon.

Marxism in the halls of ivy was also the subject of *FIGHTING YOUTH* (1935). Charles Farrell was the All-American football player and patriot who triumphs over the subversive ideology of co-ed Ann Sheridan, a Communist Party agent who matriculates only for the purpose of organizing rebellious activities.

In their inimitably witty style, Ben Hecht and Charles MacArthur gave campus radicals a hilarious thumping in *SOAK THE RICH*, which they wrote, directed, and produced in 1936. Here the story is a deliberate lampoon, with the students' revolution satirized as just another growing pain, to be reminisced about in later years along with goldfish-gulping, tearing down goalposts, and panty raids. The plot, such as it is, describes a tycoon's daughter who enrolls in her father's alma mater, which is largely supported by his gifts. She falls for the chief campus radical who is leading the protest against the dismissal of a professor. This liberal pedagogue has written a pamphlet supporting a proposed "soak the rich" tax bill. To the horror of her father, the girl joins the anticapitalist movement. But Hecht and MacArthur are, after all, only kidding, and the movement is deflated by a happy return to academic normalcy — until the next fad.

A more serious look at young people in rebellion occurred in an unexpected film for director Cecil B. DeMille, *THIS DAY AND AGE* (1933). The youths here are high school students who take the law into their own hands. During Boy's Week in a city these youngsters become "district attorney," "chief of police," and other officials. They use this role-playing to apprehend a murderous gangster. Exercising their own concept of due process of law they kidnap the gangster, bind him, and give him their version of the third degree — lowering him into a pit filled with rats — until he signs a confession. The suggestion of this film that the democratic system of government could tolerate this kind of solution to the problem of crime has disturbing implications.

THIS DAY AND AGE provides an interesting comparison to *GABRIEL OVER THE WHITE HOUSE* and *THE PRESIDENT VANISHES*. All three films condone flaunting of existing legal procedures guaranteed by the Constitution

Fury (Metro-Goldwyn-Mayer)

to achieve expedient answers to pressing social problems. Is it more justifiable when a high-handed President uses illegal methods to combat criminals than a gang of high school students?

The cancerous effects of a lawless mob are elucidated in two of the most outspoken message films of the decade, *FURY* (1936) and *THEY WON'T FORGET* (1937).

FURY is about an attempted lynching in a Midwestern city. In the United States, where 6,000 lynchings had occurred over the previous half-century, this was not an unusual happening. Perhaps the film's director, Fritz Lang, who had recently left Nazi Germany in protest against its repressive government, was struck by the realization that America, too, had its pockets of group insanity. In *FURY*, "Joe Wilson" is an innocent suspect of a kidnaping; he is picked up by the police and placed in jail pending his arraignment. Through the psychology of rumor the town converts Wilson into a hardened criminal and "judges" him guilty. A mob storms the jail, overcomes the sheriff and his deputies, and set the building afire. The mob is unaware that Joe had escaped being burned alive. Later the leaders of the mob are brought to trial for his "murder"; and Joe, although hearing the report of the trial on the radio, keeps his silence and actually enjoys his ironic vengeance. Just as they would have killed him irrationally, Joe, now, has become a "blood brother" of those who slaughter in wrath.

Forty years before *FURY* the noted French social psychologist, Gustave Le Bon, had written that modern industrialized society is epitomized by "crowd assemblages" — gatherings in which the conscious personalities of individuals are submerged even as their subconscious minds become collectively active. These gatherings-turned-into-mobs seem almost to be seeking those rumors which can fan the fire of their latent fears. At that point they are susceptible to a demagogic leader who invariably emerges from their midst.

Claude Rains (front) in *They Won't Forget* (Warner Brothers)

FURY reveals Fritz Lang's affinity for Le Bon's theories by showing us the metamorphosis of the good townspeople of Strand, Illinois, into a raging mob crying out for Joe Wilson's life. Expanding Le Bon's insights, Lang explores the necessity of the guilty citizens to rationalize their aberrant behavior. The "responsible" community leaders give themselves (and the town) a political rationale; the clergy provide a moral cop-out . . . "some things are better forgiven and forgotten."

Equally condemnatory of a mob psychology that instigates lynchings was *THEY WON'T FORGET*, directed by Mervyn LeRoy, who had made *I AM A FUGITIVE FROM A CHAIN GANG* a few years earlier. Inspired by the inflammatory Leo M. Frank case, the film is an extremely forthright accusation of those who cannot control their own prejudices and intolerance of others. The story is set in a small Southern city where a politically ambitious public prosecutor (Claude Rains) seizes upon the murder of a co-ed to advance his career. In his attempt to solve the crime, and at the same time aggrandize himself, he investigates several suspects: the scion of old Southern gentry, a Negro janitor who discovered the girl's body, and a Northern schoolteacher who was on the staff of the local college. Robert Hale — the stranger from up North — represents the most politically expedient opportunity for the prosecutor.

The press is used to exploit sectional bigotry, and the case hits the national headlines. Hale is convicted, and to save him from a lynch mob he is rushed by train to another city. The crazed mob is not to be denied its prey; they board the train, drag Hale off, and hang him. The film ends with the prosecutor doing a post-mortem on the case with a reporter crony. "Now that it's over," ponders the reporter, "I wonder if Hale really did it?" Looking out the window, the prosecutor has to consider at that moment what he has wrought. He merely says, "I wonder."

THE PRISONER OF SHARK ISLAND (1936) is another depiction of the vindictive fury of the mass mind, this time on a larger canvas as a vengeful nation seeks a scapegoat in the aftermath of President Lincoln's assassination. In this film director John Ford employed the historical metaphor to show how the ideals of a democracy are challenged and corroded when hysteria overtakes reason. The film tells the true story about Dr. Samuel Mudd, the physician who, unaware that Booth had shot Mr. Lincoln, set his broken leg during his escape. Dr. Mudd is accused of being Booth's accomplice and is tried before a military tribunal. In a mockery of a trial he is found guilty and sentenced to life imprisonment in the penitentiary known as "Shark Island."

Throughout his career John Ford made many message films, such as the previously mentioned *FOUR SONS* and, of course, the great ones to come like *THE GRAPES OF WRATH* (1940). As early as 1936 he affirmed his interest in making films that "say something." When asked in an interview whether he believed in including in his pictures his viewpoint about "things that bothered him," Ford replied, "What the hell else does a man live for?"[7] As Lindsay Anderson points out in his excellent monograph, in *JUDGE PRIEST* (1934) Ford wanted to include an antilynching sequence, but it was excised to shorten the film. However, the persistent Ford found the opportunity to insert a similar sequence in his 1953 film *THE SUN SHINES BRIGHT*.

Detroit, Michigan, in the Thirties was a microcosm of the fears and frustrations of an industrial society fighting its way out of the Depression. That it was a hotbed of racial prejudice was apparent in the xenophobic broadcasts of Father Coughlin. When a secret antilabor, antiminority organization in Detroit murdered unionist Charles Poole, the city's undercurrent of ugliness splattered the front pages of the nation's press. These events were the basis of another hard-hitting social drama, Archie Mayo's *BLACK LEGION* (1936). Humphrey Bogart, in an offbeat role, was a factory mechanic who is embittered because a foreign-born worker is chosen over him as the new foreman. He becomes the easy dupe for a violent group of black-hooded super-patriots. Like the Ku Klux Klan the Black Legion flogs, beats, and bombs the targets of their 100% American bigotry — "the undesirable aliens who are taking our jobs." Trapped in the membership of the Legion, Bogart is coerced into murdering his best friend, who had opposed the robed terrorists. At an investigation and subsequent trial for the killing, Bogart recants his allegiance and exposes the despicable night riders. Along with the others he goes to prison for life. Before the judge sentences the Black Legionnaires he delivers a lengthy oration in the courtroom on the Constitution and its Bill of Rights, in essence underscoring the message of the entire film. Such overt didacticism is not uncommon in Hollywood's message films; in order to ensure that audiences "get the point" a judge or equally prestigious character often becomes the editorial voice of the film's creators.

Violent labor strife in the Thirties was, of course, not restricted to the large industrial centers. Turbulence in the coal-mining areas was frequently reported in the day's news. Among the sensational stories of the period was the

The Prisoner of Shark Island with
Warner Baxter
(Twentieth Century-Fox)

Humphrey Bogart (center) in
Black Legion (Warner Brothers)

murder of Mike Shemanski, a coal miner beaten to death by the company police at Imperial, Pennsylvania. One of the prosecutors in the trial of the three company policemen charged with the murder, Michael Musmanno, wrote an account of the event which became the source for *BLACK FURY* (1935), directed by Michael Curtiz. Paul Muni, perhaps the actor who is most identified with the American message film, played Joe Radek, a coal miner whose rapport with his fellow workers is exploited by racketeers who want to dominate the miners' union. The film urges responsible unionism to join with enlightened management, and shows that extremism on either side leads to deprivation of the workers and useless violence.

A majority of the message films produced during the Thirties were made by the Warner Brothers/First National studio. Even as each major company

Paul Muni in *The Life of
Emile Zola* (Warner Brothers)

generally had its own distinctive film style, the Warner films were recognizable
by their topicality and reflection of the quickly moving events that dominated
the headlines. There is little doubt that Warners was the most socially conscious studio of the period. *I AM A FUGITIVE, THE MAYOR OF HELL, BLACK
LEGION,* and *BLACK FURY* were all Warner productions. The studio also had
its cadre of directors whose careers are closely linked to the social-problem
film, such as Michael Curtiz, Archie Mayo, Raoul Walsh, Alfred Green, William
Dieterle, and, before he went to MGM, Mervyn LeRoy. Although many studios
in the Thirties were making biographical films about such figures as Abraham
Lincoln, Ziegfeld, Alexander Graham Bell, Cardinal Richelieu, and Pancho
Villa, Warner Brothers used the biographical genre as a frame for message
films, as typified by *THE LIFE OF EMILE ZOLA* (1937) and *THE STORY OF
LOUIS PASTEUR* (1936), both starring Paul Muni and both directed by Dieterle.

PASTEUR* was an extraordinarily moving account of the French scientist's
battle against ignorance and rigidity in the medical circles of his day. If, as
Thomas Carlyle posited, "the history of the world is but the biography of great
men," Louis Pasteur was among the half-dozen scientists who most advanced
medicine and effected the lives of generations to follow. By dramatizing Pasteur's fight against the ritualized stupidities of his contemporaries, the film
expressed a viewpoint which is relevant to every age: society's True Hero is the
man who struggles, initially alone, against the Nay-Sayers, the smug, the Haves,
and the complacent.

This message was also at the heart of *THE LIFE OF EMILE ZOLA* —

THE
CELLULOID
WEAPON

58

 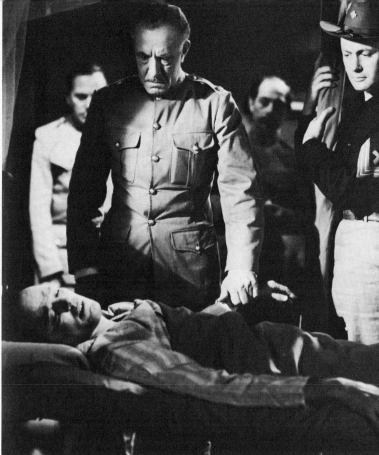

for the True Hero, the renowned novelist Zola, could have rested on his literary laurels and enjoyed his later years in quietude. But the moral imperative of the Dreyfus case, with its noxious overtones of anti-Semitism and intolerance in its varied aspects, aroused this elderly man to challenge the Goliaths of his age and to defeat them.

Donald Woods and Paul Muni in
The Story of Louis Pasteur
(Warner Brothers)

Yellow Jack with Henry Hull,
Lewis Stone, and Robert Montgomery
(Metro-Goldwyn-Mayer)

The struggle of the individual against entrenched and stultifying interests was seen in several other films dealing with medical science. Besides *PASTEUR*, the Thirties saw *ARROWSMITH* (1931), *YELLOW JACK* (1938), and *THE CITADEL* (1938). Each of these films reiterated the theme that institutions do not change unless men of courage and persistence challenge them.

Despite the many socially committed films of the Thirties, there were issues that were rarely touched upon. Examination of prejudice against racial and religious minorities — blacks, Jews, Indians, Chicanos, and Asiatics — was for the most part avoided. This neglect was not necessarily an oversight. As Fritz Lang has recalled, while making *FURY* he intended to include a scene in which a group of Negroes are sitting in a broken-down Ford listening to the radio reports of the lynching trial. As they hear the district attorney summarize the many lynchings that take place in America each year, an old Negro nods his head knowingly. Studio head Louis B. Mayer had this scene, and others like it, deleted because — as Lang says of Mayer — "at that time even he was convinced that Negroes should be shown only as bootblacks, or carhops, or menials of some description."[8]

Daniel Haynes (center) in
Hallelujah!
(Metro-Goldwyn-Mayer)

Since the nickelodeon days, the Negro had been characterized as an inferior and clearly a second-class human being. In such early films (circa 1910) as the "Rastus" series and *COON TOWN SUFFRAGETTES* the treatment of blacks was patently racist. *THE BIRTH OF A NATION* exacerbated the stereotype. Although Negroes in post-World War I films were never overtly ridiculed, nevertheless they were demeaned by portrayals as merely happy crap-shooters, faithful servants, and totally irresponsible, lovable "darkies."

It wasn't until 1929, when King Vidor's *HALLELUJAH!* appeared, that the first of a subsequent handful of films with an all-Negro cast was even attempted. Unfortunately, this well-meaning film contributed little to the blacks' struggle for recognition on the American screen. In its attempt to be sincere *HALLELUJAH!* leaned too far toward the tradition of the folk-Negro with its episodes of spiritual singing, baptismal religious fervor, and work chants in the cotton fields. Even though it was not intended to be controversial, *HALLELUJAH!* faced difficulties in securing bookings in theaters. Southern theater managers didn't want the film because they feared it would attract too many Negro patrons; nor did it fare much better in Chicago. There it was shown in a major theater only after its favorable reception in a small side-street theater.

A film in which blacks figured importantly in the plot and which held promise for serious probing of the Negroes' problem was *IMITATION OF LIFE* (1934). Derived from Fannie Hurst's novel of a white woman and her black servant who become partners in a pancake business, the film only hinted at the unrest of a young black girl, the daughter of the servant, who is resentful of the invidious obstacles that hold her back socially. Light-skinned and rebellious, the girl is unwilling to reconcile herself to her mother's meek philosophy that Negroes "should know their place."

In *SO RED THE ROSE* (1935) the treatment of the Negro took a step backward. The climax of this post-Civil War drama is the revolt of Negro slaves against a plantation owner. Without going into any examination of the causes of the uprising, the film shows the black leaders merely as crazed opportunists.[9]

THE EMPEROR JONES (1933), the film version of Eugene O'Neill's play, had a memorable performance by Paul Robeson as the Pullman-car porter who becomes the dictatorial "King" of Haiti. The film neither patronizes nor glorifies Brutus Jones; instead it shows the full emotional range of the man, including his megalomania.

If anti-Semitism existed in the Thirties (which it clearly did), the Hollywood film seldom took cognizance of it. Although *THE LIFE OF EMILE ZOLA* underscored prejudice against Jews, the subject was discussed in a historical frame of reference rather than a contemporary one. Raoul Walsh's *THE YELLOW TICKET* (1931) also looked back in history in its theme of anti-Semitism. The locale was Russia under the Czar, and the film's main character is a Jewess who survives the pogrom only by obtaining a "yellow ticket" — the identity card of prostitutes — which guarantees her immunity from arrest.

Among the scores of "little," low-budget films that come and go with virtually no critical or public notice, there are, from time to time, a few that quietly deal with social problems in a meaningful way. Such a film was *VICTIMS OF PERSECUTION* (1933). The protagonist is a Jewish judge who loses his chance for the gubernatorial nomination by refusing to compromise his principles. A Negro has been sentenced to death by a lower court and the appeal comes before the judge. His determination to give the man a fair trial incurs threats against his life. After his home is bombed his family and friends plead with him to drop the case, but his devotion to high ideals prevails.

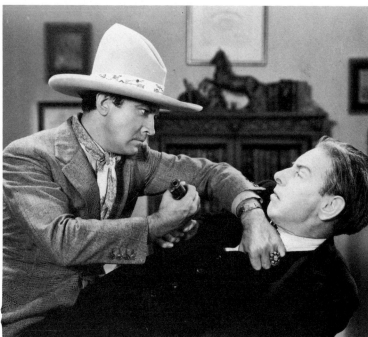

Loretta Young and Don Ameche in
Ramona (Twentieth Century-Fox)

Richard Barthelmess (left) in
Massacre (Warner Brothers)

Prejudice against Indians was the subject of *LAUGHING BOY* and *MASSACRE*, both released in 1934, and another remake of *RAMONA* (1936). Of these films, all of which were concerned with the white man's exploitation of these indigenous Americans, *MASSACRE* is most angry in its protest. Although unduly melodramatic, *MASSACRE* does reveal the inequities fostered on the redman by whites who govern their reservation. A college-educated Indian (Richard Barthelmess) returns to his tribe, assumes its leadership, challenges the malefactors, and becomes the Federal representative at the reservation.

One of the very few films of the Thirties with a Mexican-American as the pivotal character was *BORDERTOWN* (1935), still another Warner Brothers production with Paul Muni as the star. Muni was Johnny Ramirez, an ambitious Chicano who goes to night school to become a lawyer. Humiliated by the Yankee judiciary and disbarred after he strikes a smirking lawyer who had laughed at his inept courtroom tactics, Ramirez achieves power by running a gambling casino. But even this is taken away from him and he returns to the poverty and squalor of the small bordertown of his youth.

If, as Calvin Coolidge once said, "The chief business of the American people is business," Hollywood films in the Thirties revealed a curious ambivalence toward entrepreneurial capitalism. While there were films in which the laboring man was the protagonist, there were also some which were sympathetic to the businessman as hero. Films like *THE WORLD CHANGES* (1933), *COME AND GET IT* (1936), and *DODSWORTH* (1936) depicted American businessmen as ambitious, likable, pragmatic, robust — and above all — human, rather than just Wall Street caricatures. It was as if the movies were saying that for America to survive the Depression the Joe Radeks of the Penn-

 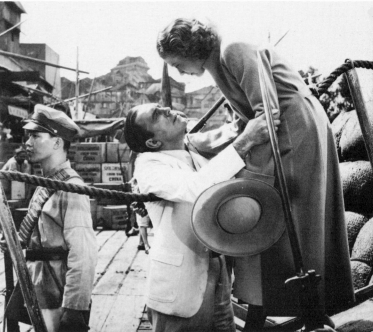

sylvania coal mines and the Sam Dodsworths of the Midwest must recognize their mutual dependence. This favorable viewpoint toward business even extended to international financiers, as in *THE HOUSE OF ROTHSCHILD* (1934), and to business institutions, as in *LLOYDS OF LONDON* (1936).

Although they endeavored to show the businessman sympathetically, films also portrayed him warts and all — in short, as a person who pays a price for success. Sometimes he learns, too late, that the game wasn't worth the candle. The life of the silver king, Tabor, was the subject of *SILVER DOLLAR* (1932). Even before Tabor is wiped out financially when the country goes to the gold standard, he has already lost the vital, human qualities which had carried him to success. *THE POWER AND THE GLORY* (1933) had a similar theme. In this film, whose story development anticipated Orson Welles's *CITIZEN KANE* (1941), a railroad magnate wins success at the cost of personal happiness. *OIL FOR THE LAMPS OF CHINA* (1935) dramatized the dedicated service of a representative of a large American oil corporation in China (Pat O'Brien). He, too, is beset by conflicts as he tries to reconcile his personal life with his almost-religious devotion to his company.

Just as in previous decades there were a few films of the Thirties whose sources were novels praised for their examination of the mores and values of American life. One of the most notable of such novels was Theodore Dreiser's *An American Tragedy* which, in its very title, is a social evaluation. *An American Tragedy* was based on a widely reported murder trial in which a young man drowned his pregnant sweetheart so that he could be free to marry a rich socialite. Dreiser's message is that the real tragedy lies in the crass materialistic values of American society which pulled the boy into the vortex of success no matter what the consequences.

Perhaps not surprisingly, this novel, with its swipe at American capitalism, was assigned to the noted Soviet director, Sergei Eisenstein, when he was brought to Hollywood in 1930. Eisenstein's fame as a filmmaker had been established in his Russian films. Indicative of the interest of many Hollywood studios in importing the best of foreign directors is this apocryphal anecdote attributed to, who else but Samuel Goldwyn. Goldwyn is alleged to have told Eisenstein via a translator, "Please tell Mr. Eisenstein that I have seen his film POTEMKIN and admired it very much. What we would like would be for him to do something of the kind, but rather cheaper, for Ronald Colman." Clearly, Eisenstein did not do anything resembling POTEMKIN (1925) for Hollywood.

At the Paramount studio Eisenstein's script for the Dreiser novel was rejected by the front office, and subsequently the project was assigned to director Josef von Sternberg. He, in turn, concentrated on the crime per se and eliminated the broad sociological elements which Dreiser had emphasized. When AN AMERICAN TRAGEDY (1931) was released Dreiser attacked it as a vulgarized adaptation of his novel. Nevertheless, the film's general tone retained some of Dreiser's bitter comment on the American bitch goddess of success.

Eisenstein, it might be added, left Hollywood a disappointed director. With the financial help of Upton Sinclair he went to Mexico to make a film on the struggling poor of that country. His intended epic, QUE VIVA MEXICO, was never fully realized. Whatever were the differences that developed between Eisenstein and Sinclair, the film reached American screens only in an emasculated version under the title THUNDER OVER MEXICO (1933). With the collaboration of Sol Lesser, Sinclair culled 7,000 feet from the 285,000 feet of film which Eisenstein had shot in Mexico.

There is a familiar adage: some are born to greatness, some achieve it, and some have greatness thrust upon them. The same may be said of certain Hollywood message films, of which John Ford's THE INFORMER (1935) is a good case in point. The film was, in the parlance of the trade, a "sleeper." Actually, halfway through the production, when Joseph P. Kennedy sold his interests in RKO, the producing company, it was dubious whether the picture would ever be completed. To many of the studio executives the picture was another backlot quickie about an Irish civil war that nobody ever heard of. THE INFORMER, of course, became one of the most famous of Hollywood films, swept the Academy Awards, and assured John Ford's place in the pantheon of American directors.

Although it focused on a man who betrayed his friends and their cause, THE INFORMER showed the poverty and despair of the Irish people and their revolutionary struggle for independence. This was not the first picture, nor would it be the last, in which Hollywood would turn to social upheavals in other countries or other times to promulgate a political message. Although John Ford has termed himself an apolitical director, THE INFORMER, perhaps malgré lui, took a political position in its sympathetic treatment of a repressed people.

An *American Tragedy* with
Phillips Holmes and Sylvia Sidney
(Paramount)

Victor McLaglen in *The Informer*
(RKO Radio)

Charles Chaplin in *Modern Times*
(United Artists)

Paulette Goddard and Charles
Chaplin in *Modern Times*
(United Artists)

Long before the youth and "hippies" of the Sixties and Seventies refuted American middle-class values, Charles Chaplin created a screen character who apotheosized the counterculture of his own day. The "Little Tramp," with his baggy trousers and his twirling cane, represented those proud "gentlemen of the road" who in all ages have preferred to live apart from the conventions of job, family, and success. Their presence is always a counterpoint to the materialistic goals which dominate so much of the American ethos. The Little Tramps are always beyond the reach of Madison Avenue, and the $20 billion spent on advertising each year might be aimed at the man in the moon as far as they are concerned.

No film of the Thirties (or since) compares with Chaplin's *MODERN TIMES* (1936) in its satiric irreverence for Machine Culture. Chaplin's early mentor, Upton Sinclair, must have been delighted when this film appeared, for in his own writings over three decades he, too, had taken on the industrial giants. In his autobiography, Chaplin describes the genesis of the idea for *MODERN TIMES*. While visiting Detroit, Chaplin was told by a reporter of the assembly-line system in the big automobile plants, and how young workers became nervous wrecks after serving the inexorable belt system after four or five years.[10] In *MODERN TIMES* the Little Tramp is lured into a factory as a worker and pits his ingenuity against the super-efficiency of the oversized gadgets. Efficiency expertise is carried to such a degree in this factory that the owners plan to use a feeding device to prevent workers from taking a lunch hour. There is no respite allowed even for relieving oneself: Big Brother appears on a screen in the toilets reprimanding the workers to stop fooling around and to get back to the Machine. After the Little Tramp battles the Machine and, of course, loses, he finds his female counterpart (Paulette Goddard) in a police paddy wagon. Together they try to survive Depression riots, strikes, and unemployment — all the social evils of modern times.

Another rich vein of social satire is the American fantasy of mobility best achieved by a poor boy marrying a rich girl, or vice versa. In a country where wealth is equated with royalty, even a show girl from Hoboken or a lowly butler can hope to marry the Crown Prince or Princess. The movies of the Thirties went along with this myth, even winked at it, primarily in the "screwball" comedies. Frank Capra's *IT HAPPENED ONE NIGHT* (1934) took an heiress and a newspaperman on a cross-country jaunt that led, naturally, to the altar. In Gregory La Cava's *MY MAN GODFREY* (1936), a wacky socialite, Carole Lombard, discovers William Powell, a hobo, while on a scavenger hunt. He becomes the family butler, teaches the maladjusted rich family how to live, and, expectedly, marries the daughter. *HANDS ACROSS THE TABLE* (1935) was another variant on the familiar theme. Here a manicurist and a destitute former millionaire, both seeking wealthy mates, end up with each other. Film after film repeated this myth. Joan Crawford, Robert Montgomery, Myrna Loy, Franchot Tone, Janet Gaynor, Irene Dunne — all of them appeared in social comedies in which a wedding band proved that love is stronger than class differences.

The films of the Thirties also explored another popular paradigm: that the very rich with all their material accoutrements are not necessarily happy, and that they have lost touch with basic American ideals. *RUGGLES OF RED GAP* (1935), directed by Leo McCarey, exemplified this theme by having an English butler teach his *nouveau riche* employers what the American Dream is really all about.

The director most consistent as a social commentator, both in comedy and serious films, is Frank Capra. His affinity for a Populist sociopolitical viewpoint is apparent in the majority of his films. Capra's belief is that the common man can and often does triumph over circumstances. As he has put it, "There is something in every man that is unconquerable by any machine,

My Man Godfrey with Carole Lombard and William Powell (Universal)

Zasu Pitts, Charles Laughton, Charlie Ruggles, and Maude Eburne in *Ruggles of Red Gap* (Paramount)

Gary Cooper in *Mr. Deeds Goes to Town* (Columbia)

by any difficulties or failures or anything else. That is the glorification, the dramatization of the individual triumph over adversity."[11]

The Capra hero, by dint of his own resources and capabilities, contends against the behemoths of modern society — political machines, powerful publishers, industrial tycoons — all the forces of the Establishment that would destroy his individuality. But although this hero is essentially a loner, he is supported by kindred spirits who recognize his incorruptible innocence and who rally to his cause in fellowship and good neighborliness. All of them bound together by goodwill and love, they can solve society's problems without the political interference of any centralized Big Government.[12]

Although his cinematic forebears appeared rough-sketch in the earlier *THE STRONG MAN* and *AMERICAN MADNESS*, the Capra Populist hero appeared in full dimensions in *MR. DEEDS GOES TO TOWN* (1936). Gary Cooper was Longfellow Deeds of Smalltown, U.S.A., tuba player and greeting-card poet, who inherits twenty million dollars and decides to give it away. Because the press makes fun of the "Cinderella man" as an eccentric (to conventional society "he is so fresh and wholesome he looks like a freak"), he becomes the target of everyone's outstretched palms. However, he commits his fortune to helping bankrupt farmers recover their land. Other would-be legatees take him to court to have the will set aside on the charge that Longfellow is insane. In one of the most delightful and "pixilated" court scenes in movie history, Deeds and Populism triumph.

If Mr. Deeds were an individualist nonpareil, imagine an entire family living his philosophy every day. Capra found them in the stage success, *You Can't Take It with You*, and brought the whole happy Vanderhof household to the screen. Tuned out from the rat race of the external world, the Vanderhofs have tuned in to the joys of individual expression. Among the Vanderhofs and their peripatetic friends are a would-be ballerina, a xylophone player, a hopeful playwright, a fireworks doodler, and, of course, the patriarch of the

The Bitter Tea of General Yen
with Toshia Mori, Barbara
Stanwyck, and Nils Asther
(Columbia)

Jane Wyatt and Ronald Colman in
Lost Horizon (Columbia)

clan, Grandpa Vanderhof, the homespun philosopher. In the final capitulation of the Wall Street lion who had opposed the marriage of his son and Vanderhof's granddaughter, Capra's social moral in *YOU CAN'T TAKE IT WITH YOU* (1938) is clear: love, not devour, thy neighbor.

Capra was equally adept in serious dramas as in comedies. Prior to *MR. DEEDS* he had directed *THE MIRACLE WOMAN* (1931) and *THE BITTER TEA OF GENERAL YEN* (1933), the first film ever shown at Radio City Music Hall. Intrigued by the faith-healing vogue of Aimee Semple McPherson, Capra attacked religious exploiters in *THE MIRACLE WOMAN. THE BITTER TEA OF GENERAL YEN* dealt with a subject that most audiences were not ready to accept during the Thirties, a love affair between a white woman and a yellow man. Because of its theme the picture was banned in England as well as the other Commonwealth nations, and was a financial failure.

In 1937 another global holocaust seemed imminent, as the Germans, Italians, and Russians were holding a dress rehearsal in Spain's Civil War; and the Japanese, firmly in control of China's major cities, were building their war planes with a covetous eye on Pearl Harbor. Indeed, as Winston Churchill put it, there was a gathering storm. It is not surprising that, consistent with his social idealism, Capra should make *LOST HORIZON* that year. Ostensibly a fantasy, James Hilton's best-selling novel was also a parable which urged readers to reflect upon the possibility that the world could consume itself if international violence and hate were not checked. Capra describes his fascination with the book after he had heard Alexander Woollcott's rave review on the radio: "I read it; not only read it, but dreamed about it all night."[13]

LOST HORIZON enabled Capra to comment on the need for human solidarity in a context that went beyond the simple humanitarianism of a small-town Mr. Deeds. The guru of Shangri-La, with his deeper wisdom, wanted to save the entire world.

IV

Cagney Turns G-Man

Probing Social Causes of Crime

"The Grapes of Wrath"

Totalitarian Threats from Abroad

An Exposé of Nazi Espionage

"Ring yourself around with steel, America!"

The Little Tramp Takes On Hitler

Poking Fun (Temporarily) at the Russians

"Mr. Smith Goes to Washington"

Fascism — in America?

Hollywood Mobilizes

A Message Film That Never Was Made

"Wilson"

"Do you realize, by the way, what really made propaganda for the American way of life? American motion pictures. Goebbels understood the enormous power of film as propaganda, and I'm afraid that even today people don't know what a tremendous means of propaganda motion pictures can be."

Fritz Lang[1]

Blockade with Henry Fonda
(United Artists)

By the end of FDR's first administration, his New Deal philosophy had permeated many facets of American thinking beyond the White House. The public accepted and supported such broad legislation as the National Industrial Recovery Act, the Tennessee Valley Authority, and the Agricultural Adjustment Act — all of them directed to benefit the unemployed, the farmers, labor, the young, and the aged, all of whom had felt the Depression most keenly. They showed their approval of the New Deal by reelecting Roosevelt overwhelmingly in 1936.

This interest of the Roosevelt administration in analyzing the roots of America's problems in order to find solutions strengthened the role of social scientists both in Academe and in the councils of govenment. Scholars like A. A. Berle and Rexford Tugwell became governmental policy makers, leaving their classrooms for Washington. Intellectuals, the public, and their Congress alike had a common goal: to attack major social ills, such as crime, with systematic and zealous effort. After the horror of the kidnaping of the Lindbergh baby, Congress gave the FBI unprecedented authority.

Hollywood, too, reflected the change in attitude toward the criminal. There was no longer sympathy for either backwater bandits like Dillinger or their more organized urban counterparts like Al Capone. FBI agents now became the heroes of the crime movies. In *G-MEN* (1935), for example, Jimmy Cagney switched allegiances from previous roles and joined the feds as they swooped down on lawbreakers. This shift in Hollywood's portrayal of the criminal was also caused by increasing demands of censorship by such organizations as the Catholic Legion of Decency with its threat to boycott films it considered morally dangerous. In 1933 the Production Code Authority of the Motion Picture Association forbade producers to further glorify hoodlums.

Crime by no means disappeared from the American screen, but now there was more of an attempt to probe the ideology of the criminal personality and the milieu that spawned him. Among the films which focused on environment and its causal relationship to lawlessness were *THE DEVIL IS A SISSY* (1936), *WINTERSET* (1936), and *DEAD END* (1937). In *THE DEVIL IS A SISSY* Mickey Rooney, Jackie Cooper, and Freddie Bartholomew were seen as young delinquents of Lower East Side tenements who become increasingly involved in crime. "It took three jolts to kill him!" Rooney cynically brags about his father who was electrocuted for murder. When the burglary of a Madison Avenue home brings the boys to juvenile court they learn the lesson that it takes a tougher guy to go straight — that, in short, the devil is the real sissy.

WINTERSET, Pandro S. Berman's production of Maxwell Anderson's play inspired by the Sacco-Vanzetti case, was a powerful story of murder and revenge against the sordid background of the tenements. Burgess Meredith, in his first screen role, acted Mio, the son of a radical who was railroaded to his death. As Mio tries to avenge his father's death he, too, is drawn toward a life beyond the law.

William Wyler's *DEAD END* delved deepest into the effect of a dismal environment on young people. The film version of the Sidney Kingsley play

Mickey Rooney, Freddie
Bartholomew, and Jackie Cooper
in *The Devil Is a Sissy*
(Metro-Goldwyn-Mayer)

Dead End with Humphrey Bogart
and The Dead End Kids
(United Artists)

retained the admonition that the crime-breeding slums recycled each suc-
ceeding generation of kids into vicious gangs. This message was emphasized
in the character of "Baby Face" Martin (Humphrey Bogart) who returns to the
neighborhood after ten years, still unrepentant and unreformed. We are left
with the grim realization that he represents the future of the *DEAD END* kids
unless some social changes can be made to improve their environment.

The critical and popular success of *DEAD END* inevitably brought its
imitators, some which shared its seriousness of tone and others which merely
exploited it. *ONE THIRD OF A NATION* (1939), taking its title from a speech
by FDR, presented a strong argument for slum clearance. In this film a decrepit
old building is the symbol of all that is pestilential and oppressive in slum life.
ANGELS WITH DIRTY FACES (1938) and *ANGELS WASH THEIR FACES*
(1939) examined the same kinds of corrosive environmental conditions as
DEAD END. The Dead End Kids, of course, were in both of these films. This
ubiquitous group appeared still again in Lewis Seiler's *CRIME SCHOOL* (1938)
and *HELL'S KITCHEN* (1939). In the latter, the boys team up with movie
ex-gangster Ronald Reagan to transform their neighborhood club into a self-
governing, responsible group.

BOYS TOWN (1938), with Spencer Tracy as Father Flanagan, was the
definitive film stressing that through love and understanding young delinquents could be returned to society and living within the law.

IV

Henry Fonda and Sylvia Sidney
in *You Only Live Once*
(United Artists)

By the end of the Thirties a different characterization of the criminal appeared, best illustrated by John Garfield's roles in such pictures as *THEY MADE ME A CRIMINAL* and *DUST BE MY DESTINY*, both seen in 1939, and by Henry Fonda in *YOU ONLY LIVE ONCE* (1937). Here the people outside the law are not the flamboyant transgressors of *THE PUBLIC ENEMY* or *LITTLE CAESAR*; they are criminals because they are victims of circumstances worsened by the Depression. If they have escaped the tenement ghettos, and even if they have been sent to the Boys Towns or liberalized reformatories, these social misfits still carry a burden of bitterness and alienation. Harboring within themselves a prevalent despondency and sadness, they sense that their destiny is defeat.

Fritz Lang's tragedy, *YOU ONLY LIVE ONCE*, is about a "born loser," Eddie Taylor (Henry Fonda). Having already served his third term for felony, he is warned that any further offense will result in life imprisonment. All that Eddie wants is to marry the girl he loves (Sylvia Sidney), get a decent job, and have a home and family. Such dreams are not to be fulfilled. Though innocent, he is sentenced to death for a fatal shooting in a bank robbery. At

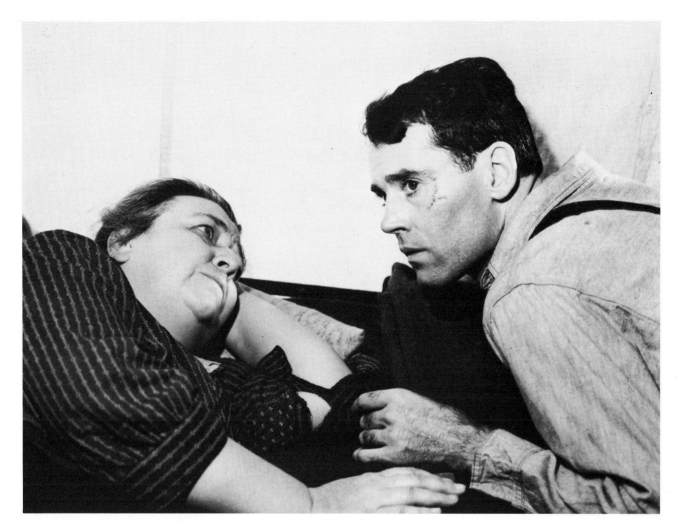

the very moment his innocence is established and a pardon granted, he breaks out of jail and in so doing kills the prison chaplain who tried to bargain with him. Eddie and his wife become fugitives, stealing food, medicine, and gas; their baby is born in a backwoods shack. In the end they are caught in a police dragnet and die in each other's arms.

One of the unquestionable triumphs of the socially conscious film in America was John Ford's *THE GRAPES OF WRATH* (1940), the odyssey of the Joad family from the dust bowls of Oklahoma to the "promised land" of California. It took considerable courage on the part of producer Darryl F. Zanuck to undertake a film which dealt so honestly and painfully with wounds that had not yet healed in the fabric of American life. John Steinbeck's novel, which was based on his own investigation of California migrant camps, had been denounced by rich landowners and was banned in many libraries. That the movie became a tremendous success proved once again to the Hollywood doubters that a controversial social film could also be profitable, if made with sensitivity and artistry. In *THE GRAPES OF WRATH* director John Ford expressed a theme that is evident in all of his major films: men can grope their

Jane Darwell and Henry Fonda in
The Grapes of Wrath
(Twentieth Century-Fox)

IV

75

way toward social justice if they stick together. The solidarity of the Joad family kept them going even when after their long trek all they found was a pot of stew instead of the proverbial pot of gold.

Despite the film's general fidelity to the Steinbeck novel their endings differed. The novel closes pessimistically with Tom Joad clubbed during the strikebreaking episode, the strikers dispersed and Casey the preacher killed. Zanuck, who had started his career as a scriptwriter, decided to give the film a more upbeat ending.[2] We see Tom leaving the family to organize a union to ameliorate the plight of the migrant laborers. He tells Ma: "Fella ain't got a soul of his own. Just a little piece of a big soul. One big soul that belongs to everybody. I'll be around. Wherever there's a fight so hungry people can eat. Wherever there's a cop beating up a guy, I'll be there. . . . And when the people are eating the stuff they raise and livin' in the houses they build, I'll be there."

Ma Joad accepts this, and her final words to her husband are hopeful: "For awhile it looked like we was beat. . . . We're the *people*. Can't nobody wipe us out. We'll go on forever 'cause we're the people."

Another John Steinbeck novel, *Of Mice and Men*, was brought to the screen the same year. Its principal characters are two wandering ranch hands who, like the Joads, seek a place to belong to; their dream is to have a little ranch of their own. Although in no sense as grand in theme or scope as *THE GRAPES OF WRATH*, nevertheless *OF MICE AND MEN* evoked much of the despair and unrealizable dreams of those without roots.

While the United States was engulfed in domestic tensions during the Depression years of the Thirties the rise of militarism and totalitarianism in Europe and the Far East created other fears. Indeed, there were many who worried that if the policies of the New Deal failed to stem the Depression a native form of fascism, perhaps led by a Huey Long, could seize political power.

Two Frank Borzage films, *LITTLE MAN, WHAT NOW?* (1934) and *THREE COMRADES* (1938), suggested the sociopolitical upheavals in Germany after the First World War which contributed to the emergence of Hitler. A more specific warning against the violent curbing of personal freedom in a dictatorial country was *ARE WE CIVILIZED?* (1934). Although the country was not named in this film, it was quite obvious that here the celluloid weapon was aimed at Nazi Germany.

The story tells of a naturalized American who returns to the land of his birth and finds it gripped in censorship, race hatred, and religious intolerance. The American tries to persuade his friend, the head of the propaganda bureau, to relent in his persecution and book burnings, but loses his life when a rock is thrown from an inflamed mob. To underscore its message that "mankind will never be truly civilized until all races become one in spirit, understanding, and brotherly love," the film used a sequence depicting the great men who had contributed to human progress — Moses, Buddha, Confucius, Christ, Mohammed, Lincoln. Perhaps naïve in terms of what was happening in Germany,

Clark Gable, Norma Shearer, and
Fritz Feld in *Idiot's Delight*
(Metro-Goldwyn-Mayer)

this independently produced film at least confronted a subject which the major
studios were generally avoiding.

If Hollywood was reluctant to reveal what was being perpetrated by German National Socialists or Mussolini's *Fascisti*, it was equally unconcerned
with events in Spain, where Hitler, Mussolini, and Stalin were testing their
new machinery of destruction.

Walter Wanger produced the first important film that dealt with the
Spanish Civil War, *BLOCKADE* (1938). Even in this film, however, the position
taken was somewhat ambiguous. Despite its being, in Wanger's phrase, "loaded
with an appeal to the conscience of the world" by its depiction of bombings of
civilians, the adversaries were never identified as either Loyalists or the forces
of Franco. Wanger himself said that the film would have died at the box office
had it not enjoyed a brief notoriety. The American Communists supported it
as a meaningful picture from their viewpoint (the script, after all, had been
written by John Howard Lawson); the Knights of Columbus and the Catholic
press, on their part, protested the film vigorously. Demonstrations in front of
Radio City Music Hall during its showing gave a promotional shot-in-the-arm
to what was essentially a glib spy thriller.[3]

Hollywood or not, the European war was at the detonation point and it
was already too late in the spring of 1939 to stop the eruption. Robert E. Sherwood's play *Idiot's Delight*, which had made a philosophical appeal for pacifism, reached the screen in February 1939. Underlying the comic aspects of
the film — Norma Shearer as a phony Russian refugee princess and Clark
Gable as a peripatetic song-and-dance man — was a witty comment on the
pointlessness of war, the idiot's delight of militarists and munitions manufacturers. Although the film was released only six short months before Germany
blitzkrieged Poland, *IDIOT'S DELIGHT* made no specific references to the
German or Italian dictators. Even as the walls of Hotel Monte Gabriele are
buckling under a pounding air raid, and while Gable and Shearer are singing

IV

farewell to a world gone mad, the aircraft are not identified. Apparently, Metro-Goldwyn-Mayer was not about to relinquish its lucrative German film market by being too partisan.

The year 1939 clearly was one in which the inevitable mortal struggle between totalitarianism and the free world was becoming more and more of a reality. Amidst their daily lives, whether they liked it or not, Americans had to acknowledge this. In such a period it was not unexpected that Warner Brothers, with its penchant for making topical social films, should release the Hal Wallis production *JUAREZ* in April 1939.

Set within a historical metaphor of the revolution led by Benito Juarez against a dictatorial emperor, Maximilian, the content of the film was cogent to a world threatened by totalitarianism. While the political philosophy expressed in *JUAREZ* is vague (Maximilian is shown in a sympathetic as well as unfavorable light; Juarez is betrayed at one point of the film by opportunistic associates), what does emerge is the inspiring story of a poverty-born peasant and his struggle to lead his people against an oppression imposed from abroad. The underlying message was never in doubt: freedom is never easy to achieve or to keep.

If *JUAREZ* was, perhaps, a veiled allusion to the dangers imposed by Nazism, Warner Brothers in *CONFESSIONS OF A NAZI SPY* (1939) made no pretense about its position. Released the same week as *JUAREZ*, this film was an exposé of the Nazi Fifth Column in the United States and was clearly intended to press the alarm button. From its inception the film created controversy. Isolationists (like the America First movement), who wanted to believe Hitler's pledge of nonaggression against America, denounced the film as warmongering. Fritz Kuhn, *gauleiter* of the German-American Bund, threatened a $5,000,000 libel suit against Warners, insisting that the Bund was loyal to the Constitution.

But Warner Brothers was not to be deterred in its distribution of the film. The plot was no paranoid fiction tapped out by a hack Hollywood screenwriter. Rather, it was based on the widely read book by Leon G. Turrou which pulled the covers off Nazi espionage activities in America. Cognizant of the journalistic impact of the *March of Time* episode *INSIDE NAZI GERMANY* (1938), director Anatole Litvak utilized a semidocumentary style in his film. *CONFESSIONS OF A NAZI SPY* provided audiences, most of whom had not gotten the message before from Turrou's book or other accounts, an extremely valuable tocsin of the insidious nature of the Nazi conspiracy within our borders.

CONFESSIONS OF A NAZI SPY not only anticipated but in many ways set the pattern for several anti-Nazi films that appeared before the events of Pearl Harbor precipitated America into World War II. *THE MORTAL STORM* (1940) told of a Jewish professor in a German university who is sent to a concentration camp because he refuses to deny the scientific fact that all blood is alike. The professor's family is divided in its loyalties for or against the Hitler regime. His two stepsons change from clear-eyed, joyous boys into

Juarez with Paul Muni (Warner Brothers)

Confessions of a Nazi Spy (Warner Brothers)

Margaret Sullavan and Robert Young in *The Mortal Storm* (Metro-Goldwyn-Mayer)

Foreign Correspondent with
Laraine Day and Joel McCrea
(United Artists)

Joan Bennett and Francis Lederer
(left) in *The Man I Married*
(Twentieth Century-Fox)

Nazi sadists; his daughter (Margaret Sullavan), who is loyal to her imprisoned father, tries to flee the country but is killed. *FOUR SONS* (1940) also depicted the dissolution of a family under the Nazi terror, this time in Czechoslovakia.

In *THE MAN I MARRIED* (1940) the fanaticism of the Nazis is seen through the eyes of an American woman who visits Germany in 1938 with her German-American husband and their small son. While she is appalled by the regimentation and screaming, idolatrous *Sieg Heils* at the mass meetings, her husband is fascinated by these activities. The credibility of the film's message was heightened by the portrayal of Germans not as brutal, congenital villains but as a people deluded and hypnotized by the chauvinistic spectacles that engulfed them.

Two 1940 films that had contraband anti-Nazi viewpoints were *FOREIGN CORRESPONDENT* and *ARISE MY LOVE*. Although Alfred Hitchcock's *FOREIGN CORRESPONDENT* was basically a spy hunt, in which an American reporter discovers a fifth-column plot against England, the last sequence exhorted America to prepare itself against an expansion of the war. We see the hero, Joel McCrea, in a London radio-studio broadcasting a news report to America. All over London the German bombs are falling as he warns: "The lights have gone out in Europe! Hang on to your lights, America — they're the only lights still on in the world! Ring yourself around with steel, America!"

Mitchell Leisen's comedy-romance *ARISE MY LOVE* also had a foreign correspondent as a principal character — this time a female (Claudette Colbert). After covering the surrender to France at Compiègne Forest she returns to America with a personal mission — to urge the United States to "arise and be strong."

Like other directors whose message films during the Thirties dealt with domestic tensions, Mervyn LeRoy and Fritz Lang turned to anti-Nazi films in the period immediately preceding America's involvement in World War II. LeRoy's *ESCAPE* (1940) described the struggle of a young man to rescue his mother, a famous actress, from a Nazi concentration camp. Nazimova, in one of her last roles, played the mother. Fritz Lang's *MAN HUNT* (1941) posed the hypothetical situation of a plot to assassinate Hitler at his mountain headquarters in Berchtesgaden. Walter Pidgeon was the English rifleman who almost succeeds. The plight of refugees fleeing before Hitler's minions was the subject of *SO ENDS OUR NIGHT* (1941). An adaptation of Erich Maria Remarque's novel *Flotsam*, it recounted the hardships of people-without-passports moving from one country to another in search of sanctuary.

In the midst of numerous films of espionage, underground activities in Nazi Germany, and escape stories, *THE GREAT DICTATOR* (1940) took a grand, comic swipe at Hitler and Mussolini. As a modern Aristophanes,

The Great Dictator with Jack Oakie, Charles Chaplin, and Henry Daniell (United Artists)

IV

Greta Garbo and Melvyn Douglas
in *Ninotchka*
(Metro-Goldwyn-Mayer)

Hedy Lamarr and Clark Gable in
Comrade X (Metro-Goldwyn-Mayer)

THE

CELLULOID

WEAPON

Chaplin used the weapon of film satire to puncture their homicidal pomposity. After a five-year absence, Chaplin reappeared on the screen — this time in the dual role of a Jewish barber who bore an exact resemblance to Adenoid Hynkel, Dictator of Tomania — and for the first time he talked. To those who had looked forward to the release of another Chaplin film (the idea for the plot, Chaplin has written, began in 1937), it was inconceivable that a comic genius would wrestle with a subject so serious, volatile, and frightening. If Adolf Hitler hadn't worn that ridiculous mustache that reminded so many people of the Little Tramp, maybe Chaplin wouldn't have been so inspired to "take him on."

Chaplin took advantage of all the rich comic possibilities that can result from a situation of mistaken identity, especially when the look-alikes are so diametrically opposed in status and outlook. When the little barber tries to escape his persecutors he is picked up at the border, mistaken for Dictator Hynkel, and given the VIP treatment. This sets up the occasion for Chaplin's stepping out of character to deliver — with spoken words now, not subtitles — an eloquent speech urging brotherhood and democratic solidarity. Chaplin was addressing his message to the audiences of the world as he said: "Now let us fight to free the world — to do away with national barriers — to do away with greed, hate, and intolerance. Let us fight for a world of reason — a world where science and progress will lead to the happiness of us all."

Chaplin's resemblance to Hitler was striking, but no more striking than Jack Oakie's Benzini Napaloni, Dictator of Bacteria, who, of course, was a parody of Mussolini. THE GREAT DICTATOR caused controversy, not only during its production but after its release. Some accused Chaplin of warmongering, others of making light of a tragic era in history. Chaplin himself has said that had he been aware of the horrors that were actually occurring in the German concentration camps he simply could not have made the film; he could not have made fun of the homicidal insanity of the Nazis. The reality would have been too overwhelming.[4]

If Hollywood, in a still neutral America, had become harshly critical of German life under Hitler, the Soviet Union (particularly after it signed the infamous nonaggression pact with Germany) also came under attack. But unlike the heavy artillery leveled against the Nazis, the celluloid weapon employed in NINOTCHKA (1939), HE STAYED FOR BREAKFAST (1940), and COMRADE X (1940) was hardly more than a playful squirt gun. These three films had a common plot situation: take a dedicated communist, expose him (or her) to blandishments of entrepreneurial materialism, toss in some sophisticated lovemaking, and the Red will be converted to capitalism. The humor was at the USSR's expense. In NINOTCHKA, for example, co-scripted by Billy Wilder, the dead-pan Comrade Garbo came up with this gem: "The last mass trials were a great success. There are going to be fewer but better Russians." COMRADE X has a Russian explain that a song being sung by a group of prisoners is "the same thing they always sing when in prison: 'We Are Free!' "

IV

James Stewart in *Mr. Smith Goes to Washington* (Columbia)

In September 1939, the European war that seemed inevitable after Chamberlain gave Czechoslovakia to Hitler in the tragic Munich meetings exploded. As it had been before the First World War, public opinion regarding America's involvement was sharply divided. Hollywood, whose power structure generally hestitates to alienate any segment of the Great Audience, was reluctant to take an overt political stance. When Frank Capra's *MR. SMITH GOES TO WASHINGTON* (1939) was released a few weeks after the German invasion of Poland, it came as a who-needs-it-now irritant to many leaders in the film industry. Capra's film about an idealist who defies his venal fellow congressmen angered those who felt that it was an inappropriate time to criticize such a venerable democratic institution as the Congress. Indeed, for some it was downright unpatriotic. Capra, in his autobiography, discusses the rumor that circulated Hollywood after *MR. SMITH* was released: that a coalition of the major film companies offered the producing studio, Columbia, $2,000,000 if it would halt any further showings of the film. Joseph P. Kennedy, then ambassador to Great Britain and himself a former movie magnate, wrote an anxious letter to Harry Cohn, president of Columbia. While professing admiration for Capra, Kennedy raised a caveat that *MR. SMITH* might do harm to America's prestige abroad. He voiced the belief that "pictures from the United States are the greatest influence on foreign public opinion of the American mode of life," and urged more cautiousness in the content of American films shown in Europe.[5]

Although *MR. SMITH* became a *bête noire* for various political factions, it was in no sense a subversive picture; in fact, by the standards of the 1970s it seems hardly more than a mild rebuke of congressional corruption. James Stewart played Jefferson Smith, Populist cousin to Longfellow Deeds, who goes to Congress as a short-term senator. The politicos had surreptitiously appointed Smith to be their patsy; they expected no opposition from him to their graft clause in a bill the senior senator was pushing into law. But Smith's naïve eyes are opened — with the help of Jean Arthur as his secretary — and he rebels. With cries of *Et tu, Brute!* the senior senator's machine frames Smith and tries to get him expelled from the Senate. In the famous climactic filibuster scene, in which Senator Smith appeals to the conscience not only of his fellow senators but also the people-at-large, he prevails. In his message films Capra is constantly telling us that good men are always on trial, always being challenged to prove themselves.

Capra's next film, *MEET JOHN DOE* (1941), has little of the "Polyanna patriotism" for which many critics have faulted his films. John Willoughby (Gary Cooper) is not a tuba-playing "Boy Ranger" from comfortable middle-class America. He is a drifter, an outsider, a mediocre baseball player who had lost his pitching arm; and he becomes an easy mark for a group of would-be dictators *American style* — big industry and big mass media in a coalition. Masters at the art of staging mass rallies and promoting pseudoevents into front-page headlines, the coalition needs a figurehead to lead their bogus Golden Rule movement (with its "Love Thy Neighbor" motto), a front for their neofascist schema. Willoughby is redubbed John Doe, the Messiah of Goodness.

Jean Arthur and Thomas Mitchell
in *Mr. Smith Goes to Washington*
(Columbia)

Mr. Smith Goes to Washington
(Columbia)

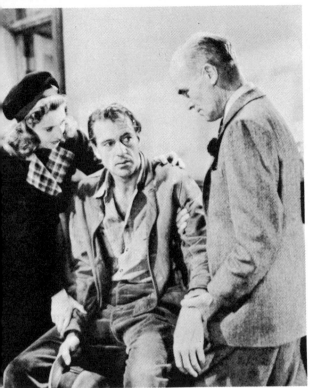

Meet John Doe with Barbara Stanwyck, Gary Cooper, and James Gleason (Warner Brothers)

Spencer Tracy and Katharine Hepburn in *Keeper of the Flame* (Metro-Goldwyn-Mayer)

At first, delighted to be eating again and with a decent suit of clothes, he goes along unquestioningly. Only when he finally realizes that the John Doe Clubs are the means by which a greedy industrialist will seize political power does John Doe fight back. But he is no match for them, and even as he tries to denounce the industrialist at a rally his microphone is cut off. Deceived even by the girl he had come to love, discredited and in deep despair, he plans to commit suicide to publicly prove his belief in the principles which the coalition had perverted. Again, the Capra hero is on trial, this time alone on the roof of a skyscraper. In this film, however, the climactic speech is made by the remorseful girl who dissuades him from jumping to his death. It is she who reaffirms Capra's social philosophy that the ideal of the golden rule is timeless and that "the little people are the hope of the world."

By March 1941, when *MEET JOHN DOE* was released, the America First movement, using Charles Lindbergh as a spokesman for their conservative Super-Patriotism, was at its height. *MEET JOHN DOE* was one of the most incisive warnings ever made in films against the forces that could destroy American democracy under the guise of nationalism. Recalling Joseph P. Kennedy's hesitancy about the content of *MR. SMITH GOES TO WASHINGTON*, one wonders what his reaction might have been to the image of America shown in Robert Riskin's script for *MEET JOHN DOE*.

The danger of a neofascistic takeover of America was also the theme of *KEEPER OF THE FLAME* (1943). Spencer Tracy acted the reporter who probes the past of a seemingly loyal American who was killed in an automobile acci-

dent. Secretly the Great Man was the leader of rightist subversives plotting a political coup. His widow (Katharine Hepburn) tries to conceal from the reporter the truth of her husband's activities.

Donald Ogden Stewart, who wrote the screenplay for *KEEPER OF THE FLAME*, recalls that the content of the film had to be concealed from MGM's Louis B. Mayer, the studio head — "it wasn't what you'd call a Republican picture." Stewart also remembers the Hollywood scuttlebutt that the first time Mayer saw the picture was at Radio City Music Hall in New York. Mayer is said to have been so angered by the message of the film that he stormed out of the theater.[6]

CITIZEN KANE (1941), one of Hollywood's most acclaimed films, had certain contraband political elements in its characters and dialogue. If Charles Foster Kane was not patterned after the career of William Randolph Hearst — as Orson Welles's lawyers publicly and repeatedly asserted — why does the newspaper tycoon in the film paraphrase one of Hearst's most famous utterances: "You provide the pictures, and I'll provide the war!"? Like Hearst, Charles Kane used the power of his newspapers to influence public opinion, in this case to get America to declare war on Spain. Nor is Kane above using his newspapers to further his political ambitions.

Preston Sturges's comedy, *THE GREAT McGINTY* (1940), also had a contraband political message. Despite Sturges's aversion to what he called "deep-dish movies," i.e., problem films, in *McGINTY* he views political morality with a cynical eye. McGinty's career personifies the old saw of the man who

IV

snatched defeat from the jaws of victory. Starting as a nobody in a breadline, McGinty ascends the political spectrum, first as a paid "repeater" at the polls, then as a party thug, an alderman, a "reform" mayor, and even governor. His falling-out with the Tammany-type bosses and his one decent, honest act precipitates his return to obscurity — and we last see him as a nostalgic bartender in a Latin-American "banana" country.

On December 8, 1941, after the "day of infamy," President Roosevelt asked Congress to declare war on the Axis powers. As in the First World War, Hollywood joined the mobilization effort. Stars like Clark Gable, James Stewart, Victor Mature, and Tyrone Power volunteered for duty, while others went on cross-country bond tours or entertained the troops at the front with USO units. Director John Ford served in the Navy in a motion-picture unit that made the memorable *THE BATTLE OF MIDWAY* in 1942; Frank Capra, as a Signal Corps officer, was in charge of the *Why We Fight* series (1943-1945) produced for military training purposes. With Hollywood mobilized, the majority of films were concerned with war themes and were aimed at the swing-shift Johnnies and Rosie the Riveters at the home front. Deanna Durbin was their lyrical spokesman in *HERS TO HOLD* (1943) when she sang "Say a Prayer for the Boys Over There" during lunch hour at a defense plant.

The war films of the period might be divided into three broad types: those that showed combat heroism — e.g., *WAKE ISLAND* (1942), *GUADALCANAL DIARY* (1943), *THE FIGHTING SEABEES* (1944), *OBJECTIVE, BURMA!* (1945); those that examined ideological differences between democracy and totalitarianism, such as *WATCH ON THE RHINE* (1943), *MISSION TO MOSCOW* (1943), and *TOMORROW THE WORLD* (1944); and those which depicted the courageous determination of people whose homelands were occupied by the Nazis, such as *THE MOON IS DOWN* (1943), *EDGE OF DARKNESS* (1943), and *THIS LAND IS MINE* (1943), which was directed by Jean Renoir, one of the many famous European filmmakers who went to Hollywood during the war years.

Since the many combat films were intended as morale builders for both the troops who saw them at their military bases and the people at home, they naturally emphasized deeds of valor. But there was also the quieter, cumulative heroism of fighting men who had become prisoners of war in the course of their duty. An outstanding example was Lewis Milestone's *THE PURPLE HEART* (1944) which told of the trial of Air Force men whose bomber had been shot down during the historic raid over Tokyo in April 1942. Despite their physical and mental torture by their Japanese captors, the men are steadfast in their refusal to disclose the origin of their dramatic flight.

Dealing with the bravery of a group of flyers on the island of Java, *PILOT NO. 5* (1943) included a strong political message. Franchot Tone acted a flyer who, as an ambitious lawyer before the war, had become unwittingly involved with a fascist-minded governor. To expose the governor he wrecked his own career. Tone undertakes a suicide mission against a Japanese aircraft carrier to settle his personal score with fascism.

WATCH ON THE RHINE, the screen version of Lillian Hellman's 1941 Broadway hit, was an articulate discourse on America's blindness to the evils of Nazism prior to our own entry into the war. When the escaped leader of the anti-Nazi underground brings his wife and children to the home of his mother-in-law in Washington, D.C., he discovers that the Nazi tentacles have reached across the Atlantic as well.

The virulent philosophy of the Nazi *ubermensch* exploited the children of the Third Reich. In *TOMORROW THE WORLD* a 12-year-old German youth is brought to America after his anti-Nazi father dies in a concentration camp, but the poison of the Hitler *Jugend* had already seeped into his personality. Although his hatred for democracy's weaknesses is finally overcome by his uncle's kindness and patience, the boy's conversion is unconvincing. Another film dealing with the legacy of Nazism was *HITLER'S CHILDREN* (1943),

IV

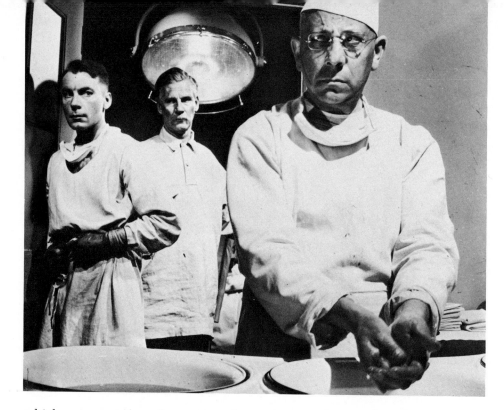

The North Star with Martin
Kosleck, Walter Huston, and
Erich von Stroheim (RKO Radio)

which commented on the matter of genetic control to produce future Aryan-pure followers of the *Fuehrer*.

The Hitler regime had propaganda value for numerous other films. Among the most persuasive were *HANGMEN ALSO DIE* (1943), whose plot was suggested by the assassination of Reinhard Heydrich, the Nazi overlord of Czechoslovakia. Directed by Fritz Lang and based on a story by Bertolt Brecht, *HANGMEN ALSO DIE* showed how the revengeful Nazis killed hostages each day in order to force the villagers to turn in Heydrich's killer. Other films of this type were *HITLER'S MADMAN* (1943), also about the slaying of Heydrich; *THE HITLER GANG* (1944), tracing the rise to power of Hitler and his cabal; and *THE MASTER RACE* (1944), which anticipated the defeat of the German war machine and raised the issue of a secret perpetuation of Nazi ideology in other countries.

No wartime Hollywood picture was more blatantly propagandistic than Warner Brothers' *MISSION TO MOSCOW*. A dramatization of the book by former Ambassador Joseph E. Davies, the film's purpose was to persuade the American public that the Russians were sincere allies. This it did with a rather heavy hand. Stalin was characterized as the kindly, wise "Uncle Joe" who omnisciently perceived what the Nazis were up to and made a treaty with them only to buy time. According to "Uncle Joe," the villains are the Trotsky faction who plotted with the Japanese and Nazis to sap Russia's strength, Britain's Neville Chamberlain, and even American isolationists in Congress. Ambassador Davies appeared at the beginning to lend credibility and immediacy to the account. After Davies explained his intentions in writing the diary, Walter Huston became his screen counterpart.

Also pro-Russian were *THE NORTH STAR* (1943), *SONG OF RUSSIA* (1943), and *DAYS OF GLORY* (1944). With a screenplay by Lillian Hellman,

THE NORTH STAR takes place in a little Russian village that is invaded by the Germans. The men become guerrillas in the hills, while the women, children, and old people burn their crops to prevent them from feeding the Nazis. The guerrillas attack the Nazi garrison and liberate the village. Despite the excessive heroics of the film, there were pivotal characters that embodied the film's message. Erich von Stroheim portrayed a Nazi surgeon who is eventually killed by the village doctor, Walter Huston. The Nazi voices his regret for his inhuman actions, to which the Russian replies in Hellmanesque terms: "I have heard about men like you — civilized men who are sorry. . . . You are the real filth — men who do the work of Fascists and pretend to themselves they are better than those for whom they work, men who do murder while they laugh at those for whom they do it."

In *SONG OF RUSSIA* pro-Soviet propaganda was accompanied by the music of Tchaikovsky. Robert Taylor was the American symphony conductor who marries a Russian girl he meets in prewar Moscow. They are separated by the war but are reunited in the girl's bomb-torn village. In the end they become Russia's musical emissaries to the United States.

DAYS OF GLORY was another pro-Russian romance — this time involving a Russian guerrilla leader and a ballerina trapped behind the Nazi lines. The film introduced a newcomer named Gregory Peck.

If Hollywood had to convince American moviegoers of the determined fighting spirit of the Russians, who were then our allies, it also reminded them that our own commitment to the struggle warranted and demanded their continued support. Films such as *JOE SMITH, AMERICAN* (1942), *THE WAR AGAINST MRS. HADLEY* (1942), *SUNDAY DINNER FOR A SOLDIER* (1944), and the splendid David O. Selznick production *SINCE YOU WENT AWAY* (1944) all showed the patriotic war efforts of American families. William

IV

Wyler's *MRS. MINIVER* (1942) — she "caught a Nazi flyer with a cup of tea"
— revealed the courage of an English counterpart of the American housewife.
King Vidor's *AN AMERICAN ROMANCE* (1944) was the story of an immigrant,
Steve Dangos, who starts as a laborer in an iron mine and works his way up
to become head of a wartime steel mill. Although the film had the unsubtle
ring of a Horatio Alger rags-to-riches tale, it nevertheless underscored the contribution of all nationalities to America's fighting strength, and stressed President Roosevelt's theme of America as the arsenal of democracy.

As mentioned previously, although the 1937 film *BLOCKADE* failed to
confront the real issues involved, it did draw attention to the Spanish Civil
War as a threat to world peace. Ernest Hemingway's popular novel of 1940,
For Whom the Bell Tolls, was more explicit in identifying the opposing forces
and in taking the side of the anti-Franco Loyalists. When the film version was
released in 1943 there was no longer any public ambivalence that the events in
Spain had been a forerunner to the death-struggle between the democratic and
totalitarian countries. Because the film focused mainly on the love of the or-

Hail the Conquering Hero with Ella Raines, Eddie Bracken, and Georgia Caine (Paramount)

phan Spanish girl, Maria, for the American volunteer, Robert Jordan, the political message of *FOR WHOM THE BELL TOLLS* was perforce muted and contraband.

A less acclaimed film, *THE FALLEN SPARROW* (1943), also made reference to the Spanish Civil War. John Garfield acted a returning member of the Lincoln Brigade, the American volunteers to the Loyalist cause. He is pursued by Nazi spies in America who are after a battle flag in his possession. Hitler himself has ordered its recovery because one of his early friends had been killed in that battle.

Devastating as World War II was, there were filmmakers who realized that humor, in its own way, was as necessary to maintaining morale as patriotic accounts of battlefront and homefront courage. Preston Sturges was a self-appointed jester of the war. Like the fictional director in his *SULLIVAN'S TRAVELS* (1941), Sturges avoided making message films — at least not "serious" ones. If his *HAIL THE CONQUERING HERO* (1944) is not intentionally a message film, nevertheless its satire contained a devilish put-down of the

Alexander Knox (center) in
Wilson (Twentieth Century-Fox)

American penchant for hero worship, particularly war heroes. Who else but Sturges would have called his ersatz hero Woodrow Lafayette Pershing Truesmith? Woodrow is a patriotic young man who joins the Marines to bring honor to his Mom and the memory of his father who had died a hero in the First World War. Unfortunately, his tour of duty is a short one — he is washed out of the service because of hay fever. To spare his mother's feelings he fabricates heroic deeds in the Solomons. When he arrives home with a chest full of bogus medals, he is met by a hero-worshiping mob who offer to run him as a candidate for mayor on a reform ticket.

Not all message films ever go before the cameras, let alone get distributed or exhibited; and even during Hollywood's patriotic fervor in World War II *Storm in the West* was never made. Written by Sinclair Lewis and Dore Schary, who also planned to be the producer, the script of *Storm in the West* was a realistic allegory of the rise to power of Hitler and Mussolini and the international skulduggery that led up to the attack on Poland by the Nazis. The background was not Europe and modern America, but the American West of 1880. The characters were symbolic: Adolf Hitler was Arnold Hygatt, Mussolini became Mullison, Chamberlain was Chambers, Stalin was Slavin, and Churchill became Chancel, while the United States was represented in the character of Ulysses Saunders.

At Metro-Goldwyn-Mayer opinions about *Storm in the West* were divided. Finally Louis B. Mayer and Nicholas Schenck decided against filming the script. Confronting Mayer, Dore Schary learned that "some executives felt there was 'too much politics' in the script and that since we were fighting a war against Naziism why should we keep talking about it?" Complaints had also been raised about the use of the hammer-and-sickle to identify Slavin as Stalin. After leaving MGM soon afterward Schary tried to buy *Storm in the West*, but the property was not for sa'e.[7]

By the spring of 1944, even before the invasion of Normandy on D-Day, the tide of the war had turned in favor of the Allies. The aftermath of the battle of Stalingrad and Montgomery's defeat of Rommel's Afrika Korps signaled the beginning of the end for the Axis powers. Consequently, films began to recognize problems that would arise in the postwar world if there were to be any lasting peace.

Henry King's WILSON (1944) utilized the biography of America's leader in the First World War to make an idealistic plea for a viable world organization to maintain peace. Roosevelt, like Wilson, was urging such a world body which would guarantee the Four Freedoms to people throughout the world. The message of WILSON was evident: unless the nations of the world were each willing to give up their special interests for the larger vision of a world community, the second global conflict of the twentieth century would not be the last one. With the catastrophic event that happened in Hiroshima in August 1945, bringing the Second World War to an end, it became apparent that if there were a Third World War it would truly be the last one.

IV

V

Other Wartime Problem Films

Ray Milland's Dipsomaniac

Postwar Adjustment: "The Best Years"

Messages in Melodramas

"Crossfire" and "Gentleman's Agreement"

A Negro-Prejudice Cycle

International Narcotics Traffic

"The Snake Pit"

Politics and Willy Stark

Another Great Screen Morality Play

The HUAC Witch Hunt: Round 1

Chaplin's Controversial Bluebeard

Anticommunism with a Vengeance

"Battleground"

"I have talked with literally hundreds of 'foreign' writers, directors, and producers. They are amazed by the freedom Hollywood enjoys from political censorship; by the fact that Hollywood is able and courageous enough to criticize our own way of life, our institutions, and even our own government. This freedom does not exist anywhere else in the world."

Darryl F. Zanuck[1]

Olivia de Havilland in *The Snake Pit* (Twentieth Century-Fox)

Cary Grant, Jean Arthur, and Ronald Colman in *The Talk of the Town* (Columbia)

From Pearl Harbor day until the hour when General Douglas MacArthur accepted the Japanese surrender on the battleship *Missouri*, the dominant concern of the American film was war. The other social issues which the films of the Thirties had vigorously explored perforce became of secondary importance to winning the war. With the end of the conflict, America again had to face problems which had been temporarily sublimated.

During the war years, however, there were a few films whose critical outlook continued the social commitment of the Thirties and in some ways anticipated the message films of the immediate postwar period. The "screwball" comedy, for example, which had reached its peak during the Thirties as a vehicle for comment, lingered on in two bright films of 1942, *THE MALE ANIMAL* and *THE TALK OF THE TOWN*.

Academic freedom was the subject of the James Thurber-Elliott Nugent comedy *THE MALE ANIMAL*. Consternation results among the conservative trustees of a small college when an English professor tells his class that he intends to read a letter by Bartolomeo Vanzetti to illustrate beautiful prose style. Despite warnings of dismissal and other threats of professional retaliation, the meek professor fortifies his courage with a few jiggers of whiskey and does read the letter to a packed auditorium. The professor's plea for tolerance and freedom of expression echoed *MR. DEEDS GOES TO TOWN* and *MR. SMITH GOES TO WASHINGTON*.

In *THE TALK OF THE TOWN* another professor takes a courageous stand at the risk of his career. Against his better judgment, a famous law professor (Ronald Colman) who is an appointee to the Supreme Court takes on the case of a zany, outspoken political activist (Cary Grant). The anarchist had broken

out of jail after being framed by the powers-that-be in a stuffy New England
town. Although this George Stevens film was light-mannered in tone, there was
the underlying serious message that civil liberties are the heritage of each
American, no matter how unpopular his cause may be.

Similar in theme to two great social films of the previous decade, *FURY*
and *THEY WON'T FORGET*, was *THE OX-BOW INCIDENT* (1943). A classic
statement against mob violence, no film ever surpassed its blunt denunciation
of what happens to men when they abandon reason. It is of small consequence
that the locale of the film is Nevada in 1885, for the message of the film is
universal. Three innocent men are picked up by an inflamed posse as suspects
for a cattle-rustling murder. Although the posse is challenged by a few thoughtful people who protest ineffectually, the mob heeds the ranting of a demagogue
who demands a triple lynching. The men are strung up, and only afterward
does the mob learn that the supposedly murdered man is still alive. They
themselves are collectively murderers.

During the war years Hollywood's examination of prejudice against Negroes was still cautious. Indeed, when a Negro even appeared on the screen it
was usually as a song-and-dance entertainer in such "segregated" films as
CABIN IN THE SKY (1942) and *STORMY WEATHER* (1943). True, in their
attempt to be authentic as to characters and events, some war films — e.g.,
BATAAN (1943), *SAHARA* (1943), and *LIFEBOAT* (1944) — had blacks in
important supporting roles. An atypical film for 1942, when the war film per se
began to dominate Hollywood's output, was *IN THIS OUR LIFE*. While it followed the pattern of other Bette Davis histrionic *tours de force*, the film had
an overt reference to blatant racial discrimination. A neurotic woman tries to

V

Beulah Bondi, Jay Gilpin,
Zachary Scott, Betty Field, and
Bunny Sunshine in *The Southerner*
(United Artists)

escape her guilt in a hit-and-run killing of a child by telling the police that it was done by a Negro youth whose mother worked for her family. What is most unusual about an otherwise prosaic film was the characterization of the black as an ambitious youngster who studies law at night school rather than a shiftless nonentity.

With the war finally won in mid-1945, the Hollywood message film was on the threshold of one of its most prolific periods. The daring of the many socially conscious films of the Thirties reemerged with even greater immediacy. Almost a throwback in subject to *THE GRAPES OF WRATH* was Jean Renoir's film dealing with sharecroppers, *THE SOUTHERNER* (1945). In this later film we see again the poverty that afflicts a family whose survival depends on the land and their fierce determination against the natural disasters of crop-destroying storms and floods. In such sequences as a child's "spring sickness" for lack of milk and fresh vegetables, director Renoir used the motion-picture camera for his realistic editorializing.

One of the most serious problems afflicting American society is alcoholism. With more than 15 million problem drinkers the consequences of this disease are almost incalculable, not only in monetary terms but in its debilitating personal effects. Hollywood, it might even be said, because it so often sets trends in fashions, courtship rituals, and contemporary manners, has contributed to the problem of alcoholism. Too often the hero, whether in a Western cantina or a Park Avenue penthouse, must prove his masculinity by belting down a couple of drinks. Apart from the $100 million spent annually for advertising

by the liquor industry, consider the more persuasive and *free* endorsement provided by a Tyrone Power or a Jean Harlow with cocktail in hand. Who'll ever forget Humphrey Bogart's "The whole world is about three drinks behind"?

Before Billy Wilder's 1945 film *THE LOST WEEKEND* only D. W. Griffith's *THE STRUGGLE* (1931) had attempted a serious portrayal of alcoholism. Indeed, even while *THE LOST WEEKEND* was in production many knowledgeable industry sources doubted that audiences would respond to a film which so unsparingly depicted the human degradation of this disease. Ray Milland gave his best performance as Don Birnam, the despondent writer who becomes a dipsomaniac. The film shows the lengths to which an alcoholic will go to acquire whiskey, even the humiliation of being caught stealing money from a woman's handbag in a bar. The delirium tremens which culminates his long binge makes him hallucinate the gruesome image of a bat devouring a mouse on his bedroom wall. His scream at the flowing blood encapsulated the anguish of millions of alcoholics like him.

The female counterpart of Don Birnam appeared in *SMASH-UP* (1947). Susan Hayward was the nightclub singer who turns to the bottle as her career declines while her husband's ascends. Lacking the perception to see alcoholism as a sickness, and relying on a pathetic, soap-opera plot, *SMASH-UP,* unfortunately, was not even a good imitation of *THE LOST WEEKEND.*

The timing of a film's release is an important factor in public reaction to a message, and particularly in regard to war films. Although the Second World

Burgess Meredith in *The Story of G.I. Joe* (United Artists)

War was drawing to a close in the summer of 1945, certainly no studio could foresee that the dropping of the A-bomb at Hiroshima would end the conflict so quickly. Three of the best films about World War II didn't reach the screen until hostilities were over. John Ford's *THEY WERE EXPENDABLE* (1945), William Wellman's *THE STORY OF G.I. JOE* (1945) with Burgess Meredith as war correspondent Ernie Pyle, and Lewis Milestone's *A WALK IN THE SUN* (1946), coming at the end of a long, grueling war, consequently did not elicit the interest they might have received even six months before. All shared a common weariness that was the lot of the fighting man — whether on a PT boat in the Pacific or dogging his way on the Salerno beachhead. Ernie Pyle's G.I. Joe personified the Kilroy who *was* there and experienced every muddy foot along the way. All of these brave men were the usable human commodities of war; some died in forgotten skirmishes and others came home for "readjustment."

The stars who had gone to war came home, too. As MGM buoyantly exclaimed in its advertising campaign for *ADVENTURE* (1945), "Gable's back and Garson's got him!" Expectedly, a series of films dealing with the returning serviceman followed. Some, of course, were romances of couples who had married hastily during the war and now had to learn to live with each other; or, like *THE ENCHANTED COTTAGE* (1945), had a disfigured veteran as a principal character. But the film that "put it all together" was William Wyler's *THE BEST YEARS OF OUR LIVES* (1946), produced by Samuel Goldwyn. If any film ever urged public understanding of the psychology of the man who comes home from war, it was *THE BEST YEARS*. In the story of three veterans returning to the same community — an Air Force captain, a middle-aged sergeant, and a sailor whose arms have been replaced by prosthetic "hooks" —

Michael Hall, Teresa Wright,
Myrna Loy, and Fredric March in
The Best Years of Our Lives

Cathy O'Donnell and Harold
Russell in The Best Years of
Our Lives (RKO Radio)

The Best Years of Our Lives with Harold Russell and Dana Andrews (RKO Radio)

we learn that adjustment to civilian life has many dimensions. As Fredric March remarked to his two buddies, "The thing I'm most scared of is everybody's going to want to rehabilitate me."

For the sergeant, with a wife, two grown-up daughters, and an executive position in a bank, the readjustment is fairly easy. But for the captain, who had been a soda jerk before the war, his future civilian life is frighteningly uncertain. For the armless sailor, who must put up with the stares and well-meaning sympathy of strangers and family alike, the return to civilian life will demand the most courage of the three. Many thousands of amputees or other physically handicapped veterans and their loved ones were inspired by the determination of Harold Russell to live as normal a life as possible. Among the many memorable scenes in this thoughtful film, none was so moving as the marriage of Russell and his "Wilma."

Director William Wyler discribed his eagerness to direct THE BEST YEARS when he was shown MacKinlay Kantor's original story. Having been in the Army himself for four years, Wyler said, "I wanted to do something I felt close to. . . . I had experienced some of the pains of readjustment, and I knew just how these fellows felt."[2] In directing his superb cast he knew how

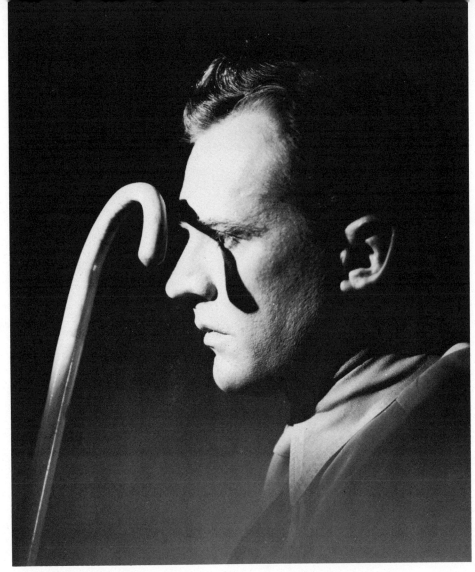

these servicemen would respond to postwar circumstances.

Other films also called the public's attention to the personal anguish of the maimed victims of the war. *THE MEN* (1950), directed by Fred Zinnemann, was the story of a paraplegic veteran, one of thousands confined to wheelchairs in VA hospitals. Marlon Brando, in his screen debut, was the ex-serviceman paralyzed from the waist down who refuses to accept the fact that he will never walk again. Mark Robson's *BRIGHT VICTORY* (1951), an equally inspiring film, showed the problems of blinded war veterans and their treatment and training at Army hospitals. The film also made a comment on racial understanding when the blind hero learns that color is of no consequence when it comes to friendship.

Although resembling *THE BEST YEARS* in that its plot revolves around three returning servicemen, *TILL THE END OF TIME* (1946) was concerned with problems other than readjustment. It was the first postwar film that touched upon the subject of racial and religious prejudice, a matter that was to become widely examined in many films during the next few years. In one scene two ex-Marines are in a bar playing a pinball machine with a Negro soldier. They are approached by a member of the American Patriots Association, a

Till the End of Time with
Robert Mitchum and Guy Madison
(RKO Radio)

veterans' organization. When one of the Marines asks him what kind of people belong to the Association, the recruiter replies, "We take all Americans, that is everybody except Negroes, Catholics, and Jews." In an obvious "message" retort, the ex-Marine grabs him by the collar and says angrily, "My best friend, a Jew, is lying back in a foxhole at Guadalcanal. I am going to spit in your eye for him, because we don't want to have people like you in the U.S.A. There is no place for racial discrimination here now!"

Ralph Waldo Emerson once said, "My idea of heaven is that there is no melodrama in it at all." The Yankee Brahmin would certainly not have found the green hills of Hollywood a paradise, for varying degrees of melodrama have always been a staple of the mass culture of the movies. The elitist critics hold their aesthetic noses when they ponder the often exaggerated situations and the *deus ex machine* solutions found in popcult. They are equally condemnatory of people who read detective thrillers when they should be reading, in their opinion, more serious, enduring literature.

Whether melodrama per se is necessarily inferior art begs the question. What is clear, however, is that in extending popular fiction or plays like *The*

"Some people carry blind, ugly HATE inside of them...like a loaded gun. And when they carry it around too long, it goes off AND KILLS... the way it killed a stranger last night!"

DORE SCHARY presents

ROBERT YOUNG · ROBERT MITCHUM · ROBERT RYAN

in

"Crossfire"

with GLORIA GRAHAME · PAUL KELLY · SAM LEVENE
Produced by ADRIAN SCOTT · Directed by EDWARD DMYTRYK
Screen Play by JOHN PAXTON

RKO RADIO PICTURES

...the hero who recovered the rage he thought he lost on the battlefield—to help avenge the killing!

...the ex-Army sergeant who thought he knew all the answers!

...the dance-hall girl who met a lot of men —but how was she to remember all of them!

...the wife who begged an alibi from her rival—to save her husband from the chair!

Count of Monte Cristo (in which Eugene O'Neill's father starred for a ten-year run), the movies very often have used the melodramatic form to sustain audience interest. The moving picture has generally stressed physical action, sudden plot reversals, and unexpected outcomes — a kind of instinctive bow to the operation of chance in human life. Certainly, on those rare occasions when a film is able to shuck the conventions of melodrama and still have the narrative pace and fluidity to hold and entertain an audience, it achieves what even the elitists begrudgingly admit is Art.

Working within the conventions of the familiar detective story, the film *CROSSFIRE* (1947) was a melodrama with a potent social message. What had been only a subtheme of racial prejudice in his earlier *TILL THE END OF TIME* emerged as the dominant theme of Edward Dmytryk's *CROSSFIRE*. It was the first film in which the problem of anti-Semitism was an integral part of the plot.

In questioning murder suspects, the police round up an ex-soldier who refers to the victim as a "Jewboy." The suspect continues to drop comments that reveal a pathological resentment to "Jewboys who lived on easy street

V

during the war while the white people fought in the front-line trenches." The audience begins to realize that here is indeed the murderer, and that his motive for the slaying was sheer, paranoid hatred.

The production history of this film reveals an interesting insight as to when Hollywood considers the time ripe for discussion of certain kinds of social issues while eschewing others. In the novel by Richard Brooks on which CROSSFIRE was based, the murder victim was a homosexual rather than a Jew. Obviously, 1947 was not a propitious time for even the use of the word "homosexual" in a film, let alone an examination of paranoid fury against homosexuals. Even with the thematic change from homosexuality to anti-Semitism, the property was held by producer Adrian Scott for two years. When Dore Schary went to RKO as production chief the decision was finally made to go ahead.

GENTLEMAN'S AGREEMENT, also released in 1947, dealt even more directly with anti-Semitism. Laura Z. Hobson's novel was one of the postwar best sellers, and when Darryl F. Zanuck decided to film the book he gave it the "quality" treatment with a top-notch cast and an acclaimed new director, Elia Kazan. Gregory Peck played the role of an investigative writer who pretends to be Jewish to gather material for a series of articles on the extent of anti-Semitism in American life. He experiences firsthand the humiliation of being denied a room at a swanky hotel, of name calling, and the other stigmata of discrimination. Kazan recalls Zanuck's determination to make GENTLEMAN'S AGREE-MENT despite the admonitions of his Hollywood friends, including rich Jews who preferred not to stir up the matter of anti-Semitism. As Kazan has remarked, "GENTLEMAN'S AGREEMENT was not terribly daring, but at the time it marked a step."[3]

Postwar Hollywood saw the burgeoning of independent filmmaking activity. Many stars who came back from the war did not return to their "studio homes." Instead, in association with agents, writers, and directors, some of them set up their own producing firms. There were new producers and directors emerging, too; and one of them was Stanley Kramer, whose new independent company made the first in the cycle of Negro-prejudice pictures, HOME OF THE BRAVE (1949). While this influx of young blood in the motion-picture industry, with its eagerness to explore new ideas, may have prodded the older, more established "majors" to make more socially conscious films, there were also other factors at work. The demography of the United States had changed considerably during the war. Hundreds of thousands of Negroes had left their agrarian poverty in the South for jobs in defense factories in Detroit, Chicago, and Los Angeles. Last to be hired, first to be fired, the blacks had exchanged one kind of ghetto for another. The dispersion of blacks across the country made it difficult to ignore the racism which previously had been blamed solely on the South.

In HOME OF THE BRAVE the central character is a Negro soldier (James Edwards) in the Pacific theater of war who returns from a harrowing mission in a severe state of amnesia and paralysis. Through the use of narcosynthesis

Dorothy McGuire, Gregory Peck, and John Garfield in *Gentleman's Agreement* (Twentieth Century-Fox)

Home of the Brave with Jeff Corey, James Edwards, Steve Brodie, and Douglas Dick (United Artists)

V

Beatrice Pearson, Mel Ferrer, and
Richard Hylton in *Lost Boundaries*
(Film Classics)

an Army psychiatrist delves into the psychogenesis of the black man's breakdown. Not only war's horror had triggered his neurosis but also the racial
prejudice of the comrade who had called him a "nigger."

That producers of message films must have an almost intuitive grasp of
when the public is ready for a dramatization of a particular social issue is
evident again in the circumstances surrounding *HOME OF THE BRAVE*. The
protagonist in the Arthur Laurents play, the source of the film, was a Jewish
soldier. Scriptwriter Carl Foreman changed the character to a Negro. Although the ravages of discrimination might have been depicted through the
eyes of a member of any minority group — Jew, Mexican-American, American
Indian — the point is that producer Kramer felt that the public was ready for
a candid film on black prejudice.

Within a year there were several other films that took up the problem
of prejudice against Negroes. *LOST BOUNDARIES, PINKY, INTRUDER IN
THE DUST*, all made in 1949, and *NO WAY OUT* (1950). Alfred L. Werker's
LOST BOUNDARIES revealed an unusual aspect of the Negroes' life in

Pinky with Jeanne Crain and
Ethel Waters
(Twentieth Century-Fox)

America. Mel Ferrer acted a Negro doctor who is so light skinned that he
is unable to practice among the blacks; he becomes a leading member of
a New Hampshire community where he and his family "pass" for white.
When the community discovers his true racial identity, its people are confronted with a crisis of conscience. Through the courage of an Episcopal
clergyman, played by a real-life minister in Portsmouth, the town makes its
decision to put brotherhood above bigotry.

Despite the threats of local Southern censorship boards which were
always opposed to any film attempting to deal frankly with blacks, producer
Darryl F. Zanuck proceeded to make his contribution to the cycle of Negro-
prejudice films. The main character in *PINKY* is a light-skinned Negro who
passes for white; the locale, however, is not an enlightened New England
community, as in *LOST BOUNDARIES*, but a small town in the Deep South.
After working as a nurse in the North, Pinky (Jeanne Crain) returns to her
Mississippi home where she encounters all the things she had tried to run
away from — police brutality, vulgar epithets, Jim Crowism in all its mani-

V

festations. Willed a legacy by an old white schoolteacher, Pinky wins the right to keep it in a tense courtroom sequence.

Mob violence with racial implications was the subject of Clarence Brown's *INTRUDER IN THE DUST,* based on a William Faulkner novel. Here the would-be victim of the mob's wrath is a black man accused of murder. *INTRUDER IN THE DUST* proved once again that within the conventions of a suspenseful thriller profound statements about human relationships can be presented. In a far cry from the ear-to-ear grinning mammies or the fawning stable boys of so many Southern plantation films, Juano Hernandez acted the accused Lucas as a dignified, proud, almost defiant man who would have preferred being lynched to denying his own human worth. As critic Richard Winnington has observed, in a sense Lucas is the conscience of the white boy Chick and his uncle, a lawyer, who despite their mixed feelings toward the black man track down the real murderer. At the end of the film the lawyer acknowledges their own racial prejudice by saying to Chick: "Lucas wasn't in trouble. We were in trouble. . . ."[4]

In Joseph L. Mankiewicz's *NO WAY OUT* racial tensions erupt in a violent confrontation between blacks and whites not seen on the screen since *THE BIRTH OF A NATION.* Sidney Poitier had his first screen role in *NO WAY OUT* as the only nonwhite doctor at a large county hospital. Assigned to the prison ward, he becomes the target of a psychopathic criminal's revenge for the death of his wounded brother, who had died while Poitier was operating on him. A race riot breaks out in the city after the hoodlum conspires with his gang to inflame the already tense racial situation. The blacks are seen fighting back at whitey in the ghetto — a graphic sequence that unwittingly forecast the events in Watts, Detroit, and Newark in the Sixties.

The range of problems treated in message films is subject to many variables, not the least of which is the censorship which the motion-picture industry imposes on itself. After the public uproar over the violent crime movies of the early Thirties and the not-too-subtle sexuality of the Mae West films, the Production Code was tightened. For twenty years Joseph I. Breen, as Administrator of the Production Code, wielded strong influence on film content. One of the taboo subjects of the code was narcotics, and it was not until 1948, with the film *TO THE ENDS OF THE EARTH,* that even drug traffic could be discussed. This film became possible only because of a special "dispensation" by the Code authority. Utilizing the semidocumentary style of filmmaking so prevalent in postwar movies, *TO THE ENDS OF THE EARTH* was a global chase film, but the hunter this time was a T-man stalking an international combine of dope smugglers. To heighten the authenticity of the picture, and perhaps to convince civic groups that this film was a serious treatment of the problem of narcotics, the real-life U.S. Commissioner of Narcotics, Harry J. Anslinger, played an integral role in the story. We see the workings of the narcotics division at the Treasury Department, and also the attempt to control drug traffic at the United Nations' council table. The film's message was clearly made: unless the sources of narcotics can be controlled the vicious drug peddlers will always have a commodity for sale. Not until 1971 was world public

Fredric March and Florence
Eldridge in *An Act of Murder*
(Universal-International)

opinion ready to put the necessary pressure on such countries as Turkey to desist from cultivating opium.

As in *TO THE ENDS OF THE EARTH*, the semidocumentary films of this period often had characters representing governmental agencies. *PANIC IN THE STREETS* (1950) was an account of the joint efforts of the New Orleans police and a doctor of the U.S. Public Health Service to prevent an epidemic of the pneumonic plague. An equally pressing matter in the film was to avoid the mass hysteria that would result should the news leak out that an infected killer was loose in the city.

Because of the dramatic potential in hospital settings, with their stark, quiet corridors, dedicated personnel, and life-against-death struggles in wards and operating rooms, there has never been a lack of hospital films from Hollywood. Long before he transferred his shingle to Television City, Dr. Kildare personified the American Doctor to millions of moviegoers from Puget Sound to Peoria. But not all hospitals are blessed with the devoted Jim Kildares and humane Dr. Gillespies, or with the most up-to-date facilities for the treatment of patients.

THE SNAKE PIT (1948), with Olivia de Havilland in an extraordinary performance, gave another view of hospitals and illness. Despite the obvious

fact that more people are being treated for mental illness than any other disease, Hollywood, up to this time, had never dealt with this matter except superficially in such films as *PRIVATE WORLDS* (1935) and *SPELLBOUND* (1945). But in *THE SNAKE PIT* director Anatole Litvak vividly illuminated the human tragedies in so many state mental institutions. Although the plot evolved around one woman's breakdown, treatment, and slow recovery to mental health, the film *in toto* is an honest disclosure of the poor facilities, limited number of doctors, and the sense of hopelessness which seem to pervade mental hospitals. By being shown such techniques as electroshock therapy, hydrotherapy, and narcosynthesis, the viewer was drawn directly into the experiences of the mentally ill. Unquestionably a daring film, *THE SNAKE PIT* avoided dwelling on the agonies of these afflicted women for sensationalism and brought to the public a sharpened awareness of the need for amelioration in this area. Producer Darryl F. Zanuck subsequently took pride in the fact that because of *THE SNAKE PIT* innovative and progressive laws regarding mental hospitals were passed in 26 states.[5]

From time to time, Hollywood will delve into a subject that by tacit understanding in our culture is seldom even mentioned, let alone confronted. *AN ACT OF MURDER* (1948) considered both the legal and moral aspects of

V

"mercy killing." A quarter of a century later, we are still barely able to discuss euthanasia in other than very emotional terms. This film concerns a judge who cannot endure to see his wife suffer an incurable disease and plans to end her life. Although she dies in an automobile accident, the broader, philosophical issues of mercy killing are openly discussed.

Since 1948 was a presidential election year, of course, in the months preceding it the public was being inundated by preconvention politicos who toured the country and released trial balloons. As goes the nation, so goes Hollywood, and a cluster of political films appeared. A trio of America's top wits — George S. Kaufman, Charles MacArthur, and Nunnally Johnson — collaborated in the hilarious *THE SENATOR WAS INDISCREET* (1947). William Powell was a hustling senator who uses every traditional technique to gain his party's nomination for President. Like Calvin Coolidge and other politicians, he even is inducted into an Indian tribe. When he loses his secret weapon, a little black book which lists the party's hidden skeletons, his hoodwinking game is over.

One of the masters of Hollywood comedies is screenwriter and director Billy Wilder. Adept at both serious dramas (*vide THE LOST WEEKEND*) as well as incisive satire, he is an admitted smuggler of messages into his films. Wilder has said, "Whatever meaning you will find in my pictures, it's all put in kind of contraband, you know — sort of smuggled in; a kind of message of, I hope, decency, of liberal thinking, whatever you want to call it, or something biting, something satirical, something poking fun at our way of life. But I never set out just to have them sit down, and then I blast a sermon at them. I just don't believe in it."[6]

Wilder's *A FOREIGN AFFAIR* (1948) is an excellent example of how to conceal a message within the frame of entertainment. With his usual keen perception of a topical situation — in this case the Cold War tensions in Berlin — Wilder tells the story of a spinster congresswoman who is a member of a committee investigating too much fraternization between the GI's and their German frauleins. Wilder's sharp pen scratched such postwar phenomenon as de-Nazification, black market operations involving GI's, and bumbling congressional investigators. If Congress and the Defense Department had taken umbrage, Wilder would always plead: Me? I'm only a satirist.

Another contraband comedy of the late Forties was *THE FARMER'S DAUGHTER* (1947). Loretta Young played the Minnesota farm girl who starts out as a maid in a Kennedy-like family in Washington, gains the confidence of the family's political machine, and finally is elected to Congress. In its good-natured way, the film made a comment on unscrupulous politicians as well as the viability of the American democratic system.

If Frank Capra's prewar Populism was essentially nonpartisan in its social idealism, his *STATE OF THE UNION* (1948) was more specific in delineating its targets. The "bad guys" are described as an "old Harding gang" of Republicans, not to mention some GOP lame ducks. Like Longfellow Deeds and Jefferson Smith before him, Spencer Tracy as the dark-horse Republican

The Senator Was Indiscreet with
William Powell and Peter Lind
Hayes (Universal-International)

presidential candidate runs headlong into the wall of cynical campaign managers and wheeler-dealer press lords. The capitalist system itself is not above
a critical swipe, as Candidate Tracy says, "Thinking about high profits instead
of high production is just playing the Communist game." Reminiscent of Wendell Willkie and his dream of "One World," Tracy's platform includes a plan
for a world government and a feasible system of atomic weapon control.

Politics is not a matter for satire or witty characters in *BOOMERANG*
(1947) and *ALL THE KING'S MEN* (1949), in fact it's downright serious business. *BOOMERANG* was based on the early career of Homer Cummings, who
later became Attorney General of the United States. The film told of a public
prosecutor who bucked the political machine to save the life of a man whom
he had come to believe was innocent of a murder charge. When public opinion
clamors for a conviction of the priest murderer, it becomes politically expedient to nail the most vulnerable suspect.

Robert Penn Warren's novel, a thinly disguised biography of Huey P.
Long, was the basis for the most scathing indictment of political demagoguery
in any American film, *ALL THE KING'S MEN*, directed by Robert Rossen.
Willy Stark, like Long, emerges from the despair of Depression days by promising the people of his state to "share the wealth." At first the sincere voice of
the downtrodden, his charisma catapults him to the governorship. But un-

V

Broderick Crawford, Mercedes McCambridge, and John Ireland in *All the King's Men* (Columbia)

fortunately, to paraphrase Lord Acton, power corrupts and Willy Stark corrupts power absolutely. Both fascinating and at the same time hateful, Willy controls the state with almost hypnotic power. The voters may be willing to smile indulgently at Willy's wenching and drunken outbursts, but those whom he has personally mangled are not so forgiving. Just as Stark is ready to make his bid for national power in what could be the first homegrown fascist dictatorship, he is assassinated in the corridors of the State capitol by a doctor whose sister he had seduced. Unlike the benevolent American dictatorships depicted in *THE PRESIDENT VANISHES* or *GABRIEL OVER THE WHITE HOUSE* of the Thirties, Willy Stark is not inspired by any archangel Gabriel or love for his country — power, sheer power, is his game. The casting of Broderick Crawford as Willy Stark was uncomfortably apt, for in physical appearance, gesture, and voice he virtually re-created the presence of Huey Long.

The unsavory career of Long was also traced in Raoul Walsh's *A LION IS IN THE STREETS*, the screen version of Adria Locke Langley's novel of the late Forties. Although production was planned before *ALL THE KING'S MEN* this film was not made until 1953. The vicious political demagogue of *A LION*

IS IN THE STREETS was flamboyantly played by James Cagney.

As previously noted, in every period of American film history there are message films which, while not commenting on specific social matters, express viewpoints which have ramifications for the whole range of social interaction. Such a film was *THE FOUNTAINHEAD* (1949), based on Ayn Rand's philosophical novel-treatise. If during the late Forties Hollywood came under the scrutiny of the House Un-American Activities Committee for alleged leftist content in films, *THE FOUNTAINHEAD* clearly expounded the ideology of the ultra-Right. Gary Cooper had the role of an architect who exemplifies Miss Rand's belief that true freedom exists only when the individual is allowed to do what he alone wills, and that any shackles on that right is the subordination of the individual to the "collective" will. After the architect destroys the building he had designed because of the betrayal of his artistic integrity, he defends himself (with pure Rand arguments) at his trial.

In *THE TREASURE OF THE SIERRA MADRE* (1948), John Huston directed a morality tale to stand beside von Stroheim's *GREED* of the Twenties. Within the convention of the long-established adventure genre, Huston stressed the psychological drives which confounded the three prospectors. Blinded by

Tim Holt, Walter Huston, and Humphrey Bogart in *The Treasure of the Sierra Madre* (Warner Brothers)

V

119

what Dr. Samuel Johnson called "the potentiality of growing rich beyond the dreams of avarice," Dobbs sees the gold for which he would commit murder swallowed up by the wind. In the immediate postwar period which saw so many excellent message films, *THE TREASURE OF THE SIERRA MADRE* went beyond pressing immediate social problems to become a classic commentary on the human condition.

The "studio system," which in the Twenties had already become the *modus operandi* of the American film industry, has been both a blessing and bane for writers and directors who have tried to "say something" in film. On the one hand, the emphasis on assembly-line entertainment makes it difficult for a serious subject to even be considered. On the other hand, the substantial box-office receipts of the musicals, Westerns, boudoir romances, and other staples of Hollywood's cupboards provide the financial wherewithal for investing in a socially daring film. The development of the Hollywood message film clearly reveals that a majority were produced by studios which had a secure economic base. Indeed, it was so-called moguls like Jack L. Warner and Darryl F. Zanuck who, in addition to making numerous successful Alice Faye-Tyrone Power-Don Ameche musicals and Errol Flynn swashbucklers, often provided the necessary front-office support and even the impetus for social-problem films. Sound and consistent corporate management of a studio can often be a guarantee that a picture that deviates from the usual mold will be completed once the commitment is made. At a studio blighted by frequent managerial ups-and-downs the unusual project is likely to get postponed or lost in the shifting fortunes of top personnel.

An example of this is Joseph Losey's *THE BOY WITH GREEN HAIR* (1948). The film started out as an allegory about racism and was begun at the RKO studios with Adrian Scott as producer and Dore Schary as executive producer. During the shooting of the film Scott was subpoenaed to appear before the House Un-American Activities Committee that was investigating alleged infiltration of subversive propaganda into motion pictures. The film was temporarily shelved, perhaps because of the upheaval that the hearings were causing in Hollywood. Losey went on to another project, Schary went to Washington to testify at the HUAC hearings, and Scott was off the picture. Schary subsequently got Losey to resume the picture, but shortly thereafter Howard Hughes gained control of RKO. Now Schary resigned, and the film was finally completed only after changes that Hughes decreed. What started out to be a plea against racism ended as a mild antiwar allegory with even a few anti-communist overtones. With RKO in such a managerial flux it is small wonder that the story of a boy who suffered discrimination because he looked "different" was not a fully realized message film.

Few events have ever disturbed the equanimity of Hollywood as much as the 1947 investigations of that congressional witch hunt known as the House Un-American Activities Committee. Actually, the 1947 hearings were a resumption of earlier investigations into Hollywood, especially of such groups as the Anti-Nazi League. The chairman of the HUAC in the early Forties was Congressman Martin Dies who, like J. Parnell Thomas, the later chairman, was extremely adept at making charges that made headlines in the afternoon newspapers. One of the committee members in the 1947 hearings who learned a lot about the political brownie points to be earned from free-swinging redbaiting was a young California congressman named Richard M. Nixon.

In October 1947, many Hollywood writers, directors, and producers were called before the House Un-American Activities Committee. Nineteen of them were "unfriendly witnesses" — they declined to answer the committee's $64 question of whether they were indeed card-carrying Communists. Among them were writers Albert Maltz, Dalton Trumbo, John Howard Lawson, Alvah Bessie, and Lester Cole; directors Edward Dmytryk and Herbert J. Biberman; and producer Adrian Scott — all of whom (along with two others) were subsequently convicted of contempt of Congress and sentenced to one-year jail terms. Thus was born the discriminatory epithet, "The Hollywood Ten."

In an attempt to establish a relationship between the alleged communist ideology of certain writers and directors and their possible influence on the content of Hollywood films, the committee resurrected such pictures as MISSION TO MOSCOW, THE NORTH STAR, and even the innocuous SONG OF RUSSIA — all pro-Soviet films that had been made during the war and while Russia was our ally in the fierce struggle against Hitler.

To protest what many thought was an unfair image of the industry the Committee for the First Amendment was organized. Humphrey Bogart, Lauren Bacall, and John Huston led a contingent of 50 Hollywoodians to Washington, but their efforts probably had a more negative than antidotal effect simply because some of them were quickly intimidated by the HUAC.

Eventually the HUAC had reaped as much press coverage at Hollywood's expense as it could and moved on to other fertile fields — until 1951, when it returned for a repeat performance. But the first hearings had already exacted a heavy toll in many sectors of Hollywood. What was most difficult to assess were the animosities among old acquaintances at studios and the endless, feckless debate of whether so-and-so was or wasn't a Commie. An atmosphere of fear pervaded the entire industry, especially at the managerial level.

Not every executive was daunted by the bad publicity which so many of their colleagues believed had turned American public opinion against Hollywood. At an industry-wide top-echelon meeting in New York's Waldorf, Dore Schary, Samuel Goldwyn, Walter Wanger, and Eddie Mannix opposed the suggestion that all suspected communists be fired forthwith. "How can you fire people who haven't been convicted of anything?" Schary asked.[7] But such voices were in the minority. Back at the Hollywood studios many creative people were indeed discharged openly while others suffered unemployment for several years through the more insidious practice of blacklisting.

The House Un-American Activities Committee's probing was not inconsistent with the general hunt for "internal enemies" that came with the first wave of the Cold War. It was a period of deep suspicion of any long-time

V

Monsieur Verdoux with Barbara
Slater and Charles Chaplin
(United Artists)

exponents of liberal causes. Inevitably, conservative factions throughout the
country began to scrutinize the career of Charles Chaplin. His 1947 film MON-
SIEUR VERDOUX became a palpable target for their political dementia. Unlike any of his previous films, *VERDOUX* was a bitter philosophical statement
(albeit not totally without Chaplin's comic skills) about war as mass murder.
While focusing on a Bluebeard who marries rich women and subsequently
murders them for their money, the picture is actually an extended contraband
message against the kind of world which legalizes mass slaughter but pun-
ishes an individual murderer. "One murder makes a villain, millions a hero,"
says Verdoux to the reporters in his prison cell. To pursue his point, Chaplin
made this program note at a public preview of his film: "Von Clausewitz said
that war is the logical extension of diplomacy; M. Verdoux feels that murder is
the logical extension of business."

MONSIEUR VERDOUX, in its mix of the serious and the slapstick, was
a complex film on which critical opinion varied. Whatever other reasons may

have accounted for its failure at the box office, certainly the political harassment of Chaplin himself did not promote the sale of tickets. The nationally influential Hearst newspapers, not to mention the *New York Daily News*, excoriated Chaplin and *VERDOUX*. Organizations like the New Jersey Catholic Legion picketed theaters showing the film, carrying signs exclaiming "Chaplin, the ingrate and Communist sympathizer" and "Kick the Alien out of the country!"[8] To add fuel to the fire, the Independent Theater Owners Organization, representing 325 theaters in the Columbus, Ohio, area, urged theater owners throughout the country to "give serious thought to the matter of withholding screen time" from *MONSIEUR VERDOUX*.[9]

In such a climate, where everyone felt the compulsion to prove his 100% Americanism, the outpouring of anticommunist political message films began.

One of the first defectors from Soviet ideology after World War II was Igor Gouzenko, a code clerk in the Russian embassy in Canada. When, in his personal account, he divulged the extent of the Soviet spy network throughout North America, the book furthered anti-Russian public opinion. Perhaps fortuitously, *THE IRON CURTAIN* (1948), based on Gouzenko's disclosures, appeared only a few months after the HUAC hearings had begun; if there were any question about Hollywood's "loyalty," this film, seemingly, bent over backward to prove otherwise. In 1939 *CONFESSIONS OF A NAZI SPY* was an eye opener; in 1948 *THE IRON CURTAIN* might have been more aptly called "Confessions of a Russian Spy." In both cases these films served to alert the public that an erstwhile ally was operating an extensive spy apparatus.

The Russians were also denounced in *THE RED MENACE* (1949), *THE RED DANUBE* (1949), *GUILTY OF TREASON* (1949), *I MARRIED A COMMUNIST* (1949), and *I WAS A COMMUNIST FOR THE F.B.I.* (1951).

THE RED MENACE tells of a disillusioned ex-GI who is duped into joining the Party because he wants to bring about social reforms. He meets the traditional types one would expect in a Party cell: the girl who converted to Marxism because of her poverty-stricken childhood, the revolutionary poet-intellectual, the Negro student who dreams of the liberation of his people, and a European refugee who joined because her father had been a member in Europe. They all have their disillusioning "darkness at noon" and try to break away, but learn that the Party can exert pressure on defectors.

THE RED DANUBE told of Soviet repression in a different setting, post-war Vienna. Although the Austrian capital was supposed to be equally governed by the four powers, the film stressed deceit in the day-to-day roundup of displaced persons doomed to forceful repatriation.

Few stories that emerged from the Cold War inflamed public opinion in the West as much as the trial on Moscow's manufactured charges against Josef Cardinal Mindszenty, the Primate of Hungary. It was inevitable that in an anticommunist cycle a film should deal with the Soviet's campaign against religion. *GUILTY OF TREASON* was based on the book *As We See Russia*, by members of the Overseas Press Club of America, which tried to dramatize published reports of what was taking place in Budapest. Cardinal Mindszenty,

V

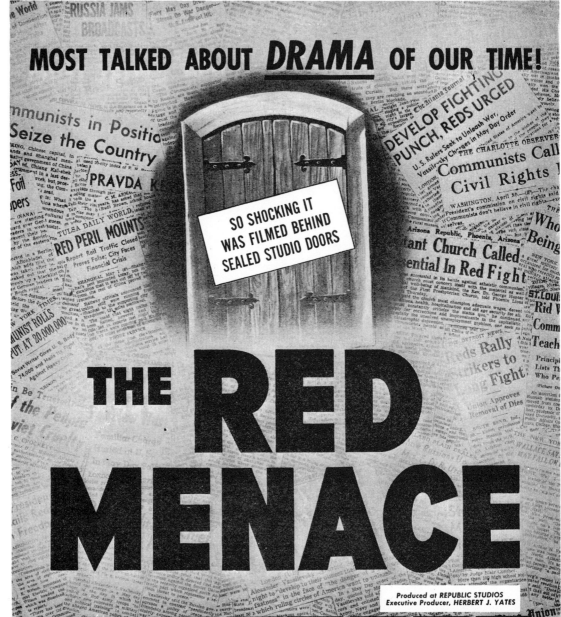

MOST TALKED ABOUT **DRAMA** OF OUR TIME!

SO SHOCKING IT WAS FILMED BEHIND SEALED STUDIO DOORS

THE RED MENACE

Produced at REPUBLIC STUDIOS
Executive Producer, HERBERT J. YATES

BILL JONES
The ex-GI who almost lost everything he fought for!

NINA
The girl who came to breed hate but instead learned to love!

SOLOMON
He gave his life rather than bend to the yoke of tyranny!

MOLLIE
The seductive party girl used as man-bait!

FATHER LEARY
The fearless, fighting priest who conquered evil with faith!

YVONNE
A power-hungry psychopathic, love-starved woman of destruction!

REACHI
MURDERED... because he defied the terroristic underground!

TYLER
Trapped in the web of violence he set for unsuspecting victims!

THE
CELLULOID
WEAPON

124

played by Charles Bickford, symbolized the resistance of the Hungarian people to a takeover by Stalinism, and the film revealed how he was discredited and imprisoned.

During the first hearings in 1947 of the House Un-American Activities Committee, not all "suspected" fellow travelers were called before the self-styled tribunal. As a result of the internecine accusations and counteraccusations that infected the various Hollywood talent guilds as well as the entire industry, the overt layoffs and blacklisting were earnestly vengeful. Director Joseph Losey, who himself was blacklisted in the Fifties, has recalled that a script for a film initially titled *I MARRIED A COMMUNIST* became a literary touchstone for determining who was or wasn't a Red. The logic (or illogic) of the ploy hardly would do credit to a hack scriptwriter like "Pat Hobby": offer the script to any director suspected of being a "pinko" and if he turned it down, QED, he was. Thirteen directors turned it down, one of whom was Losey himself.[10] The film was finally made at Howard Hughes's RKO studio, but its title was eventually changed to *THE WOMAN ON PIER 13*. In this film the communists were instigating labor strife on the San Francisco docks. Again there was the repetition of the theme of brutal retribution against a Party member who "tries to get out of line."

If the anticommunist message had not been hammered home enough by the Jack L. Warners and other Hollywood moguls to prove to the paying public that they were all indeed patriotic Americans, any lingering doubt was dispelled by *I WAS A COMMUNIST FOR THE F.B.I.* Here Warner Brothers used the celluloid weapon like a battering ram, wildly and even irresponsibly. What was reprehensible in this film was not its fawning approbation of the HUAC hearings, but rather the vicious stereotyping of schoolteachers, Negroes, and laborers as easy targets for communist proselytizers. It was unfortunate that during a period when such films as *CROSSFIRE, PINKY,* and *GENTLEMAN'S AGREEMENT* were urging rationality in social interaction such a divisive film should be released. Movies like *I WAS A COMMUNIST FOR THE F.B.I.* are naturals for the Inspiration Hour at annual conventions of the John Birch Society.

The caution which pervaded Hollywood in the final years of the Forties and the reluctance to treat any subject which might incur the pointed finger of the HUAC were illustrated in *ALL MY SONS* (1948). When Arthur Miller's stage play about war profiteering was brought to the screen the emphasis was shifted to the indictment of one culpable individual rather than the broader guilt of a social system which encourages the "blood money" acquired in wartime. Even in its muted form, however, Miller's antiwar viewpoint was unmistakable in the character of the greedy industrialist (Edward G. Robinson) who sells defective war goods to the Air Force.

A criticism of war that was less obvious (and consequently less controversial) than Miller's began to appear in films that looked at World War II retrospectively. *BATTLEGROUND* in 1949 was what the publicity pundits called *THE BIG PARADE* of the Second World War. *BATTLEGROUND*

V

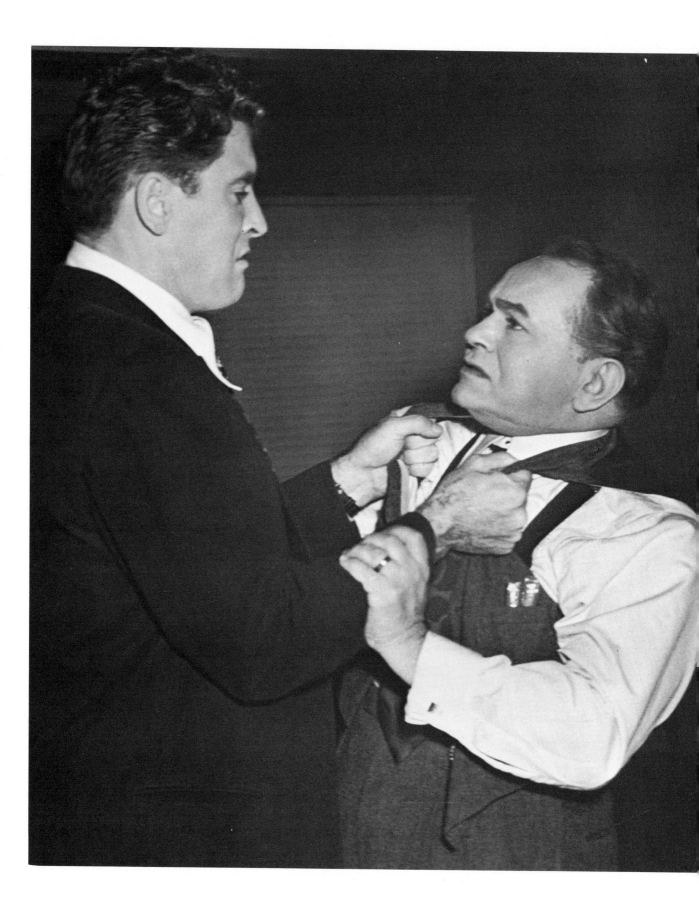

had its measure of the heroics that marked so many of the films of the war years themselves, but the overall effect went far beyond an *ACTION IN THE NORTH ATLANTIC* (1943) or *BACK TO BATAAN* (1945). In its dramatization of the circumstances of the Battle of the Bulge, *BATTLEGROUND* did not deny the hardship and sterility of war. The sage of the GI, stripped of patriotic slogans and slugging it through the winter mud, was in no sense a glorification of military exploits. Implicitly *BATTLEGROUND* asked of all warring nations, Why?

As critic Pauline Kael has aptly remarked, it's unfortunate that pacifism always flourishes between wars. True, the antiwar viewpoint in *BATTLEGROUND* did not have the persuasive force of *ALL QUIET ON THE WESTERN FRONT* or *THE CASE OF SERGEANT GRISCHA*, but the winds of public opinion, to which the mass media are so sensitive, precluded the introspection that marked these older films. Even while *BATTLEGROUND* was being shown in theaters, the United States had already had a confrontation with the Russians in Iran and Berlin, and within a few months we would be engaged in another large-scale war, in Korea.

V

All My Sons with Burt Lancaster
and Edward G. Robinson
(Universal-International)

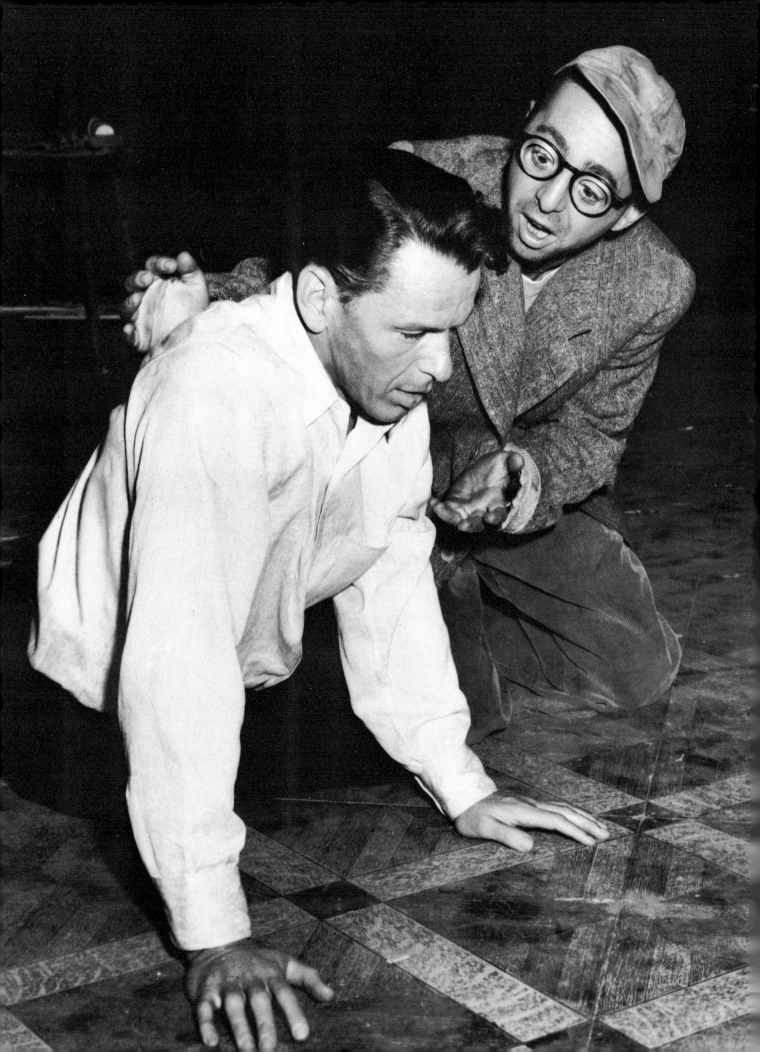

VI

The A-Bomb and Sci-Fi Messages

The HUAC Witch Hunt: Round 2

Anticommunism — John Wayne Style

The Return of the Mobsters

"On the Waterfront"

Biberman's "Salt of the Earth"

Chaplin vs. McCarthyism

Examining Prejudice Against Nisei and Chicanos

Negroes in Films of the Fifties

"The Defiant Ones"

Indians and "Broken Arrow": A Turning Point

Drugs

Alcoholism

Juvenile Delinquency

The "Blackboard Jungle" Controversy

Counterfeit Youth Movies

"Of course art has a social function. We are social
beings and live in a society. If you don't want to
recognize that then you have to live without the
products of society, without any obligations to
society and without any obligations on the part of
society to you. Anyone who feels that strongly
that art has no social function should go to the
proverbial desert island."

Joseph Losey[1]

Frank Sinatra and Arnold Stang in
The Man with the Golden Arm
(United Artists)

129

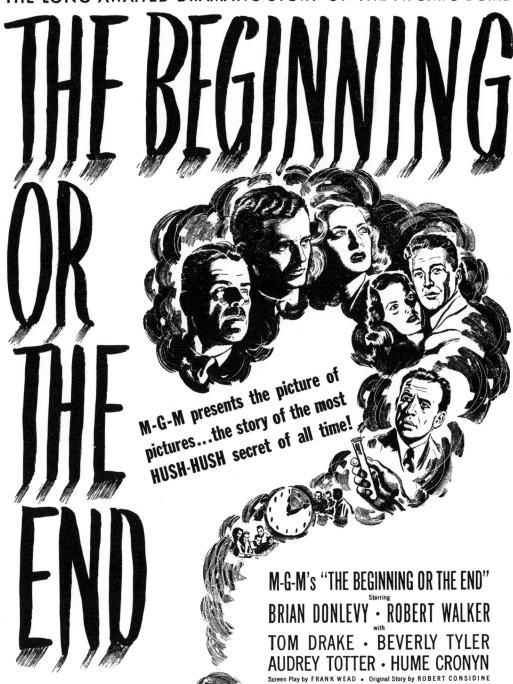

THE LONG-AWAITED DRAMATIC STORY OF THE ATOMIC BOMB

THE BEGINNING OR THE END

M-G-M presents the picture of pictures...the story of the most HUSH-HUSH secret of all time!

Look into the forbidden city! Meet the girl who lost her identity—the only girl who knew the world's most terrifying secret!

M-G-M's "THE BEGINNING OR THE END"

Starring

BRIAN DONLEVY · ROBERT WALKER

with

TOM DRAKE · BEVERLY TYLER
AUDREY TOTTER · HUME CRONYN

Screen Play by FRANK WEAD · Original Story by ROBERT CONSIDINE
Directed by NORMAN TAUROG · Produced by SAMUEL MARX
A METRO-GOLDWYN-MAYER PICTURE

World War II ended abruptly with the dropping of the A-bomb on Hiroshima and Nagasaki. For as long as man lives on this planet the connotations of that day in late summer of 1945 will cast a pall on human existence. Though more than 200,000 people died in Japan from two relatively small nuclear bombs, so far, in his bumbling, groping way man over the past quarter of a century has managed to avoid repeating such an act of horror. As Albert Einstein, the scientist whose theories fathered the atomic age, warned, if civilization is not entirely wiped out in a future nuclear war, at least two thirds of the world's population would die.

For the Hollywood filmmaker the subject of the atomic bomb and its human consequences is both provocative and fascinating, while at the same time it defies congruence with the basic pleasure principle of the American film. Moreover, the fact that in nearly three decades so few films have even been made referring to atomic destruction may be because writers, directors, and producers (like people on the *other* side of the screen) are reluctant to consider The Bomb's implications.

The first film that dealt with the atomic bomb was *THE BEGINNING OR THE END* (1947). Within a fictional framework, not without a romantic subplot of a young scientist and his bride, the film was a reenactment of the development of the A-bomb, from the signal by FDR to begin the Manhattan Project, the mustering of science and industry to make the bomb, its first test at Los Alamos, and finally its being unleashed over Japan. *THE BEGINNING OR THE END* took no sides in the controversy that has always surrounded the decision to drop the bomb; its message was as problematical as its title — man must harness atomic energy for the betterment of human life or be hounded by the possibility of total global annihilation.

Another nuclear bomb is dropped in the futuristic *FIVE* (1951), with the awesome aftermath predicted by scientists. Arch Oboler's film hypothesized a situation in which only five people are left after a global holocaust. Even this microcosm of man's society cannot live together for mutual survival; there is the usual bickering, jealousy, and mistrust, and even racist elements in their relationship. The sole Negro of the group is killed by an arrogant, hateful mountain climber. In the end only two are left, a young girl and an idealistic young man — the symbolic Adam and Eve of the Brave New World. Although his typologies were somewhat obvious, Oboler's film was the first of the "bomb psychology" movies to contemplate what the world would be like after an atomic Apocalypse.

After the war Science became the new Delphic oracle. On one hand, scientific accomplishments offered a vision of conquering age-old diseases, of a better environment through the control of natural forces, and a materialistic well-being hitherto undreamed of. On the other hand, since it was the scientists themselves who had created the atomic bomb and were working in the secret laboratories of germ and chemical warfare, their very probing into the unknowns of the universe engendered anxiety on the part of the ordinary citizen. Because he had little if anything to say about the direction of science,

VI

the everyman Joe Smith, American, often turned to science fiction. Even if he couldn't solve a quadratic equation, he could at least pick up the jargon of the Scientific Conversation.

A dominant theme of science fiction is the notion that the universe contains distant planets inhabited by beings of superintelligence who are far ahead of mere earthlings in both material and spiritual wisdom. In *THE DAY THE EARTH STOOD STILL* (1951), one of these superior out-of-space creatures (Michael Rennie) is an emissary to Washington whose mission is to inculcate political morality and peaceful coexistence on this planet. To prove that other planets will not tolerate an Earth whose atomic fuse is already glowing, the soft-spoken, intellectual Martian temporarily neutralizes the world's electric power. The message is patently clear: Shape up, Earth!

Another vein of the science-fiction message film was *THE NEXT VOICE YOU HEAR* (1950). Far from the fantasies of Jules Verne or H. G. Wells with their souped-up flying saucers, ray guns, and Buck Rogers decor, *THE NEXT VOICE YOU HEAR* was closer to the writings of C. S. Lewis as a unique religious-philosophical parable. In the film a Voice is heard over the radio one night which says, "This is God. I will be with you for the next few days." The medium of radio thus becomes the new Tower of Babel in reverse; this time all peoples of the world hear the message in their native tongue. Incredulity sets in. Is Orson Welles loose again on the airwaves? Is this a super-colossal Madison Avenue ad campaign? Even science can't explain this phenomenon, and the people of the world are fearful. When the Voice is heard the following night, they accept it as truly God speaking to them. He admonishes the world's people that they have abandoned the principles of mutual trust, *caritas*, and brotherhood. "You are like children going to school," God says. "You have forgotten some of your lessons. I ask you to do your homework." After the six-

The Next Voice You Hear with
James Whitmore
(Metro-Goldwyn-Mayer)

day series of "broadcasts," the people resolve to turn away from divisive
hatred and build a better world. Seen against the social malaise of the Fifties
— with its international tensions — this Dore Schary production was a one-
of-a-kind message film.

In 1951 the House Un-American Activities Committee, now with tough
competition for newspaper headlines from the Joe McCarthy and Pat McCarran
investigative committees, came back to Hollywood for a reprise performance.
The events of the Korean war — actually the first time that American soldiers
faced communists in open conflict — as well as the trial of Julius and Ethel
Rosenberg for wartime espionage on behalf of the Russians strengthened public
support of such congressional probes. During the 1951 go-round the HUAC
was not concerned so much with obviously pro-Russian films as *MISSION TO
MOSCOW* as with any film which had the slightest contraband political element. In its annual report for 1951, the committee said, "We are less interested
in a film that has Communist context, where a few hundred people will come
and see it. We are more interested in an ordinary John-and-Mary picture where
there is only a drop of progressive thought in it." By the end of the hearings in
1952, a list of 324 names denounced as communists was made public. The
American Legion provided 56 additional suspects, and later 300 more names.
The majority of these people were blacklisted and barred from employment
at the studios.

Some of the Hollywood people accused on one or another of the "lists"
went abroad to continue working in films; others like scenarists Nedrick
Young, Waldo Salt, and Dalton Trumbo went "underground" and sold scripts
under pseudonyms. When "Robert Rich" won the Academy Award for the
best screen story of 1956, *THE BRAVE ONE*, the hypocrisy of blacklisting was
exposed, since everyone knew that "Rich" was really Dalton Trumbo.

VI

As the second round of HUAC hearings began, it was not long before another wave of anticommunist political message films reached the nation's theaters. Leo McCarey's MY SON JOHN (1952) was in its own emotional, super-patriotic way a worthy bedfellow to the earlier I WAS A COMMUNIST FOR THE F.B.I. The film centered on a mother who suspects her intellectual son of being a communist solely through "guilt by association." Helen Hayes and Dean Jagger were the distraught parents eaten with paranoid guilt that they may have nurtured a traitor to their 110% Americanism. They (and the film) equate being good citizens with an ultra-right stance that included distrust of intellectuals (especially those on the East Coast), support of flag-waving Legionnaires, and literal, fundamentalist belief in the Bible. The boy, of course, learns too late that his parents' fears were well-justified, and he meets a violent death at the steps of the Lincoln Memorial in Washington.

Lest there be any misunderstanding that the House Un-American Activities Committee had its friends and supporters in Hollywood, BIG JIM McCLAIN (1952) should dispel any doubts. The film was a panegyric to the intrepid congressmen of the committee. It began with a narrator's voice over footage of the Capitol intoning a tribute to the antisubversive work of the HUAC and the congressmen who are "undaunted by the vicious campaign of slander launched against them." McLain was an investigator for such a committee who goes to Hawaii to uncover a communist plot. The part of "Big Jim" was, of course, a natural for John Wayne, not only because the Duke was just the man to land that Sunday punch on the communist's kisser, but also because it expressed his own political ideology. Wayne was, after all, a president of The Motion Picture Alliance for the Preservation of American Ideals, which had been formed to counter the pinkos in the industry.

A more substantial look at Soviet-inspired subversion was WALK EAST ON BEACON (1952). Suggested by J. Edgar Hoover's report The Crime of the Century, the film detailed the operations of the FBI in apprehending a master spy from Russia and his Washington cohorts. Although essentially an FBI dragnet opus, it avoided the hectoring and name calling of MY SON JOHN.

That denunciation of the communist totalitarian philosophy need not be a maudlin, simplistic recital of warmed-over espionage plots filled with snarling spies, counterspies, and double agents was evident in Robert E. Sherwood's screenplay for MAN ON A TIGHTROPE (1953). Set in Soviet-dominated Czechoslovakia, this film was about a Czech circus group trying to escape from the state's grip. In its strong avowal of the freedom of thought and movement which is stringently curtailed behind the Iron Curtain, MAN ON A TIGHT-ROPE made a sober commentary on political repression.

The gangster and crime film generally has fluctuated between a virtual flood of releases and a mere trickle. The genre came into being when Prohibition spawned the era of the bootleggers (which in turn brought on the first big organized gangs), and it reached its peak in the early Thirties. After the strictures of the Production Code against glorifying criminals, the "big mob" movies were gone. To be sure, there have always been criminal personalities in films

Robert Walker and Helen Hayes in
My Son John (Paramount)

— Duke Mantee in the 1936 *THE PETRIFIED FOREST* was like a predatory refugee from the age of Little Caesar — but he was alone. Although the small-time hood still hung around the tenements of *DEAD END*, by 1937 the mobster was already being seen in retrospect, as in *THE LAST GANGSTER*. Indicative of what had happened, in this film Edward G. Robinson acted a once-powerful gang lord who upon his release from prison tries unsuccessfully to make a comeback. *THE ROARING TWENTIES* (1939), was an even more stylized chronicle of a bygone period. James Cagney, who had symbolized the curled-lip gangster, again met a violent death. "What was his business?" a cop asks as he bends over the gunned-down Cagney on the steps of a church. "He used to be a big shot," Gladys George replies. Parenthetically, Cagney did not appear again as a gangster until *WHITE HEAT* (1949), having in the meantime romanced Bette Davis in *THE BRIDE CAME C.O.D.* (1941), played George M. Cohan, and worked as a French underground leader in *13 RUE MADELEINE* (1946).

After World War II Big Crime was again much in the public mind. With such corporate titles as Murder, Inc., "the Syndicate," and an organization

VI

135

The Set-Up with Audrey Totter
and Robert Ryan (RKO Radio)

J. Carrol Naish and Gene Kelly
in *Black Hand*
(Metro-Goldwyn-Mayer)

THE

CELLULOID

WEAPON

that communicated gambling information under the high-sounding name Continental Press Service, postwar organized crime gave the public a new kind of crime directory. Names like "Legs" Diamond, Al Capone, "Bugs" Moran, and Roger Touhy were replaced in the Forties by Joe Adonis, the Anastasia brothers, and Louis "Lepke" Buchalter. The change from open gang violence to more white-gloved racketeering was reflected in the films of the period.

Abraham Polonsky's FORCE OF EVIL (1948) dissected the numbers racket. The story dealt with a lawyer (John Garfield) who gets involved with a policy racket gang to help his brother, and then becomes a frightened victim of the underworld himself. This film, like so many others, connected the racketeer with greedy politicians and corrupt law officials — "the links in the system," as D. W. Griffith had described such palm-greasing in his THE MUSKETEERS OF PIG ALLEY.

Organized crime also "muscled" its way into sports events, including the fixing of boxing matches, bribery of players in professional and even college athletics, and the perennial bookmaking on horse races. Among several postwar boxing films was Robert Wise's THE SET-UP (1949), a highly effective, low-key narrative of a fading boxer who refuses to throw a fight. Because the racketeers have wagered heavily on his opponent, he is mercilessly beaten up by them after the bout.

In 1951 Estes Kefauver's Special Committee to Investigate Crime in Interstate Commerce became true-to-life "Gangbusters" on television screens, and the number of crime movies again increased. In excoriating the nationwide Syndicate his committee was investigating, Senator Kefauver pointed out that it was a "loosely organized but cohesive coalition of autonomous crime 'locals' which worked together for mutual profit." Behind these local chapters was a vague home office known euphemistically as the Mafia.

BLACK HAND (1950) described the Mafia terror in a neighborhood of Italian-Americans. The setting was not contemporary New York, however, but the first decade of the century. Through the framework of the past we see what was still happening in the Fifties — extortion, beatings, and the web of fear encompassed by the black hand.

A rash of "confidential" exposés of organized crime followed: THE RACKET (1951), HOODLUM EMPIRE (1952), THE CAPTIVE CITY (1952), in which Kefauver appeared in the epilogue, KANSAS CITY CONFIDENTIAL (1952), THE MIAMI STORY (1954), THE PHENIX CITY STORY (1955), and INSIDE DETROIT (1956). Most of them were based on actual events which had received wide coverage in the press, and all had in common a crusading inquiry into the crime network in America. Phil Karlson's THE PHENIX CITY STORY, for example, took as its subject the real-event murder of Albert Patterson, an anticorruption crusader in an Alabama city, who at the time he was murdered was running for Attorney General of the state.

One of the prime targets for investigation by the Kefauver committee was labor racketeering on the docks of New York City. Waterfront crime and its

VI

Rod Steiger and Marlon Brando in
On the Waterfront (Columbia)

tie-up with the Mafia were sharply brought to the public's attention by *New York Sun* reporter Malcolm Johnson, who won the Pulitzer Prize in 1949 for his series. Johnson's articles motivated Budd Schulberg to write the script for one of the best films of the Fifties, *ON THE WATERFRONT* (1954), directed by Elia Kazan.

Marlon Brando was Terry Malloy, the not-too-bright ex-prizefighter who unwittingly becomes the tool of the mob which controls the longshoremen's union. Duped by his brother, the shady lawyer for mobster Johnny Friendly, Malloy becomes the patsy when a rebelling longshoreman is murdered. However, when the brother himself is slain by the mob, Malloy testifies before an investigating commission and is instrumental in freeing the union from its criminal yoke. Malloy, the stumblebum who loved pigeons, was a far cry from the usual Hollywood hero; but he is kin to the many inarticulate John Does of the world who find within themselves the courage and strength to fight back against evil.

Labor and unionism were the subject of two other films of the Fifties, *THE WHISTLE AT EATON FALLS* (1951) and *SALT OF THE EARTH* (1954). Produced by Louis de Rochemont, *THE WHISTLE AT EATON FALLS* made a plea to both labor and management for mutual consideration of each other's interests. A union leader becomes the president of a New England mill in severe economic straits. Faced with dual loyalties, he must reconcile the in-

Salt of the Earth
(Independent Production Corp.)

stallation of automated devices with an attendant reduction of union personnel. When the mill is temporarily closed, his old cohorts are angry. His credibility is restored (perhaps in too much of a *deus ex machina* that dodges the real issue) when a new gadget that can be manufactured by these new machines proves highly marketable. The unemployed men are rehired, and the community returns to its former prosperity.

A more polemic depiction of laborers' problems was Herbert J. Biberman's *SALT OF THE EARTH*, the only film produced completely by a team of creative people blacklisted after the HUAC proceedings. Although the basis for the plot was a 1951 strike of Mexican-American zinc miners in New Mexico, the dramatic emphasis was on the factionalism within the miners' union, as the miners' wives themselves struggle for the right to participate in the strike with their husbands. Heavily propagandistic in its support of the union, the film scored mine operators who take advantage of the Chicano labor force and the tactics of brutal strikebreaking police. Although the exploitation of the Chicanos in Silver City, New Mexico, could easily be documented, *SALT OF THE EARTH* tried too hard to proselytize, with the result that in its own way it was as haranguing and overheated as *MY SON JOHN* on the other end of the political spectrum.

However controversial its political message, the reported circumstances surrounding the production and distribution of this film are appalling. Given

VI

139

that the film was sponsored by the International Union of Mine, Mill, and Smelter Workers, which had been expelled from the CIO in 1950 as being communist-dominated, and given the fact that the credits included such blacklistees as Michael Wilson and Paul Jarrico as well as Biberman, the film deserved its fair place in the "free marketplace of thought." This it clearly did not receive. During the shooting of the film the company was harassed by self-appointed vigilantes, and the actress who played the lead, Rosaura Revueltas, was arrested as an "illegal alien." Biberman has described the virtual impossibility of finding laboratories to develop, print, and cut the film. When the film was finally ready for showing, union theater projectionists refused to screen it.[2] Biberman's Independent Productions Corporation brought an unsuccessful suit against Loew's Incorporated and 67 other defendants charging violation of the antitrust law in hindering distribution of the film.

By the mid-Fifties the inquisitional fervor that characterized Senator McCarthy at the height of his power had abated. McCarthy himself had suffered a humiliating censure from his fellow senators and was no longer newsworthy. The House Un-American Activities Committee also ran out of steam. Its "reign of terror" was relegated to the extremist right-wingers of the John Birch Society and allied organizations. In the aftermath of McCarthyism, however, several films appeared with themes generated by the troublesome political issues the senator had inflamed.

STORM CENTER (1956) suggested the cancerous effects of national political hysteria on a typical American town. The victim of this local witch hunt is a middle-aged, widowed librarian (Bette Davis) who refuses to remove a book called *The Communist Dream* from the stacks of her library. Typical of the tenor of the times, she is labeled a "Red" by the community and put on "trial" by the town council board. The ending of the film is frighteningly symbolic of what had happened in Nazi Germany as the library is set afire by a youth goaded by his bigoted father.

Among the many innocent targets of McCarthy's free-swinging charges was a civilian employee of the Navy named Abraham Chasanow, who lost his job because he was branded a "security risk." The Chasanow case, which became the basis of another Pulitzer Prize-winning investigation, represented the dilemma of those whose loyalty was impugned by unidentified accusers. *THREE BRAVE MEN* (1957) was a fictionalized treatment of l'affaire Chasanow, and showed how one man fought back and eventually cleared himself.

The last word on the *yahooism* of the McCarthy reign was, perhaps fittingly, Charles Chaplin's *A KING IN NEW YORK*, made in England in 1957 after vituperative finger pointing goaded him to leave the United States. Despite Chaplin's telegram to the HUAC stating, "I am not a Communist, neither have I ever joined any political party or organization in my life," he was not immunized against the winds of xenophobic hatred that blew so strongly in McCarthy's wake. Just as he had taken on the absurdities of Hitler and Musso-

lini in *THE GREAT DICTATOR*, Chaplin now made congressional committees his satiric bull's-eye.

Charlie played the refugee King of Estrovia who comes to America when a revolution upsets his throne. Penniless, his only source of income is making television commercials. Eventually he takes under his wing a runaway boy whose parents are being investigated because of their political affiliations. Through "guilt by association" with the boy, King Shahdov himself is subpoenaed to testify. In a devilish put-down of the hypocritical pomposity of many congressional investigations, Shahdov turns the hearings into a shambles by aiming a firehose at the inquisitors. The film ends, however, on a muted, sardonic note. The boy, advised that it will help his parents, "cracks" and divulges the identity of their political confreres — the old Hitler *Jugend* technique. Like the disillusioned Chaplin himself, King Shahdov is so saddened by the hatred and distrust in America that he goes to Europe to make his home.

At certain anxiety-ridden times the voice of one particular subgroup in the United States seems to drown out competing opinions. The witch hunting of a J. Parnell Thomas, Pat McCarran, of Joseph McCarthy, however, were not new to Americans who remembered the "red scare" of the early Twenties. It is not too unlikely, considering the variance of American society, that the face of a new congressional demagogue could dominate the wall-sized TV screens of the 1980s.

Social irresponsibility that threatened the life-blood of a community was a repeated theme in many films of the Fifties. Just as *BLACK LEGION* uncovered a hooded organization that terrorized Detroit in the Thirties, *STORM WARNING* (1951) examined the problem of ultra-right, racist groups like the Ku Klux Klan which also existed in the Fifties (as indeed they do today). In *STORM WARNING* the Klan is a vicious gang of intimidators in a small Deep South locale. When the district attorney brings a trigger-happy Klansman to trial for murdering an investigative reporter, he has to overcome the mores of the community on which the Klan thrives.

The recurrent subject of earlier films like *FURY, THEY WON'T FORGET,* and *THE OX-BOX INCIDENT* in the Thirties and Forties emerged again in *TRY AND GET ME*, released in 1951. Here again a lynch mob takes its vengeance in an atmosphere of social irrationality. The victims in this case, however, are themselves violent hoodlums — one of them had brutally killed a youth they kidnaped. Criminals as these men are, the film does not condone the action of the mob which denies them due process of law. Violence is a social disease, stresses the film; it can be solved only by reason and understanding.

Although lacking the importance of the initial cycle of antiprejudice films of the late Forties, such as *CROSSFIRE* and *LOST BOUNDARIES*, the numerous movies with similar themes in the Fifties explored a wider spectrum of interracial relationships.

Like *HOME OF THE BRAVE*, several films which stressed understanding and tolerance of other races and nationalities had a war background. *GO FOR*

BROKE (1951) paid an overdue tribute to the 442nd Regimental Combat Team made up of Nisei who fought with great distinction in the European campaign. Their bravery under fire earns them the respect and plaudits of their fellow soldiers, even the bigoted Texas lieutenant who was out to test their mettle. *THREE STRIPES IN THE SUN* (1955) also revealed changed attitudes toward the Japanese. Set in postwar Japan, the film was based on the true story of M/Sgt. Hugh O'Reilly of the Bronx who overcomes his wartime hatred for the enemy and is the spearhead in establishing a home for Japanese orphans. A subtheme dealt with the interracial marriage of O'Reilly and a Japanese girl.

In King Vidor's *JAPANESE WAR BRIDE* (1952) the marriage between an Asiatic and a white American took on primary emphasis. A Korean war veteran brings his lovely Nipponese bride home to the Salinas country in California. The long-standing racial animosities, on both sides, between Americans and Japanese threaten their marriage — a problem which many service marriages

Mitsuko Kimura and Aldo Ray in
Three Stripes in the Sun
(Columbia)

VI

Marlon Brando, Red Buttons, and
Miyoshi Umeki in *Sayonara*
(Warner Brothers)

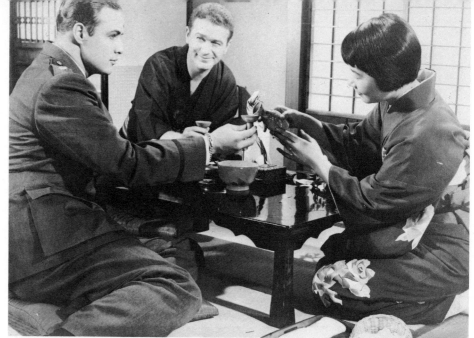

Spencer Tracy and Ernest Borgnine
in *Bad Day at Black Rock*
(Metro-Goldwyn-Mayer)

Trial with Dorothy McGuire, Katy
Jurado, Rafael Campos, Glenn
Ford, and Arthur Kennedy
(Metro-Goldwyn-Mayer)

THE

CELLULOID

WEAPON

144

faced. SAYONARA (1957), an updated "Madame Butterfly," showed that interracial love matches could end in tragedy because of prejudice. When Sgt. Kelly (played superbly by Red Buttons) is officially denied the right to take his Japanese bride home to America, they both commit suicide.

Wartime prejudice within our borders was the basis of an outstanding message film of 1955, John Sturges's BAD DAY AT BLACK ROCK. Spencer Tracy, a lame-armed veteran, arrives at a whistle-stop desert town in California to deliver a medal to the Japanese father of one of his men who had died a hero. When told that the father, too, is dead, Tracy probes the hostility which the townspeople barely conceal. He uncovers the entire unsavory circumstances in which the Japanese farmer had been slain, and which the whole town is equally guilty of covering up. Tracy, too, must now face the fury of the corrupted community.

Even before Cesar Chavez drew the eyes of the nation to the plight of the Chicano migratory farm laborers who comprise the majority of Mexican-Americans, Hollywood dealt with prejudice against them. In the 1950 Joseph Losey film THE LAWLESS a young "fruit tramp" is hunted down by a hate-filled mob in a northern California community after the boy had hit a cop in a dancehall scuffle. The literal persecution of the Chicano is symbolic of the larger antagonism toward all Mexican-Americans in the town. In this picture, as in many others dealing with prejudice, there is a young, idealistic, liberal "outsider" — a reporter, editor, or lawyer — who takes up the cause of the oppressed and himself incurs the wrath of the bigots. In THE LAWLESS it is the editor of the town weekly who serves as the conscience of whatever vestige of decency is left among the townspeople to ensure the boy a fair trial.

A Mexican-American farm laborer is also the pivotal character in MY MAN AND I (1952). Chu Chu Ramirez, who has a simple faith in the goodness of people, is cheated consistently of his wages and even railroaded to jail, and before he is finally vindicated he has learned at firsthand the consequences of prejudice.

The irrational violence of the mob against a Mexican-American youth is also depicted in TRIAL (1955). The setting is again a California town, where a young Chicano is accused of assaulting a teenage girl, thereby causing her fatal heart failure. In one of the several messages of the film, the community reveals its hysteria when the townspeople attempt to lynch the boy. To intensify the racial theme, the judge who presides at the trial is a Negro who refuses to be coerced by any faction. An anticommunist message is also included in the character of a lawyer who is ostensibly defending the boy, but only wants to make him a martyr to further the communist cause at a New York rally. Through the efforts of a calm, methodical law professor who also serves on the defense team, the communist lawyer's ulterior motive is exposed, the boy is given a fair trial, and the town grudgingly is forced to acknowledge its own culpability.

Other films which dealt with animosity toward Mexican-Americans were RIGHT CROSS (1950), THE RING (1952), both about exploitation of Chicanos

VI

Dorothy Dandridge, Philip
Hepburn, and Barbara Ann
Sanders (front) in *Bright Road*
(Metro-Goldwyn-Mayer)

in boxing, and *MAN IN THE SHADOW* (1957) in which Orson Welles acted
a despotic rancher responsible for the fatal beating of a Mexican worker.
GIANT (1956) contained a contraband subtheme about a kind of Jim Crowism
which treated Chicanos as second-class Texans. A memorable scene occurs
in a roadside cafe where "Bick Benedict" defends the right of his Mexican
daughter-in-law to eat there.

The Negro as seen in the immediate postwar film had certainly come a
long way from the shuffling Uncle Remus types, obsequious servants, and
tapdancing shoeshine boys whose hearts belonged to Dixie. It might have appeared that *NO WAY OUT* in 1950 was the beginning of an even franker and
more substantive inquiry into America's deepest problem, racial inequality.
But in retrospect it becomes clear that *NO WAY OUT* was the end of that
particular cycle represented by *HOME OF THE BRAVE, PINKY,* and *LOST
BOUNDARIES.* True, *NO WAY OUT,* with its crazed gangster who inflames a
racial outburst, was somewhat contrived, but the shift in locale to the Negro
ghetto was a recognition that there were sterner realities of the issue demanding attention.

This is not to say that Hollywood abandoned making films during the
Fifties in which Negro-white relationships were central to the plot. On the
contrary, there was an increasing number of such films, all of them refuting
the canard that Hollywood was color blind. What is most evident in the racial-
prejudice films of the Fifties is that it was no longer an anomaly to see Negroes
as integral characters. The Fifties was the decade in which a black actor,
Sidney Poitier, began to establish himself as a box-office star.

The Well (United Artists)

In some early films of the Fifties, Negroes were actually principal characters, notably in *THE JACKIE ROBINSON STORY* (1950), *NATIVE SON* (1951), *BRIGHT ROAD* (1953), with Dorothy Dandridge, and *THE JOE LOUIS STORY* (1953). Whether depicting a famous sports figure, a black schoolteacher, or an angry black man in revolt, these films had in common the need for audiences to experience racial prejudice through the black man's eyes.

Alfred E. Green's *THE JACKIE ROBINSON STORY*, with Robinson himself in the lead, did not sidestep the vehement bigotry within the Great American Sport. Even after Branch Rickey broke the color barrier and brought Robinson to the major leagues, the hecklers in both the grandstand and competing teams never let him forget the color of his skin.

Native Son, considered by many the greatest novel concerning the Negro experience in America, had the unique circumstance of having its author, Richard Wright, play the leading role in the screen version. Lacking the artistry of the novel, *NATIVE SON* nevertheless attempted to show a black man's rebellion against white society. Although Bigger Thomas is seen in the squalid South Side ghettos of Chicago, the film overemphasized mere verbal anger and unlike the novel provided little understanding of the socioecomonic pressures that forge the black man's bewilderment and outrage. Primarily because it was released through a small, independent distributor, *NATIVE SON* was exhibited in relatively few theaters.

An interesting dramatic situation, which obviously drew upon the Cathy Fiscus tragic news event, was the basis for *THE WELL* (1951). In this film, however, the child who has fallen into an abandoned well is a small Negro

VI

147

girl. Before the townspeople discover her whereabouts, inflammatory rumors that a white man had molested her have spread throughout the town's Negro section. Violence breaks out, but when the child is discovered in the well both black and white citizens work together to rescue her.

The stigma which Western society has generally attached to miscegenation, particularly involving blacks and whites, was treated in several films of this decade. They ranged from the historical antebellum *RAINTREE COUNTY* (1957) and *BAND OF ANGELS* (1957) to the World War II setting of *KINGS GO FORTH* (1958) and to contemporary times as in *THE VIEW FROM POMPEY'S HEAD* (1955) and *ISLAND IN THE SUN* (1957).

In *RAINTREE COUNTY* Elizabeth Taylor was the heroine obsessed with fear that she is part Negro; but in *BAND OF ANGELS*, Yvonne De Carlo actually learns (upon the death of her father) that she has Negro blood. Subsequently, she is sold into slavery and becomes the mistress of a New Orleans millionaire who buys her. Natalie Wood is caught in the web of negative attitudes toward mixed marriage in *KINGS GO FORTH*. She is an American-born girl living in France, and although her American Army lover learns that her father was a Negro he overcomes his bias.

Philip Dunne's *THE VIEW FROM POMPEY'S HEAD*, set in a Georgia town, concerns the efforts of a proud Southern belle to conceal from the world the fact that her husband, a famous novelist, has part-Negro ancestry. *ISLAND IN THE SUN* has a rich white planter, also with some black forebears, in addition to two interracial love affairs *plus* overtones of politically inspired racial tensions.

Two films of 1957, Martin Ritt's *EDGE OF THE CITY* and Richard Brooks's *SOMETHING OF VALUE*, both had main characters of different pigmentation who develop a close friendship. In *EDGE OF THE CITY* Sidney Poitier is murdered while defending John Cassavetes, his longshoreman buddy, during labor strife. *SOMETHING OF VALUE* tells of a white settler and his black

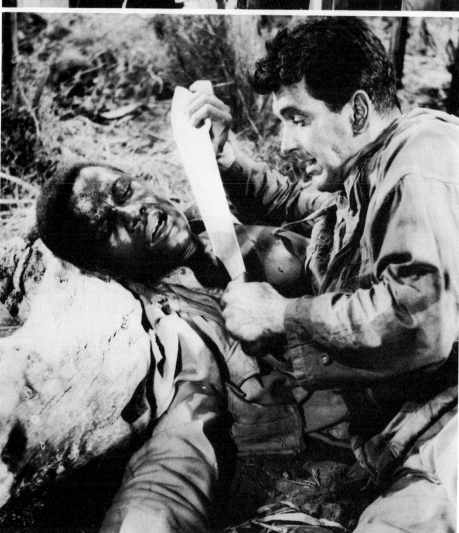

Edge of the City with John
Cassavetes and Sidney Poitier
(Metro-Goldwyn-Mayer)

Something of Value with Sidney
Poitier and Rock Hudson
(Metro-Goldwyn-Mayer)

VI

149

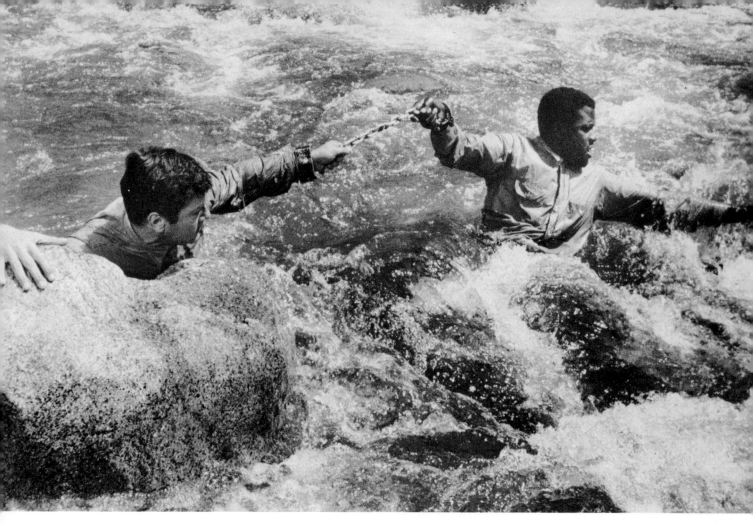

Tony Curtis and Sidney Poitier
in *The Defiant Ones*
(United Artists)

Kenyan friend during the Mau-Mau uprising. The forces of social injustice and oppression of the black natives drive them into warring camps. Poitier was also in this film, and opposite him was Rock Hudson.

This theme of the bond of brotherhood, despite color differences, was best expressed in Stanley Kramer's *THE DEFIANT ONES* (1958), with Tony Curtis and again Sidney Poitier. Through the simple plot situation in which two convicts who are shackled together escape from a prison camp, we see their relationship evolve from mutual hatred to mutual trust. Joined together at the wrists by unremovable chains the two outcasts must survive together or not at all. That the film was intentionally symbolic was made clear by its coscenarists Harold Jacob Smith and Nedrick Young in a letter to film critic Bosley Crowther, of the *New York Times:* "The real triumph, insofar as an author may be able to state it, lies in the two men overcoming a set of moribund mores learned from an abnormal social superstructure, which had originally made them think they were enemies."[3]

The acclaim accorded *THE DEFIANT ONES* contributed in large degree to the decline of the blacklist. Like many other "proscribed" writers who had gone underground, Ned Young used the pseudonym of Nathan E. Douglas on this script, for which "Douglas" received the Academy Award. By this time Hollywood filmmakers such as Kramer were fed up with the hypocrisy of the industry that purchased the scripts of blacklisted writers but denied them

screen credit under their real names. Kramer exposed the charade in an ironic "filmic" way. In the opening sequence of *THE DEFIANT ONES* there is a prison van transporting the shackled prisoners; Kramer cast the coscenarists as the drivers of the truck. The names Nathan E. Douglas and Harold Jacob Smith were superimposed under their faces when they appeared on the screen — to the delight of the cognoscenti.

Like Poitier, Harry Belafonte was the black protagonist in films whose plot situations depended on interracial relationships. In *ODDS AGAINST TOMORROW* (1959) Belafonte and Robert Ryan are smalltime criminals who plan and execute a robbery. Their partnership is far from amicable, however; the bigoted Ryan is verbally brutal in his scorn of his black accomplice. *THE WORLD, THE FLESH, AND THE DEVIL*, also released in 1959, had Belafonte as the survivor of a worldwide catastrophe caused by radioactive salt. In the deserted streets of Manhattan he meets another survivor — a white woman (Inger Stevens) — and together they manage to exist in the destroyed city. A love triangle develops with the introduction of another white character (Mel Ferrer), and the plot becomes a matter of who shall have the girl. The issue is evaded, however, and at the end the film opts for a threesome as Belafonte, Stevens, and Ferrer walk hand in hand down Wall Street.

With the exception of only a few films, Hollywood's treatment of the American Indian had been predicated on the familiar saying, "When a white

Odds Against Tomorrow with Harry Belafonte, Ed Begley, and Robert Ryan (United Artists)

VI

151

man wins it is a battle; when the Indians win it's a massacre." In the Westerns of the Fifties, however, the redman began to receive a fuller and fairer depiction — sans any disgruntled "Indian Defense League" or star-studded rally in Madison Square Garden to raise money for good public relations. *BROKEN ARROW* (1950) was the turning point, for in it, as in many films that followed, the Indian is shown more favorably than the white man. In *BROKEN ARROW* Cochise, always previously portrayed as a bloodthirsty Moloch of the Apaches, emerges as a gifted leader whose intelligence and dignity are taxed by the hate-filled settlers in Arizona. Taking a white man as his blood brother, he tries to make peace with the Army.

The Indian is also the victim of the white man's voracious landgrabbing in *DEVIL'S DOORWAY* (1950). Robert Taylor had an unusual role as the Shoshone who after serving with distinction in the Confederate army goes home to raise his cattle in peace. He suffers at the hands of doubledealing white traders and their unjust laws which deprive him of his land.

In several of these pro-Indian films a white man lives among the Indians and becomes a mediary for understanding between the antagonistic races. *THE SAVAGE* (1952), for example, has Charlton Heston as the white adopted member of the Sioux tribe threatened by the encroaching white settlers. Sometimes, as in *THE LIGHT IN THE FOREST* (1958), the pivotal agent for racial understanding is a youngster who had been captured by the Indians in a frontier raid and lived among them.

In its zeal to redress the wrongs done against the Indians, *SITTING BULL* (1954) played fast-and-loose with actual history to get across a pro-Indian message. After the battle of Little Big Horn, Sitting Bull meets with President Grant to make a treaty of peaceful coexistence for his people. In truth, however, Sitting Bull fled to Canada after the Custer debacle.

Paula Raymond and Robert
Taylor in *Devil's Doorway*
(Metro-Goldwyn-Mayer)

James Mason in *Bigger Than Life*
(Twentieth Century-Fox)

Marriage between a white man and an Indian woman was treated openly and sympathetically in *BROKEN LANCE* (1954). Here a cattle baron favors his halfbreed son over the children of his previous marriage to a white woman. As in similar films it is the Indian mother who is the calm, stabilizing "peacemaker" in the divided family.

If these numerous pro-Indian films attempted to give a more balanced view of Indian-white relations, even to the point of overstatement, it is apparent that most of them were concerned with America's frontier past. They did not show the contemporary Indian on the reservations with his problems of ill-housing, poor education, and exclusion from the mainstream of American life. The only film of the Fifties that approached depicting an Indian in a contemporary milieu was Michael Curtiz's *JIM THORPE — ALL AMERICAN* (1951), the biography of the noted Olympic champion.

The Fifties brought some major revisions in the motion picture Production Code, changes which permitted treatment of previously forbidden subjects. In regard to narcotics there had been less stringent rulings in such pictures as *TO THE ENDS OF THE EARTH* in the late Forties, but no film was permitted to show the addict himself caught in the half world of drugs. As

long as the emphasis was on the lawman tracking down narcotics rings and
not on the lawbreaker who used drugs, the Production Code Authority was
willing to nod an approval. Otto Preminger's *THE MAN WITH THE GOLDEN
ARM* (1955) was another matter — the central character was a "junkie" and
the film showed him in the actual procedure of taking drugs. This independently produced film was denied the Code's seal of approval, but this did not
deter theater owners from showing the film, or its becoming a box-office success. Faced in the mid-Fifties by the fierce competition from television, and
the influx of foreign films with candid, realistic themes, other Hollywood producers saw the economic handwriting on the wall. The Production Code was
soon altered to allow a broader treatment of narcotics and other formerly
taboo subjects.

    THE MAN WITH THE GOLDEN ARM was quickly followed by three
other films which also revealed the pitiful existence of the drug addict, *BIG-
GER THAN LIFE* (1956), *MONKEY ON MY BACK* (1957), and *A HATFUL OF
RAIN* (1957). James Mason was the schoolteacher who becomes hooked on
cortisone in *BIGGER THAN LIFE*. Although not concerned with the usual
"hard drug" kind of addiction this film, which was based on a real-life account

VI

155

Eva Marie Saint and Don Murray
in *A Hatful of Rain*
(Twentieth Century-Fox)

The Country Girl with Grace
Kelly, Bing Crosby, and William
Holden (Paramount)

by Berton Roueché, showed that even nonprescription drugs can be addictive. *MONKEY ON MY BACK*, a dramatization of boxer Barney Ross's struggle to overcome his morphine addiction, went beyond the sensationalism of Preminger's film. The film drew upon Ross's cure at the Federal hospital in Lexington, Kentucky, to indicate that this increasing social ill can be effectively treated. This film was one of several biographies of well-known personalities whose personal problems were widely publicized. *THE GENE KRUPA STORY* (1959), as another example, was about the famous jazz drummer's fight against the drug habit.

Fred Zinnemann's *A HATFUL OF RAIN* was probably the most sensitive picture about drug addiction, emphasizing the anguish it causes a junkie's family. His pregnant wife as well as his father are bewildered by the addict's behavior, for they are unaware of his habit. Only his brother knows that Johnny Pope had become addicted to morphine during his hospitalization while fighting in Korea.

The problem of alcoholism, which had received its definitive depiction in *THE LOST WEEKEND* a decade before, was also the subject of several films in the Fifties. *I'LL CRY TOMORROW* (1955), *THE HELEN MORGAN STORY* (1957), and *TOO MUCH, TOO SOON* (1958) were all fictionalized biographies of actresses whose careers were seriously blighted by alcoholism. Susan Hayward, who had played a similar role in *SMASH-UP*, gave a convincing performance in *I'LL CRY TOMORROW* as Lillian Roth, whose 16-year bout with whiskey leads her to an attempted suicide. Three other well-intentioned films about alcoholism during this decade were *COME BACK, LITTLE SHEBA* (1952), George Seaton's *THE COUNTRY GIRL* (1954), and *VOICE IN THE MIRROR* (1958). Bing Crosby had one of his best roles in *THE COUNTRY GIRL* as the middle-aged musicomedy actor who turns to drink to bolster his ego when his career begins to slip. Based on Clifford Odets' searching stage play, *THE COUNTRY GIRL* examined alcoholism essentially through the eyes of a loyal wife who is determined to save her marriage.

Whether movies, radio, comic books, or television, the mass media and their effects on young people are a perennial topic for scrutiny by one anxious group after another. Their prime source of worry is whether there is a casual relationship between delinquent behavior and violence, in its many forms, shown in the media. As early as 1900, when the comic strip medium was merely five years old, aroused citizen groups were protesting the violent antics of a popular comic strip character, "The Yellow Kid." During the Thirties the philanthropic Payne Fund underwrote a series of research studies by social scientists exploring the influence of movies on young people with such titles as *Movies and Conduct; Movies, Delinquency, and Crime;* and *Motion Pictures and the Social Attitudes of Children.*

After World War II, with its rise in juvenile crimes, a national clamor was again heard. Senator Estes Kefauver, riding the crest of his earlier highly publicized Big Crime investigations, turned his Senate Judiciary Committee to films and their possible link to juvenile delinquency. Because Kefauver

VI

Marlon Brando (center) in *The Wild One* (Columbia)

avoided demagogic rantings, Hollywood did not fear this investigation as much as it had the HUAC probes. Although the committee's report chastised the film industry for excessive brutality and killings (especially in Westerns) and advertisements for films that emphasized violent illustrations and copy, it rejected external censorship and urged stronger adherence to the self-regulating Production Code.

As juvenile delinquency became more and more a fact of life in the Fifties, Hollywood turned again to films about young offenders. To some it might have appeared that the leather-jacketed ruffians on their motorcycles were the old Dead End Kids transported from the tenements of New York's East Side to the neon paradise of California. But many of the adolescent delinquents who were beginning to appear in the movies of the Fifties had other faces, too. If they shared a middle-class background with an earlier Andy Hardy, the rift with their parents was far deeper than a youthful spat. Indeed, these middle- and upper-class delinquents had troubles that went beyond winning the Friday night basketball game or getting a date for the Senior Prom. In the Fifties the "kids next door" — whether on garbage-strewn Delancey Street or maple-lined Main Street, Arcadia — were wielding switch-blade knives, trafficking in narcotics in high school corridors, and engaging in sexual promiscuity which would have made the wild youth of the Jazz Age blush.

The motorcycle gangs that were roaming California's Highway 101 came to the American screen in THE WILD ONE (1953). Openly contemptuous of law and order the young hoodlums terrorize a small town. Because the local police seem helpless against these marauders, a group of angry citizens become vigilantes and beat up the leader of the bike cult. There was little attempt in the film to give insight into the causes of the vicious antisocial behavior of the central character, played by Marlon Brando. "What are you rebelling

Glenn Ford (right) in *Blackboard Jungle* (Metro-Goldwyn-Mayer)

against?'' a girl who has obviously fallen for the psychologically unbalanced gangleader asks him. "What have you got?" replies Brando. At the end the girl convinces her father, a cop, to let the youths go, and the cyclists roar out of the town.

Another snarling adolescent gang are the troublemakers in *MAD AT THE WORLD* (1955). In the course of their nomadic thrill seeking they throw a whiskey bottle and kill a baby. As in *THE WILD ONE* the police are ineffective in controlling the hooligans, so that the father of the dead child is forced to track them down.

If the many news reports about tension and even violence in the schools of many American cities had not brought this plight home to the public, *BLACKBOARD JUNGLE* (1955) dramatized this problem with a loud alarm. The vocational-school setting of the shocking Evan Hunter novel was a microcosm of the convulsions that were disrupting the classrooms in many large cities. The unruly kids in *BLACKBOARD JUNGLE* added their own "r" to the traditional reading, 'riting, and 'rithmetic — rampage. (Even a Mr. Chips or a Miss Bishop, great teachers as they were, might have thrown up their hands in despair.) Their teacher, Mr. Dadier — soon dubbed "Daddy-O" by his charges — never had a course in teachers' college that told him how to fend off a student attacking him with an open knife. In contrast to the real-life experiences of many teachers who had been molested and brutalized in the rundown city schools in interstitial neighborhoods, Dadier finally manages to establish some rapport with his students.

Because of the negative view it gave of a major American institution, public education, *BLACKBOARD JUNGLE* aroused criticism on the part of those who were concerned with the image of America abroad. Edward R. Murrow, then head of the United States Information Agency, and Norman Cousins

VI

of *Saturday Review*, among others, expressed fears that foreign audiences might draw a false generalization about American life from the movies Hollywood exported. Clare Boothe Luce, then our ambassador to Italy, denounced *BLACKBOARD JUNGLE* as flagrantly unrepresentative of American public schools.

In an interview Richard Brooks, the director of the film, was asked if he thought he had the right to show America in such an unfavorable light. He replied: "The point is not 'Do I have the right?' but 'Is it the truth?' America is a million things, and this is one of them, a small thing. If it's bad, let's correct it. If it's a lie, no one will go to see it anyway. If you don't want to tell the truth, that's when you're in trouble." Brooks recalls that the day the picture opened in New York a teacher was stabbed and thrown off a roof.[4]

The anatomy of movie-hero worship is often more than star-system grooming, engineered press releases, and contrived "fan" campaigns. Frequently a movie newcomer establishes a screen image that, whatever the sociological chemistry, is identifiable with the behavior of a large segment of the audience. Such cultural empathy may account for the popularity of James Dean with many young people during the mid-Fifties. If adolescents were having difficulties at home in "communicating" with their parents (and the "generation gap" was not an invention of the twentieth century), James Dean in Nicholas Ray's *REBEL WITHOUT A CAUSE* (1955) was the spokesman for their familial frustrations. The fact that Dean was killed at the age of 24 in his speeding Porsche a few weeks before the film was released added an aura of romantic morbidity for the blue-jean cult that already idolized him.

Although the "rebels" in this film are children of well-to-do parents, they are as sullen, sadistic, and prone to violence as the ghetto kids in *BLACKBOARD JUNGLE*. The "chicken run" episode (taken from an actual news report[5]) is symbolic of their death-wish orientation and their sense of *anomie* with the world. The film is quite specific in laying the blame for the young people's bitterness on their parents. Jim's father is an apron-wearing Milquetoast completely dominated by his mother; Judy's hang-up is that her dad is unable to return her affection, and as for Plato, his father had virtually abandoned him and his mother had turned his rearing over to a maid. With his uncertain, melancholy, half-articulate mannerisms, James Dean was the prototype of the many youthful anti-heroes in numerous films that came after *REBEL WITHOUT A CAUSE*.

Lack of mutual understanding between parents and their children was also examined in *TEEN-AGE REBEL* (1956) and *THE YOUNG STRANGER* (1957), both of which were obviously influenced by the James Dean mystique. In *THE YOUNG STRANGER* James MacArthur was the adolescent boy trying to establish a proper relationship with his father. Unlike *REBEL WITHOUT A CAUSE* this film ends optimistically — but not before a lecture to the neglectful father by a detective.

Judging from films like *BLACKBOARD JUNGLE* and *REBEL WITHOUT A CAUSE*, whose message was like touching a third rail, one might have ex-

JAMES DEAN

The overnight sensation of 'East of Eden'

A portrayal of surpassing impact -- the story of a teenage kid caught in the undertow of today's juvenile violence...

"REBEL WITHOUT A CAUSE"

WARNER BROS. PRESENT IT IN CINEMASCOPE AND WarnerColor

James MacArthur and James Daly
in *The Young Stranger* (RKO Radio)

pected they would have inspired other films which seriously explored the problems of juveniles. If the young people of America were indeed undergoing an identity crisis, these two films had at least touched on their complex socio-psychological traumas in stories and situations to which they could relate. But, unfortunately, the films that came after *BLACKBOARD JUNGLE* and *REBEL* merely increased the dosage of violence and crime and decreased the necessary elements for understanding the social disenchantment of the young. Except for *DINO* (1957) and to some extent *BLUE DENIM* (1959), the youth movies of the late Fifties were cynically counterfeit, passing themselves as being "where it's at" but actually being a gross exploitation of young people. There were a raft of pictures whose titles indicate their trite, sordid content: *HOT ROD GIRL* (1956), *MOTORCYCLE GANG* (1957), *YOUNG AND DANGEROUS* (1957), *EIGHTEEN AND ANXIOUS* (1957), *THE COOL AND THE CRAZY* (1958), *HIGH SCHOOL CONFIDENTIAL* (1958), and *JUVENILE*

JUNGLE (1958). Knowing the patterns of Hollywood, however, such films should not have surprised anyone. If there were no Gresham's Law (bad art drives out good art), Hollywood would have invented it. In the message film, as in other types of Hollywood's movies, one box-office success breeds imitation which in turn breeds another imitation *ad nauseam*.

Other factors were also at work during the Fifties which hindered additional serious youth films even if there had been producers who wanted to make them. It was a period of severe economic upheaval in the film industry. In the wake of television's usurpation of America's leisure hours, theater attendance fell off from a peak of 80 million weekly in 1945 to about half that number. As *Life* magazine aptly put it, "Now it's trouble that's super-colossal in Hollywood."

Attempting to win back the lost audiences who had defected to the 21-inch screen, Hollywood held up the carrot of the superscreens of Cinerama and Cinemascope. Productions from the major studios hit a 40-year low point in 1954. Compared to 1935, for example, there was a 60 percent decrease in the number of films released by the major companies. The need to fill the screens of neighborhood and drive-in theaters that were still keeping afloat was met to a large extent by quick-buck productions that capitalized on youthful violence and the more "frank" films permitted by the relaxation of Production Code strictures against certain sexual themes, drugs, and other titillating keyhole subjects.

VI

VII

A Cynical Shot of Vinegar

Dreiser in the Fifties

"High Noon" — Anticapitalist Western?

TV Message Dramas on the Big Screen

Kazan: "Lonesome" Rhodes and Zapata

Ecological Themes

In the Tradition of "I Am a Fugitive"

Capital Punishment

Korean War Films: What the (bleep) are we doing here?

"Paths of Glory"

Graham Greene Rewritten

Atomic Dust over Australia

"I take a very dim view as to the ultimate effect of a
single film on the spectator. I don't think it can
change anyone's mind, even though it does have
the effect of perhaps inspiring two people to come
out of the theater and have one say to the other,
'I never thought of it in quite that way before.' But
I cannot change their viewpoint, and I'm not trying
to. I am trying, occasionally, to provoke them to a
certain extent to think about a situation, or to look
at it in a way in which they didn't look at it before."

Stanley Kramer[1]

Gary Cooper in *High Noon*
(United Artists)

Ace in the Hole (Paramount)

Despite the myriad pressures on Hollywood in the Fifties, ranging from congressional investigations of political content in films, economic voices of doom, and a dropout of a major portion of its audience, there were many films which commented on contemporary social problems with vitality, and in some cases did it courageously. As usual, of course, the majority of Hollywood movies played it close to the vest and tried to compete with television for the old (but now fragmented) audience in such mass-entertainment forms as musicals, Westerns, and wide-screen historical spectacles. Still, there were also films like THE MAN WITH THE GOLDEN ARM which, for whatever motives Otto Preminger had for making it, took a franker look at the social problem of drug addiction than had ever been attempted before. If Preminger hadn't tested not only the Production Code but also the readiness of audiences for so stark a subject, the subsequent (and better) A HATFUL OF RAIN would probably never have reached the screen.

As in other decades in the development of the American message film, there were, naturally, films of the Fifties which did not deal with a specific social problem, but commented rather on the nature of man *sui generis* and the false values that any society constructs for itself.

If Huston's THE TREASURE OF THE SIERRA MADRE was the Forties' counterpart of von Stroheim's GREED, Billy Wilder's ACE IN THE HOLE was its mutation in 1951. A mordant illustration of Wilder's special kind of cynicism, the plot was suggested by what happened to Floyd Collins, a real-life speleologist who was trapped in a cave. In the film a totally ruthless newspaper reporter capitalizes on the accident by turning it into a major headline story which carries his exclusive byline. Even Leo, the trapped victim, enjoys the morbid publicity drummed up by the reporter: "My picture in the paper? No kidding?" The cave site becomes a freak show which attracts thousands of gawking rednecks, hot-dog and soda-pop vendors, and all the tawdry trap-

pings of a midway. There is even a cowboy singer who warbles a ditty to the thrill-seeking spectators:

> We're coming, we're coming, Leo,
> Leo, don't despair —
> While you're in the cave a-hopin'
> We are up above you gropin'
> And we soon will make an openin'
> Oh Leo![2]

Since all this is lucrative for local businessmen, the sheriff is only too glad to cooperate with the conniving reporter to slow down rescue operations. The victim's wife, too, goes along with the reporter's promises of money and notoriety. The portrait of Americans as Yahoos which Wilder painted in *ACE IN THE HOLE* was unrelenting in its Swiftian blackness.

ACE IN THE HOLE is a good example of a motion picture in which the message was unpalatable to the public, for it failed at the box office. After initial showings it was retitled *THE BIG CARNIVAL*, but even the name change didn't entice ticket buyers into theaters. As Wilder has stated in reflecting upon the fate of the film, "My mistake was in coaxing the American public into the theater with the idea that they were going to get a cocktail, whereas instead they got a shot of vinegar."[3] Perhaps Wilder learned a lesson about audiences from this film's weak financial performance, for when he made social comments in his subsequent films he did so in a contraband, smuggled-in manner.

The rationale to remake any film, especially one like *AN AMERICAN TRAGEDY*, can only be a matter of speculation. It could not have been because von Sternberg's version in 1931 was either a critical or box-office success. Nor, in 1951 when George Stevens' *A PLACE IN THE SUN* was released,

VII

was there any particular revival of interest in Theodore Dreiser's work. One
can easily understand the remake of a *RAMONA* (four times!) or even a *BEN-
HUR* with their broad popular appeals no matter what decade. But the decision to re-do a downbeat story of a young man who is executed for a crime
that he only *willed* is "a puzzlement." Director George Stevens, however, must
have thought that there was an audience that would respond to Dreiser's
severe morality play of a youth who was tragically thwarted in his grasping
for "a place in the sun." Perhaps Stevens recognized that the universality of
Dreiser's theme — that the false values of society can crush sensitive individuals — was as appropriate to the Fifties as the early Thirties. Whatever may
have been the "other" explanations for this film's huge success, e.g., the perceptive casting of Montgomery Clift, Shelley Winters, and Elizabeth Taylor,
the fact is that a message film done with great artistry and integrity can find
an audience in any period.

Interpretations of *HIGH NOON* (1952) are as numerous and differing as
there are film critics. Robert Warshow, for example, saw it as being in the tradition of the classic Western, a worthy companion to the earlier Gary Cooper
film *THE VIRGINIAN* (1929), and if a social drama at all, one of very low
order.[4] Pauline Kael also regarded *HIGH NOON* as "primer sociology" — a
sneak civics lesson in which the frontier town was used as a "microcosm of
the evils of capitalist society."[5] Andrew Sarris saw *HIGH NOON* as typical of
the post-1945 "antiwestern Western" which uses the genre to express "dis-
gruntlement with some aspect of the human condition, be it cowardice, pug-
nacity, prejudice or just plain mob hysteria."[6] For self-appointed film critic
John Wayne, who boasts that he helped run Carl Foreman, the blacklisted
scenarist of *HIGH NOON*, out of the country, the film was the most un-American thing he had ever seen. The scene that irritated the Duke most was, as he
expressed it, "ole Coop putting the United States marshal's badge under his
foot and stepping on it."[7]

Whether approving or not, these and other critics recognize that *HIGH
NOON* is more than the story of four killers out to gun down the town marshal,
and that some contemporary social comment was intended. As in many postwar films *HIGH NOON* has a core situation of a community in crisis. Instead
of the townspeople rallying to the support of their marshal to maintain the
laws that protect them, they shrink back through cowardliness and moral
apathy. Each has his own rationalization for doing so. They are not unlike the
people who can be aroused into a mob that tries to lynch a Chicano fruit-
picker, follows a Willie Stark's promises of an easy American paradise, allows
the intimidations of a Ku Klux Klan, or engages in a witch hunt against a
liberal smalltown librarian. They have their urban counterparts even today in
the people who turned a deaf ear to the screams of Kitty Genovese as she was
being murdered outside their cozy apartments in the Queens section of New
York City.

Elia Kazan's *A FACE IN THE CROWD* (1957), another collaboration with
Budd Schulberg, was in its own way one of the most devastating criticisms

Van Heflin and Everett Sloane
in *Patterns* (United Artists)

A Face in the Crowd with Andy
Griffith (Warner Brothers)

of the all-accepting idolization of personalities who are created and promulgated by the mass media. Are indifference and apathy a concomitant aspect of
America's mass society? *A FACE IN THE CROWD* would seem to respond,
Yes! "Lonesome" Rhodes (Andy Griffith), a guitar-playing tramp who becomes a national idol via network television, is a two-faced scoundrel with a
thirst for political power. His true feelings about the suckers who watch him
in millions of living rooms throughout the land are inadvertently "broadcast"
when his erstwhile girlfriend throws a switch that opens a studio microphone.
Finally the crowd — so aptly termed "the booboisie" by H. L. Mencken —
must accept the truth: their hero is a throat-cutting opportunist.

If the Hollywood rightists could see "subversion" in *HIGH NOON*, they
evidently looked the other way when *A FACE IN THE CROWD* was released.
Evidently Elia Kazan's willing cooperation with the House Un-American Activities Committee in 1952 had enabled him to continue to make hard-hitting
social films without being blacklisted.

Although television by the mid-Fifties was Hollywood's major economic
headache, it cannot be overlooked that the new electronic medium was a fertile training ground for many new actors, writers, and directors whose creative
talents subsequently enriched the movies. In the so-called Golden Age of
"live" TV drama, many writers dealt with social problems; and some, especially Reginald Rose, Tad Mosel, Robert Alan Aurthur, Horton Foote, and Rod
Serling, later wrote for films. Directors such as John Frankenheimer, Sidney

12 Angry Men (United Artists)

Lumet, Franklin Schaffner, Fielder Cook, Ralph Nelson, and Robert Mulligan shifted their talents from the small video screen to the big theater screen.

Sidney Lumet's *12 ANGRY MEN* (1957), written by Reginald Rose, is a case in point of an incisive television drama that became an equally forceful movie. The theme of the film was the responsibility of jurists to overcome their personal prejudices and emotional sets to render a just verdict on an 18-year-old youth charged with the stabbing of his sadistic father. The twelve veniremen comprise a cross section of American citizenry fulfilling their obligations to the American legal system. They are truly a mixed bag, with the flippant salesman eager to "get it over with" so that he can go out to the ballpark; the bigoted garage owner; the equivocating advertising executive; and the European-born watchmaker who believes in the importance of the jury's deliberations. Through the persuasive tenacity of one juror the others change their minds from a guilty decision, and together they reach a more enlightened verdict.

PATTERNS (1956), written by Rod Serling and directed by Fielder Cook, was another excellent television-to-Hollywood transfer. Here again was the recurrent view of American business as an abrasive social institution that will settle for nothing less than a man's essential identity. As in *THE POWER AND THE GLORY* of the Thirties, so in *PATTERNS* the intrigue and in-fighting that typify rising mobility in corporate life are vividly shown. A similar theme was the basis of *EXECUTIVE SUITE* (1954) where an internecine struggle ensues

VII

Marlon Brando (right) in *Viva Zapata!* (Twentieth Century-Fox)

among second-level executives for the presidency of a furniture-making corporation.

Although *THE MAN IN THE GRAY FLANNEL SUIT* (1956) also had a Big Business *gestalt,* its main character, Tom Rath, is a lower-echelon executive who is caught in the status trap of so many of his briefcase-carrying contemporaries — faces seen every day in the lonely crowd that rides the commuter trains from Westport to Manhattan. Nevertheless, Rath refuses to let the corporate system rob him of his family life or of his personal values.

If political strife, particularly stressing the struggle of have-nots versus the haves, was a sensitive subject during the Fifties in view of the climate of McCarthyism and its aftermath, Hollywood could always turn its cameras southward to the revolutions which were constantly on the periphery of Latin American countries. As in *JUAREZ* in the late Thirties, and *WE WERE STRANGERS* (1949) set in Machado's Cuba, the struggle for social justice in Latin America was the theme of two films of 1952, *VIVA ZAPATA!* and *THE FIGHTER.* Both of these films dealt with peasant revolts in Mexico in the early years of the twentieth century. *VIVA ZAPATA!,* directed by Elia Kazan and with a screenplay by John Steinbeck, was a biography of the Mexican Indian who led the agrarian uprising in southern Mexico while Pancho Villa was

Juliette Greco and Trevor Howard
in *The Roots of Heaven*
(Twentieth Century-Fox)

arousing the northern provinces. Although the lesson was drawn that power
corrupts, *ZAPATA* was a flattering portrait of this Mexican revolutionary.
Again one can speculate that had this film about political repression been
made by one of the "Hollywood Ten" and not by a cooperative witness like
Kazan, it probably would have been investigated by the HUAC. Clearly, films
that take the side of political underdogs are not *ipso facto* communist-inspired,
but in the climate of the witch-hunting McCarthy era a film like *VIVA
ZAPATA!* might otherwise have been suspect.

Without any stars of the Brando magnitude in the cast or spectacular production values, *THE FIGHTER* was a cogent, independently produced film
about a Mexican prizefighter in El Paso who uses his winnings to further the
cause of the rebelling peasants back home. *THE FIGHTER* was directed by
Herbert Kline, whose credits include the famous Mexican film *THE FORGOT-
TEN VILLAGE* (1944).

Several years before the general public even became aware of the word
"ecology," two unusual films of 1958 attempted to deal with the urgent necessity to restore some balance to the natural environment. One of them was
Darryl F. Zanuck's production *THE ROOTS OF HEAVEN*. A principal character is the zealous Morel (Trevor Howard) who launches a crusade to pre-

serve the elephant from extinction in French Equatorial Africa. Part moralist, part conservationist, disillusioned with man's civilization, Morel attempts to affect legislation to stop ivory hunters from distroying the great animals. Unfortunately, the intended message got sidetracked somewhere among the adventure aspects of the film, its fuzzy philosophical allegory, and Pan-African politics.

WIND ACROSS THE EVERGLADES also had a conservationist premise. In this film about wildlife preservation in Florida, Christopher Plummer was the ecologist whose major enemy was not nature but man in the guise of "poachers," who were destroying natural balance by killing the heron and snowy egret for their plumes. Despite the film's turning into yet another action-adventure story, the implicit plea to save rare species of birds was not completely subverted. One might visualize Mr. Average Moviegoer leaving the neighborhood Bijou and nudging his wife, saying, "You know, Alice, those poachers were really doing a terrible thing to those birds."

Although the films of the Fifties touched upon new problem areas such as drugs and ecology and explored more fully the dimensions of racial prejudice, the decade did not neglect other social concerns that had been treated by the movies since the silent period. One of these subjects was prisons — those black flowers of civilized society, as Nathaniel Hawthorne described them — and inhumane vs. humane treatment and rehabilitation of convicts. Films of the Fifties which went back to the tradition of *THE HONOR SYSTEM* of 1915 and *I AM A FUGITIVE FROM A CHAIN GANG* of the Thirties were *CAGED* (1950), *MY SIX CONVICTS* (1952), *RIOT IN CELL BLOCK 11* (1954), *DUFFY OF SAN QUENTIN* (1954), and *UNCHAINED* (1955).

Better than most of the scores of pictures about women in prison was John Cromwell's *CAGED*. Some of the usual elements were, of course, again trotted out: the humane woman warden who is thwarted by venal politicians, the indoctrination of minor criminals into hard-core deviates, and sadistic guards. Where *CAGED* excelled over most of its banal counterparts was in the verisimilitude of its characters, probably due to the conscientious research by scriptwriter Virginia Kellogg. She had arranged to be "sentenced" to four state prisons for women to gather firsthand information.

Don Siegel's *RIOT IN CELL BLOCK 11* was an equally strong argument for an understanding of the tensions that are endemic in prison life. Although dramatically exciting, the climactic riot was more than just an exercise in screen violence; the anatomy of a riot in Folsom Prison was an understandable consequence of the conditions within the institution — poor food, pervasive boredom, and the inmates' sense of despair.

That prison detention can be a transitional experience between recidivism to criminal ways or a useful life was the thesis of *UNCHAINED*. Based on the book *Prisoners Are People* by Kenyon J. Scudder, then supervisor of the Chino (California) Institute for Men, this unpretentious film showed the viability of the honor system in a "prison without walls."

Susan Hayward in *I Want to Live!*
(United Artists)

Bradford Dillman, Dean Stockwell,
and Orson Welles in *Compulsion*
(Twentieth Century-Fox)

Stalag 17 with Robert Strauss and
William Holden (Paramount)

THE

CELLULOID

WEAPON

176

Few legal questions generate more sound and fury than the value of capital punishment as a deterrent to crime. Those who oppose it in the United States point out, for example, that Wisconsin, which eliminated legal executions, has only a 1.9 murder rate per 100,000 population while Florida, which electrocutes convicted murderers, has nearly five times as many murders, proportionately. More than 20 nations throughout the world, including West Germany, Sweden, Norway, New Zealand, Austria, Australia, and Brazil have eliminated capital punishment by law. The debate about capital punishment reached its height in the Fifties with the Caryl Chessman case. *CELL 2455, DEATH ROW* (1955) drew upon Chessman's writings while in prison and fighting for a retrial. However, a more substantial film on this issue was Robert Wise's *I WANT TO LIVE!*, released in 1958, and also drawing on a true case. Susan Hayward was Barbara Graham, the B-girl who was condemned to death in the gas chamber for a murder which many people still believe she did not commit. If, as the opponents of capital punishment point out, society itself becomes a premeditated killer by inflicting on the condemned the mental torture of awaiting execution as well as the ultimate dropping of the gas pellet, *I WANT TO LIVE!* was certainly a persuasive argument for their viewpoint. Seldom has the celluloid weapon made such bold social comment as this film produced by one of the veterans of Hollywood's message films, Walter Wanger.

COMPULSION (1959) examined the issue of capital punishment by dramatizing a sensational case of the Twenties, the Leopold-Loeb trial. Unlike *I WANT TO LIVE!* the murderers are spared execution, partly because of their youth, but primarily because of the eloquent final argument of their lawyer, "Jonathan Wilks" (in real life, Clarence Darrow). In many pictures the courtroom is the dramatic *locus* for a clear enunciation of a film's message, probably because here words are the primary means of persuasion. One of the most famous of such scenes occurred in *COMPULSION* as Orson Welles made a long, impassioned plea for leniency while the press and public alike clamored for execution.

The only form of legalized killing, other than capital punishment, is, of course, war; and there is no decade of the American cinema without pro- or anti-war films. Like *BATTLEGROUND* in 1949, many films of the Fifties looked back at World War II as something less than a spectacle of heroics and glorified slaughter.

Although the bravery of the U.S. Marines is graphically presented in *HALLS OF MONTEZUMA* (1950), there is also the tone of questioning against war and its price in human terms. We see the personal hell of the men who have to do the fighting. A lieutenant keeps going only through large doses of medicine to relieve his mental pressures. In words that recall the ending of another Lewis Milestone film, *ALL QUIET ON THE WESTERN FRONT*, a dying soldier cries out, "War is too horrible for human beings!"

In *STALAG 17* (1953), despite its many hilarious comedy scenes, the master of contraband, director Billy Wilder, interwove a number of sardonic comments on the shabbiness of wartime existence in a POW camp and the

VII

Wendell Corey, Edmond O'Brien, and Paul Newman in *The Rack* (Metro-Goldwyn-Mayer)

scheming avarice of the prisoners. There is nothing ennobling about the cynical, fast-talking Sefton, who is a master of self-aggrandizing rackets and in dickering with the Germans for special favors. Even the Geneva Conventions and the Red Cross are targets for Wilder's black humor.

Another wartime heel appears as an officer in *ATTACK!* (1956), which may account for the refusal of the Defense Department to cooperate in its production. Eddie Albert was the cowardly captain whose competence is doubted by his men during the Battle of the Bulge. The platoon is so torn with dissension and breakdown of discipline that the accomplishment of their dangerous mission is jeopardized. Robert Aldrich, the director of *ATTACK!*, has stated that his main antiwar argument in the film was not the usual "war is hell," but "the terribly corrupting influence that war can have on the most normal, average human beings, and what terrible things it makes them capable of — things they wouldn't be capable of otherwise."[8]

The films of the Fifties that looked at World War II retrospectively from time to time showed that the enemy also suffered the *angst* of war-weariness.

THE YOUNG LIONS (1958) had Marlon Brando as the proud *Wehrmacht* lieutenant who becomes disillusioned with the "Sieg Heil" bravura and whose death comes almost as a release from a cause he no longer believes in. In *A TIME TO LOVE AND A TIME TO DIE* (1958) a German soldier returns from the Russian front to his devastated city. Although the film's source was another novel by Erich Maria Remarque, it fell far short in its attempt to make a pacifist statement as enduring as *ALL QUIET ON THE WESTERN FRONT*.

On June 25, 1950, the festering Cold War turned hot. Ironically, it did not erupt in Berlin or Greece or other tense areas where Americans and Russians were glaring at each other, but in the remote Korean peninsula. Most Americans had to turn to their atlases to find out where their sons would soon be sent.

Before the Korean "police action" was over in the summer of 1953, more than 50,000 Americans had lost their lives at such places as Pork Chop Hill, the retreat from the Yalu River, and North Korean prison camps. The Korean War — as well as the Vietnam War a decade later — left many unresolved questions not only among diplomats, historians, and even some generals themselves, but also on the part of Americans on the home front. It was probably the first war that did not have the enthusiastic support of most Americans, and as such it engendered much public debate, not only about America's involvement in Far Eastern civil wars, but indeed the efficacy of war as a solution to any problem.

Although they were relatively few in number, there were films of the Fifties that supported the Korean War effort. *I WANT YOU* (1951) was made in the first flush of patriotic fervor. The sentimental war propaganda of the film sounded hokey, especially when an over-aged Dana Andrews volunteers so that he'll be able to face his children when they ask him, "What were you doing, Daddy, when the world was shaking?" In *THE GLORY BRIGADE* (1953) American troops fight side by side with a unit of Greek volunteers to show the joint efforts of several nations in fighting Communism. Apart from *THE BRIDGES AT TOKO-RI* (1954) and John Wayne in *BLOOD ALLEY* (1955) the rest of the pro-Korean War films were run-of-the-mill action-and-battle pictures.

Unlike the films of the Second World War, which supported the war effort totally and never showed the fighting man in anything less than a heroic light, there were some Korean War films that took a critical position, even while the war was in progress. Indeed, the first film that dealt with the Korean War, Samuel Fuller's *THE STEEL HELMET* (1951), did not drum up any enthusiasm for the old flag-waving adage, "*Dulce et decorum est pro patria mori.*" The lieutenant who leads the American infantry patrol hides his insecurity in arrogance, the men he leads are themselves confused and ill-trained, the Korean populace are hostile — in short the tone of this picture could be summarized in GI lingo as, "What the (bleep) are we doing here?"

The spirit of the fighting man in Korea is also depicted as something less than indomitable in *THE RACK* (1956), *TIME LIMIT* (1957), and *PORK CHOP*

HILL (1959). In the entire tradition of American war films there was never a theme of an army officer on trial for collaborating with the enemy until *THE RACK*. Originally a television play by Rod Serling, the film's situation was the court-martial of a captain who while a POW in Korea cracked under the brainwashing techniques of his captors. The only excuse he can give was his own despair and loneliness. Paul Newman as the tormented captain vividly reenacted the personal agonies which a number of real-life officers suffered in the Korean War. *TIME LIMIT* also examined the pressures of the Korean War that caused an Army major to breach the military code by collaborating with his North Korean captors to the point of becoming a propaganda broadcaster. In the court-martial that follows his repatriation at the end of the war it is made clear that he became a turncoat to save the lives of his fellow prisoners. The film raised the questions: How much can a soldier endure under brainwashing? Should there be a "time limit" on heroism?

With *PORK CHOP HILL* director Lewis Milestone was again at the front. The antiwar tone which is so dominant in his *ALL QUIET ON THE WESTERN FRONT*, *A WALK IN THE SUN*, and *HALLS OF MONTEZUMA* is also apparent in his Korean War film. Although the American soldiers fight with desperate bravery at Pork Chop Hill, the irony lies in the fact that the audience knows that this costly battle was futile. The soldiers are well aware of military foul-ups at regimental headquarters. Moreover, they know that a political settlement of the very war itself is underway at Panmunjon even as they are dying for a few hundred yards of soil.

Required to put his life on the line for America while at home his people were struggling for their full rights as citizens, a black soldier in *PORK CHOP HILL* also questioned the value of our involvement in a far-off Asiatic war. Woody Strode acted the soldier who was reluctant to fight, and in one scene he refuses to obey the command of his white superior officer. "But all the boys are fighting," the officer tells him. Strode replies, "You ought to see where I live back home. You sonfabitch, I wouldn't die for that and I be goddam if I'm going to fight for Korea."

In many ways John Huston's *THE RED BADGE OF COURAGE* (1951) best expressed the feeling of war's futility, no matter what historical period or whether the battlefields on which young men die are the hills of Korea, the fortress of Monte Casino, the Argonne forest, or the banks of the Rappahannock in 1862. Audie Murphy was The Youth who epitomized the fears and confusion that all young soldiers experience as they wait for their first battle. Like Paul in *ALL QUIET ON THE WESTERN FRONT*, the bewildered Youth (who might well have stepped right out of a Matthew Brady photograph) dies in an inconsequential skirmish.

Of all the films of the Fifties that showed war in its most dehumanizing aspects, none showed the feculent absurdity of military philosophy more than Stanley Kubrick's *PATHS OF GLORY* (1957). The story was based on a true incident from the First World War, wherein a French division is accused of cowardice in attacking an impregnable German position. The commanding

The Quiet American
(United Artists)

general, who was using this battle to further his military ambitions, knew that the division was doomed from the beginning. Since the military machine requires scapegoats for this blot on its escutcheon, three soldiers are picked at random and marked for death by execution. ("Troops are like children," says the spit-and-polish General Broulard, "they need discipline. We must shoot a man now and then.") Despite the efforts of a colonel to rescind the execution orders, the military code is followed to the last jot and tittle and the three are shot, truly sacrificial lambs in war's inexorable slaughter. The significance of *PATHS OF GLORY* as a classic antiwar film is its difference from other films of this genre which emphasize the destruction caused by war, the moral and physical breakdown of its fighting men, and the devastation of cities and the people trapped in them. *PATHS OF GLORY* goes right to the heart of the problem by exposing the military mystique which must perpetuate itself no matter what the human cost.

Nor did the military power elite loosen its hold on the destinies of nations at the end of World War I, World War II, or even the Korean War. As the leak of the Pentagon Papers in 1971 revealed, the valence of the military-industrial entente was again at work in shaping United States policy vis-à-vis a civil war in Vietnam. When *THE QUIET AMERICAN* was released in 1958 cities such as Saigon or Hanoi were merely exotic locales "somewhere East of Suez." The average American, even if he had read about Dien Bien Phu (where the Communist insurgents had roundly defeated the French colonial force), could not have dreamed that within a decade nearly 50,000 U.S. soldiers would also die in the Indochinese jungles.

Unfortunately, Joseph L. Mankiewicz's screenplay for *THE QUIET AMER-ICAN* vitiated the intentions of Graham Greene's novel which attacked the bungling American foreign policy that finally involved this country in the Vietnam conflict. Whereas in the novel "the American" is a CIA agent, in the

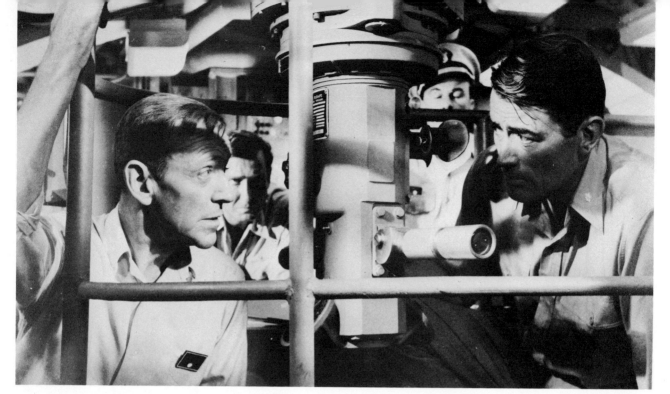

film version he is working for a private U.S. aid mission. His idea of a Third Force standing between communism and French colonialism is represented as merely his own rather than any official Washington line. In short, what could have been an insightful film about the political machinations that often undergird war, ended up as a movie that dodged the salient issues.

As T. S. Eliot wrote in his poem *The Hollow Men*, "Between the potency and the existence / Between the essence and the descent / Falls the Shadow." Overriding the commentaries about war and peace in so many films of the Fifties was the shadow cast by the doomsday weapon of nuclear bombs. It was perhaps fitting that the decade's final comment on the patent insanity of war was Stanley Kramer's *ON THE BEACH* (1959).

Premiered simultaneously in the key cities of the world, this film employed the futuristic metaphor of an atomic apocalypse. This final war started, a cynical scientist in the film says, "when people accepted the idiotic idea that peace could be maintained by arranging to defend themselves with weapons they couldn't possibly use without committing suicide." After all the other inhabitants of the world are dead from the impact of nuclear warfare and subsequent radioactive fallout, the sole survivors are a group of people in Australia. They, too, are doomed to annihilation within a few months as a lethal cloud of atomic dust drifts slowly toward them. But even as they wait for death, they cling tenaciously to the things that belong only to life — the company of loved ones, preparations for the birth of a child, the pleasures of cherished possessions.

To paraphrase D. W. Griffith, sometimes the celluloid weapon must show the evil and the negative to depict the good and the affirmative. By revealing the ultimate horror of atomic catastrophe *ON THE BEACH* eloquently urged men to abolish war and to take the utmost care to preserve the wonder of life.

183

VIII

≪Auteurs≫ and Social Comment

Two Notable "Trial" Films

"Spartacus" — Historical Spectacle with a Difference

Politics in the New Frontier Era

The Absurdity of War

Atomic Terror

A Man and a Message for All Seasons

Mental Retardation

Alcoholism, Drugs, and Criminal Recidivism

Mr. Muni and Mr. Newman

"Cheyenne Autumn"

Blacks and the Civil Rights Movement

The Southern Town as Villain

Sidney Poitier Comes to Dinner

"The thing is that people don't want to be preached
to. They want to be entertained. So that if you have
something to say, then I think it's incumbent on
you to try to make it successful so that you can say
it to a lot of people. Otherwise, if you say it only to a
handful of people, then your message is ineffective."

William Wyler[1]

In the Heat of the Night with
Rod Steiger and Sidney Poitier
(United Artists)

For some film critics the *auteur* theory, which recognizes the director of a film as its true "author," is sheer Gallic metaphysics concocted in Paris's *Cahiers du Cinema* and promulgated in the United States by its most ardent disciple, Andrew Sarris. Those who are anti-*auteur* in their critical stance insist that a film is primarily a collaborative art involving producers, writers, cameramen, and, oh yes, actors. The incessant, often petulant, bickering as to which approach to the study of film is most aesthetically *de rigueur* leads many film fans to echo Mercutio's curse, "A plague o' both your houses!"

A historical overview of social comment in the Hollywood message film reveals, however, that there is stronger support for the *auteur* approach than its detractors would care to admit. This is not to overlook the social comment in the work of producers such as Walter Wanger, Dore Schary, and Darryl F. Zanuck, or scenarists such as Sidney Buchman, Nunnally Johnson, Dalton Trumbo, and Dudley Nichols. Yet when one considers that several prominent producers subsequently also became directors (e.g., Joseph L. Mankiewicz and Stanley Kramer) and that many writers also turned to directing (e.g., Billy Wilder, John Huston, and Preston Sturges), there seems to be a tacit acknowledgment among moviemakers that the dominant artistic force in the shaping of a film is indeed the director.

The early Sixties saw movies by directors whose works indicate a consistent use of film as a celluloid weapon. Among the several splendid message films of the new decade was Stanley Kramer's *INHERIT THE WIND* (1960), a reenactment of the famous "monkey" trial of John T. Scopes in 1925. The central theme was whether fundamentalist dogma and doctrinaire provincialism were to smother the freedom of the inquiring mind. Darwinism came to Tennessee only through the courage of a young teacher who was arrested for imparting these "scandalous" theories to his pupils. The trial that ensued brought two famous lawyers into an intellectual death struggle. Although Fredric March and Spencer Tracy had fictitious names in *INHERIT THE WIND* they clearly portrayed William Jennings Bryan and Clarence Darrow; Gene Kelly played the newspaper reporter who was equally obviously the screen counterpart of H. L. Mencken. As was Kramer's earlier *THE DEFIANT ONES*, the script for this film was written by Harold J. Smith and "Nathan E. Douglas" (Nedrick Young). Insofar as any film can present ideas in a compelling and entertaining way, this movie, with superb performances by Messrs. March and Tracy, did so.

JUDGMENT AT NUREMBERG (1961) was yet another instance of Kramer's predilection for delving into important social issues. This composite version of the post-World War II trials at Nuremberg raised some thorny moral questions: Can the individual be held personally accountable for war crimes he has committed on orders from the State? and, What is the extent of guilt on the part of those who acquiesce and condone such crimes by offering no outcry? Again using the trial situation for a dramatic confrontation between a Nazi judge and the victims of his judicial rulings, Kramer kept a good balance between the emotionalism of the Nazi horrors and the need for intellectual

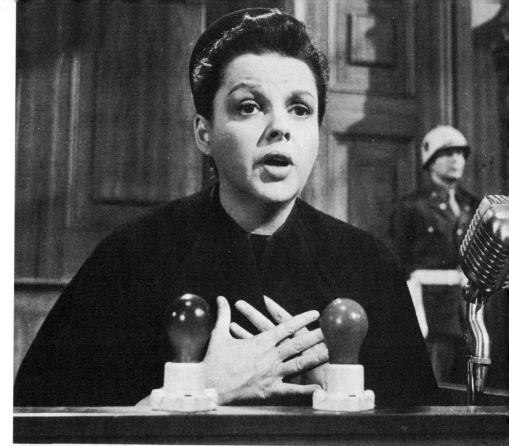

Judy Garland in *Judgment at Nuremberg* (United Artists)

Maximilian Schell and Richard Widmark in *Judgment at Nuremberg* (United Artists)

THE
CELLULOID
WEAPON

Montgomery Clift in *Judgment at Nuremberg* (United Artists)

Marlene Dietrich in *Judgment at Nuremberg* (United Artists)

VIII

Wild River with Jo Van Fleet and
Lee Remick
(Twentieth Century-Fox)

detachment if fair judgments were to be made. If there were still German people in the Sixties who could claim ignorance of the Nazi concentration camps,
enforced sterilizations, and unthinkable genocidal acts, this thought-provok-
ing film — shown widely in West Germany — had to be an eye opener. Perhaps where other means might fail, the film can be an agent in the mirroring
of a society. When a film helps society to examine itself and to recognize its
deep-rooted problems — and even, sometimes, to respond in an ameliorative
way — it utilizes the essential power of the celluloid weapon.

The year 1960 brought another film by Elia Kazan, who, like Kramer, had
begun his important work in post-World War II Hollywood. In its theme of
economic survival and the controversial building of the Tennessee Valley
dams, WILD RIVER seemed very much a film of the Thirties. A young government engineer tries to convince a stubborn old woman (Jo Van Fleet) to leave
her island home which would soon be flooded because of the TVA projects.
Her resistance, even though she is aware of the eventual benefits the dams
will bring to the whole region, is symbolic of thousands of other families in
the valley who feared dislocation from the land their forebears had cleared

and tilled. While the film empathizes with people like old Ella Garth, in the end it stresses that the collective benefits for a society must outweigh the personal sacrifices.

The Apartment with Fred MacMurray and Jack Lemmon (United Artists)

If the lukewarm reaction to *ACE IN THE HOLE* had dampened Billy Wilder's enthusiasm to make social comments too explicitly, *THE APARTMENT* (1960) was more in the vein of his sly, satiric comedies. Beyond the antics of the all-American schmo, played by Jack Lemmon, and what on the surface might pass for a sentimental romance, Wilder took advantage of every opportunity to portray the moral ambivalence of business executives and the semi-pro secretaries who get passed around with the same *sangfroid* as the key to Lemmon's apartment. In his ability to depict the malady of the world bounded by Madison, Park, and Lexington Avenues, Wilder sugar-coats the sick with the slick (who else could turn an attempted suicide into a comedic situation and get away with it?) and leaves the audience laughing but also a little skeptical about these skyscraper people. Wilder has stated that in *THE APARTMENT* and *ONE, TWO, THREE* (1961) he wanted to say: "How corrupt we are, how money-mad we are! How shaky all our convictions are!" This

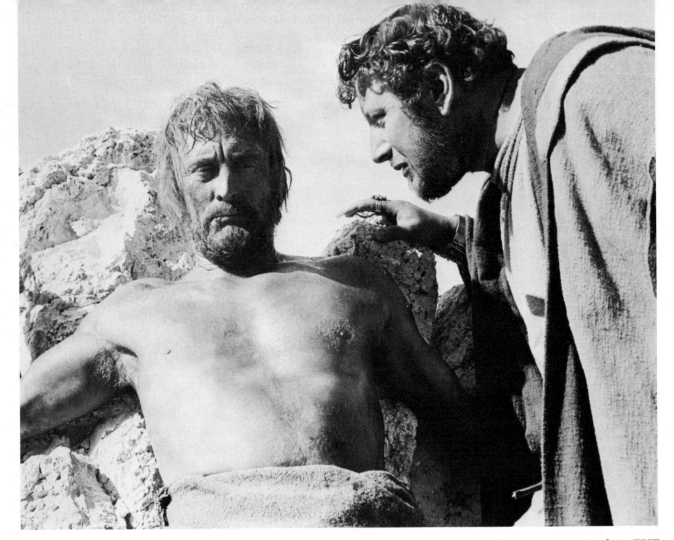

Spartacus with Kirk Douglas and
Peter Ustinov
(Universal-International)

same Wilderian view of men, manners, and morals was epitomized in *THE FORTUNE COOKIE* (1966), particularly when someone caustically remarks, "People will do anything for money. Except some people. They will do *almost* anything for money."

The early Sixties was again a period when Hollywood was not reluctant to criticize the workings of politics, government, and the pressures of the military establishment on both domestic and international affairs. It is unlikely that films such as *SPARTACUS, ADVISE AND CONSENT, SEVEN DAYS IN MAY,* or *DR. STRANGELOVE* would have been made during the conservative Fifties with the House Un-American Activities Committee and McCarthy looking for communist content in any film that scrutinized American social institutions. Even after the anti-Red paranoia had subsided, the residue of caution generally persisted for the rest of the decade. Indeed, it was only in 1960 that the blacklist was finally a dead issue and a writer like Dalton Trumbo no longer had to use an alias in getting screen credits. Perhaps it was the election of a young, liberal, intellectual, charismatic personality to the White House that encouraged filmmakers to be a little more bold. The early days of John F. Kennedy's New Frontier were reminiscent of the optimism that an earlier New Deal had promised in the Thirties. That there were soon to be dark clouds to overcast the new Camelot, with the Bay of Pigs fiasco, the Cuban missile crisis,

and the final terrible weekend of November 1963 could not be anticipated in the first months of JFK's political love affair with the American people.

In contrast to the numerous wide-screen historical films of the Fifties, e.g., *THE ROBE* (1953) and *THE SILVER CHALICE* (1954), that mixed spectacle with calendar art religiosity, Stanley Kubrick's *SPARTACUS* (1960) added the element of political revolution to the historical epic. Based on Howard Fast's thinly veiled revolutionary tract, *SPARTACUS* was the story of the great slave uprising against the Roman Empire in the First Century B.C. Within the context of the historical metaphor, the film deals with the oppression of the have-nots by a power-corrupted patrician few, and sympathetically shows the moral imperative of the slaves' rebellion. Even though Spartacus (Kirk Douglas), the leader of the revolutionaries, is executed along with 6,000 of his followers, the film makes clear that this uprising against the decadence of Rome will not be the last one, and that an empire that is two-thirds slave is already doomed. It is interesting to note that in the late Sixties a small group of antiwar activists led by Daniel and Phillip Berrigan called their burning of draft files in Catonsville, Maryland, "Operation Spartacus."

Unlike Dore Schary's production *SUNRISE AT CAMPOBELLO* (1960), whose political aspects were focused on an inspirational biography of Franklin D. Roosevelt during the trying period when he contracted infantile paralysis,

Ralph Bellamy and Greer Garson in *Sunrise at Campobello* (Warner Brothers)

VIII

Otto Preminger's *ADVISE AND CONSENT* (1962) was acrimonious in its depiction of Washington in-fighting. The cloakroom machinations of unscrupulous senators and even the President in *ADVISE AND CONSENT* are uncontested by any Jefferson Smith kind of political idealist. In the Senate debate on the confirmation of the President's appointment of a new secretary of state, we see a microcosm of the political rivalries that come from sectional and ideological differences. Nobody emerges too savory from Preminger's "lifting the dome of the Capitol." The secretary of state designate tells "a Washington kind of lie" when he denies under oath that he had ever been a member of a Communist cell while a professor at the University of Chicago; the Communist witch-hunting Southern senator promotes a smear campaign against the appointee, and the President himself is willing to overlook this perjury to push through his nomination. Although fictional and what at first may seem too contrived, *ADVISE AND CONSENT* would not seem far-fetched to Presidents Lyndon Johnson or Richard Nixon, both of whom suffered humiliating defeats from the Senate in some of their nominations for the Supreme Court.

The films of Otto Preminger almost invariably deal in some manner with contemporary social issues. Sometimes he comes to grips with these problems, as in *ADVISE AND CONSENT* and *THE MAN WITH THE GOLDEN ARM*: but other times, as in *EXODUS* (1960), he takes a situation as significant as the struggle for Israeli independence and turned it into a cowboys-and-Indians fracas. This mercurial director can give audiences a sequence in *THE CARDINAL* (1963) that attacks the racism of the Ku Klux Klan with genuine force, while in his *HURRY SUNDOWN* (1967) the social and racial tensions in a Georgia town are merely exploited for whatever box-office draw they have for the moment. Unfortunately, it too often appears that Mr. Preminger reads current events no further than their sensational headlines.

If there is little room for political idealism in *ADVISE AND CONSENT*, there is even less honor among politicos in *THE BEST MAN* (1964), from the play by Gore Vidal. The colosseum for the political gladiators is a presidential nominating convention. Their warclubs are sewed-up delegates, promises of overflowing pork barrels, and character assassination. In *THE BEST MAN* even an egghead intellectual is not above using an ugly whispering campaign to defeat his rival for the nomination. In this case he had chanced upon a worse "sin of youth" than his opponent could dig up on him.

Whether dealing with racial prejudice, juvenile delinquency, or crime, the genre of the thriller has often been a structural device for social commentary. During the Sixties a melodramatic variant began to appear — the thriller *cum* politics. Although the "political thriller" dates back to such isolated films as *THE PRESIDENT VANISHES* in the Thirties it was not until *THE MANCHURIAN CANDIDATE*, *SEVEN DAYS IN MAY*, and *FAIL-SAFE* that the genre began to proliferate.

THE MANCHURIAN CANDIDATE (1962), directed by John Frankenheimer, was a bizarre blend of political fanaticism, international espionage, and a

VIII

Frank Sinatra and Laurence Harvey
in *The Manchurian Candidate*
(United Artists)

quasi-Orwellian nightmare. A brainwashed sergeant in Korea (Laurence
Harvey) is returned to the American lines by his communist captors. Shaw
has been conditioned to kill once he is triggered by a certain phrase. Back in
the United States, he is turned over by the Russians to their American agent
— who turns out to be his own mother! She, in turn, is going to use the robot
assassin to shoot the presidential nominee at a Madison Square Garden rally to
clear the way for her husband's takeover of the White House. At the climax,
just as he prepares to pull the trigger, Shaw's mind is freed by Major Marco
(Frank Sinatra), a fellow prisoner who had managed to dispel a similar brainwashing control. Acting consciously, Shaw kills his mother and stepfather and
then turns the gun on himself.

   Apart from its implications of brainwashing as a means of manipulating
not only individuals but a whole society, *THE MANCHURIAN CANDIDATE*
was an attack on McCarthyism. As Frankenheimer has stated, "This country
was just recovering from the McCarthy era and nothing had ever been filmed
about it. I wanted to do a picture that showed how ludicrous the whole
McCarthy Far Right syndrome was and how dangerous the Far Left syndrome
is. . . . It really dealt with the McCarthy era, the whole idea of fanaticism, the
Far Right and the Far Left really being exactly the same thing, and the idiocy
of it."[2] The film made it fairly obvious that Shaw's stepfather who vehemently
attacks the secretary of defense was patterned after Senator Joe McCarthy.

   Frankenheimer's next film, *SEVEN DAYS IN MAY* (1964), also dealt with

à plot to seize political power in the United States. This time, however, the
conspirators are not foreign agents, communist or otherwise, but the right-
wing militarists of the Pentagon. The leader of the incipient military coup is a
popular Air Force general (Burt Lancaster) serving as head of the Joint Chiefs
of Staff. He rationalizes his own political ambitions by accusing the President
(Fredric March) of treason because the latter has negotiated a nuclear disarma-
ment treaty with the Russians. Cryptic messages are delivered to top military
commanders all over the world to collaborate in the seizure of the government
on a certain Sunday in May. The President becomes aware of the planned
rebellion, and with the help of some trusted friends, especially a colonel who
unwittingly learned of the cabal, he forces the general to resign just as May
Day is approaching.

Again, the political message in this film was consciously intended. Frankenheimer pointed out his conviction that the voice of the military was too
dominant in Washington affairs and that SEVEN DAYS IN MAY was "the
opportunity to illustrate what a tremendous force the military-industrial complex is." Well aware that the Pentagon wouldn't be exactly ecstatic about this
film, the producers didn't even bother to ask for its cooperation. They did receive cooperation, however, from the White House, Pierre Salinger, then
President Kennedy's press secretary, arranged permission for a riot scene to
be photographed in front of the White House, and also to study the President's
office and other rooms so that they could be duplicated in the studio sets.[3]

Burt Lancaster and Fredric March
in *Seven Days in May* (Paramount)

VIII

Two other films of 1964 lent credence to the suspicion that Hollywood had declared "war" on the Pentagon. Although *FAIL-SAFE* and *DR. STRANGELOVE OR: HOW I LEARNED TO STOP WORRYING AND LOVE THE BOMB* were perhaps unintentional copycats, in that they both underscored the awful consequences of nuclear warfare, they differed strongly in their approach to the subject.

Stanley Kubrick's *DR. STRANGELOVE*, a misanthropic nightmare comedy, went beyond any previous film satire in its depiction of man as self-destructor. Communist-hating General Ripper of the Strategic Air Command (with a paranoid delusion that the Reds were fluoridating the American water supply to pollute the body fluids of loyal Americans) sends a wing of aircraft loaded with nuclear bombs toward Russia. All efforts of President Muffley to recall the bombers, including a hotline telephone call to the Russian premier, prove futile. ("No, Dimitri, no . . . you couldn't be more sorry than I am."). Moreover, the Russians have an instant retaliation Doomsday device which is triggered by the U.S. bomb. As a visual counterpoint to the strains of a saccharine ballad, "We'll meet again, don't know where, don't know when," we see cascades of billowing atomic clouds. *DR. STRANGELOVE* is at once a hilarious but bone-chilling critique of a world that is closer to madness than it kens.

The characters in *DR. STRANGELOVE* are malevolent bumblers and snafu-masters. General Turgidson, for example, when challenged by President Muffley that the attack on Russia is an unauthorized error, responds with hurt

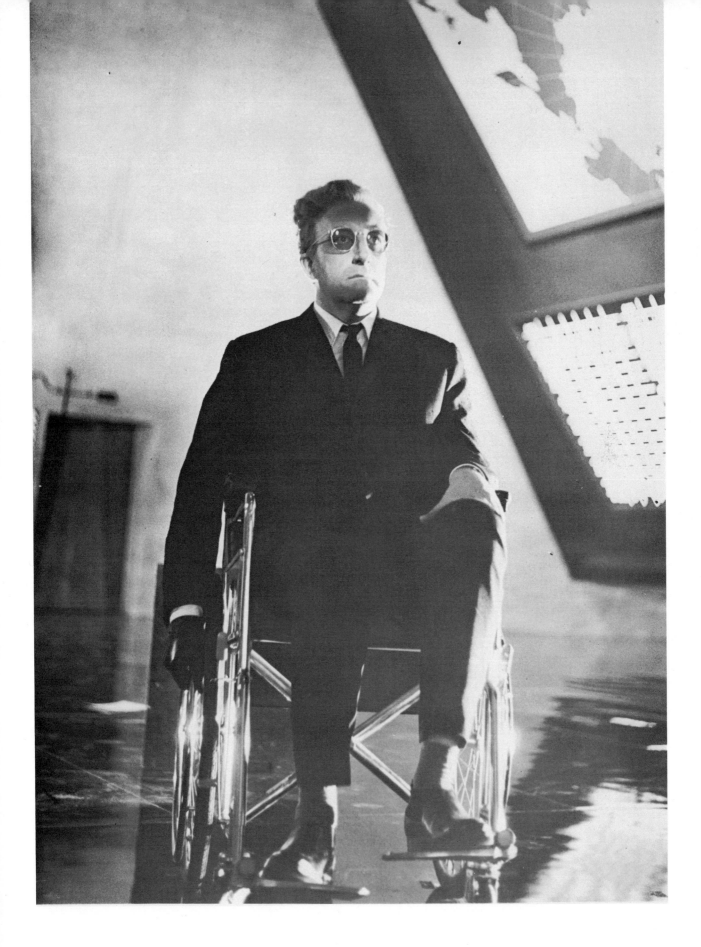

Sterling Hayden in
*Dr. Strangelove or: How I Learned
to Stop Worrying and Love the
Bomb* (Columbia)

pride: "I don't think it's fair to condemn a whole program because of a single slip-up." As grotesque as are the war rooms with their electronic maps of atomic targets, their throw switches lettered Auto-Destruct, and file cabinets labeled "World Targets in Megadeaths," who can deny that similar horror chambers exist today in the varied Pentagons throughout the world?

Stanley Kubrick started to work on the screenplay for *DR. STRANGE-LOVE* with the intention of making the film a serious treatment of the problem of nuclear warfare. As he kept trying to imagine the way in which things would really happen, Kubrick recalls: "Ideas kept coming to me which I would discard because they were so ludicrous. I kept saying to myself: 'I can't do this. People will laugh.' But after a month or so I began to realize that all the things

I was throwing out were the things which were most truthful." He decided then on his final black-comedy approach because of his belief that "satire exploits truth's backside in the hope that it is more recognizable than its prim front."[4]

In contrast to the irresponsible loonies that comprise the Hieronymus Bosch-like world in *DR. STRANGELOVE*, reasonable men try to avert a global atomic holocaust in Sidney Lumet's *FAIL-SAFE*. The situation in this film is similar to *DR. STRANGELOVE*: a flight of bombers loaded with atomic destruction are on their way to Moscow, and they cannot be recalled. Here, however, no mad General Ripper gave the command; instead a mechanism in the Omaha headquarters of the Strategic Air Command malfunctions and inadvertently sets off the code message that instigates the flight. This time a cool, competent President uses the hotline telephone to warn Moscow of the advancing American bombers. Nevertheless, one U.S. plane gets through the Russian defense webs and Moscow is totally leveled. To prevent this machine-spawned disaster from developing into a full-scale atomic war, the President offers retribution to the Russians by ordering an American plane to drop a nuclear bomb on New York City. In the nuclear age it would appear that the biblical maxim "an eye for an eye" has become "a city for a city." What *FAIL-SAFE* disturbingly suggests is that in an era of *homo cyberneticus*, where giant computers can usurp man's decisionmaking abilities, not even reason can prevent atomic destruction.

A more conventional antiwar film was *THE VICTORS* (1963). Despite its viewpoint that all military victories are essentially pyrrhic, *THE VICTORS* was hardly more than a pastiche of *WHAT PRICE GLORY?*, *BATTLEGROUND*, and *PATHS OF GLORY*. The level of the antiwar argument in this film about World War II seldom rose above so trite a scene as the execution of an American deserter on Christmas Day to the soundtrack accompaniment of "Jingle Bells."

With the release of *THE VICTORS, FAIL-SAFE; SEVEN DAYS IN MAY*, and *DR. STRANGELOVE* a faint echo of the HUAC communist witch hunting again rumbled from rightist circles. The John Birch Society and the Daughters of the American Revolution alleged that *THE VICTORS* was unfavorable to the United States, noting that its producer-director-writer, Carl Foreman, was a blacklisted émigré to England. A group that took the name Cardinal Mindszenty Foundation said that these films were communistic because they "peddled the Communist line that nuclear war is so terrible that the U.S. should appease, retreat, and even surrender rather than risk it." The Foundation charged *THE VICTORS*, in particular, as being "a massive sordid anti-military film slanted to shock us into believing soldiers defending our country are cruel fools, black marketeers, and murderers."[5]

Throughout the Sixties there were other, less auspicious films which had antiwar elements, either in their depiction of the military or in their implications of a future nuclear calamity. *HELL TO ETERNITY* (1960) and *BEACH RED* (1967), for example, reiterated the cost in human life and values — on both sides — denounced in earlier postwar films. In *BEACH RED* producer-

The Americanization of Emily
with Julie Andrews and James
Garner (Metro-Goldwyn-Mayer)

director-actor Cornel Wilde tried to give the Japanese foe a dignity which had
been lacking in previous Hollywood movies, for which he received an ap-
preciative press in Japan. As Wilde put it, "In this picture the Japanese are
not the grinning villains that they have always been pictured. War is the
villain in *BEACH RED*."[6]

"So long as valor is a virtue, we will have soldiers," says James Garner in
THE AMERICANIZATION OF EMILY (1964), another caustic spoof of the
absurdity of war. Garner played the wheeler-dealer, cynical aide to an American admiral in London during World War II. An anti-hero, at best, he is a
master of the military spoils system; he knows where the best broads, booze,
and beds are to be found. Although he would rather be a living coward than a
dead hero, he unwittingly becomes a fighting man when he is sent to Omaha
Beach during D-Day and emerges, *mirable dictu*, a living hero.

Despite the armistices that separate the shooting wars, the clandestine
maneuvers of spies continue as much, or even more, during peacetime lulls.
To deflate the glamour of the trench-coated spy hero in countless espionage
films, *THE SPY WHO CAME IN FROM THE COLD* (1965) showed the collusive
treachery and cynicism that comprise the life (and death) of agents in the Cold

War. Richard Burton played the weary, seedy spy who was on his last mission before retiring from British Intelligence. But the spy, too, like a soldier at the battlelines, is expendable. No one would expect the spy game to be a graduate seminar in ethics, but the fact that there is little moral difference between the British and the East German Intelligence administrators is the film's scornful revelation.

The unthinkable thermonuclear war, which was the underlying concern of *ON THE BEACH*, *DR. STRANGELOVE*, and *FAIL-SAFE*, was also treated in two little-noticed but meaningful films of the early Sixties, *PANIC IN YEAR ZERO* (1962) and *LADYBUG, LADYBUG* (1963). While on a holiday in their trailer, a Los Angeles family in *PANIC IN YEAR ZERO* learns that the "enemy" has exploded nuclear bombs over key American cities. Similar to *FAIL-SAFE* the Limited General War is waged on the exchange principle: a city for a city, until one side surrenders. "There are no civilians," says the President in a radio broadcast. "We are all at war." The family's struggle for survival is not only against hunger but mainly against the looters, rapists, and killers in what has become a lawless society. Unlike *ON THE BEACH*, which foretold the annihilation of all humanity via atomic fallout, *PANIC IN YEAR ZERO* sug-

Richard Burton in *The Spy Who Came In from the Cold* (Paramount)

VIII

Ladybug, Ladybug (United Artists)

gested that some people will survive if they are brutal enough to withstand the collapse of civilization.

LADYBUG, LADYBUG examined the intriguing notion of the reactions of a group of children in an American rural elementary school after an alert signals an imminent atomic attack. The film implies that even among children only the ruthless would survive. That the yellow alert turns out to be a false alarm does not alleviate the film's pessimistic view of human nature under the stress of nuclear death.

Oscar Wilde once astutely observed that "Laughter is not at all a bad beginning for a friendship." Believing that comedy could serve a good purpose in reducing international animosities and in promoting communication between cultures, Norman Jewison directed *THE RUSSIANS ARE COMING, THE RUSSIANS ARE COMING* in 1966. When a Russian submarine is grounded off the coast of New England and the crew comes ashore for help, the people of the provincial little Cape Cod town think they are being invaded. Misunderstandings proliferate and tensions rise to the boiling point as the local militia under the bumbling leadership of Jonathan Winters prepares another 1776 stand at "Concord bridge." When the Russians finally make it clear that all they want is some power equipment to free their submarine from the shoal, the "little war" is resolved with some mutual toasts of good will.

Brian Keith and Alan Arkin in
*The Russians Are Coming, The
Russians Are Coming*
(United Artists)

Lee Marvin and Vivien Leigh in
Ship of Fools (Columbia)

In every period of Hollywood's history there are a few films which uniquely comment on the whole spectrum of human folly. They do not carp at society per se but rather at the weaknesses of man himself. Their common theme might be epitomized by Pogo's astute observation, "We have met the enemy and he is us." During the Sixties *SHIP OF FOOLS* (1965) was one such film. On one level the vessel was a floating miniature world of the early Thirties with all its crosscurrents of prejudice, chauvinism, and impending war. Yet in their mutual loathing, their corruption, and morbid cynicism the passengers on the German ship sailing from Veracruz to Bremerhaven might just as well have been journeying up the River Styx to a Dantean inferno. Aboard are a virulent anti-Semitic German businessman, a fading countess addicted to morphine, the completely disillusioned ship's doctor who becomes her cruise lover, a loudmouthed Texan never-quite-made-it baseball player, and an embittered divorcee. Despite excellent performances, the film was so pompous in its attempt to be philosophically Important that the ship merely lumbered along, slowed down interminably by its self-conscious earnestness. As film critic Andrew Sarris has remarked, "the Big Subject is as often a trap as an opportunity."[7] *SHIP OF FOOLS* is a conspicuous example of ideology overwhelming art.

Whether it be an Alexis de Tocqueville in the nineteenth century or an Evelyn Waugh in the twentieth, it would appear that foreign visitors have the necessary detachment to anatomize American culture. In 1947 Waugh visited Hollywood and out of his experiences and observations in Los Angeles wrote his wickedly satiric novel *The Loved One*. Perhaps because of the satiric demolition of *DR. STRANGELOVE* and its box-office success, the producers of *THE*

LOVED ONE (1965) probably thought audiences would respond equally to the pioneer black humor of Waugh's twenty-year-old novel. Advertised as "the motion picture with something to offend everyone," the film took ribald swipes not only at the macabre commercialism of the Great American Death Ritual but at the hallowed targets of Momism, patriotism, and religion. By adding all these sacred cows and blasting away at them with a shotgun intermixture of slapstick, shock, and now and then a little bit of Waugh, this satire of California mores was more confusing than illuminating. That confusion was king during the making of *THE LOVED ONE* was evident in the roster of writers who at various times tried to adapt Waugh's novel for the screen. Included were such diverse talents as Luis Buñuel, Elaine May, Christopher Isherwood, and finally Terry Southern (who had co-scripted *DR. STRANGELOVE*). In comedy-satire, too, the Big Subject can also be a trap.

The struggle of the individual to preserve his integrity against those forces in society which would diminish him — whether tyrant kings, political demagogues, or labor racketeers — has been a continuing dramatic subject in the American message film. Quite often it is the use of the historical metaphor that facilitates expressing this theme of the individual conscience versus constrictive pressures toward conformity. Just as it would have been easier for Emile Zola to ignore the scapegoat trial of Alfred Dreyfus, it would have been more expedient for Sir Thomas More to go along with Henry VIII's establishment of the Church of England with the King himself as head. Fred Zinnemann's *A MAN FOR ALL SEASONS* (1966), although set in the sixteenth century, raised moral and political questions that are not alien to this century. Men like Pastor Dietrich Bonhoffer in Nazi Germany, Cardinal Mindszenty in postwar Hungary, and the brothers Berrigan, in the bitter moral debate in the United States on Vietnam, also faced crises of conscience even as Sir Thomas did in Renaissance times.

The cycle of youth films, exemplified during the Fifties by such films as *REBEL WITHOUT A CAUSE* and *THE YOUNG STRANGER*, continued into the Sixties. By the end of the decade they would become one of the dominant types of films on the American screen. Typical of the youth movies in the early years of the decade were *SPLENDOR IN THE GRASS* (1961) and *THE EXPLOSIVE GENERATION* (1961). Warren Beatty became for many young people the James Dean of the Sixties in *SPLENDOR IN THE GRASS* with his portrayal of the frustrated adolescent rebelling against the hypocritical morality of his rich father. The setting of the film, written by William Inge and directed by Elia Kazan, was a small Kansas town in the late Twenties, not unlike the middle-America described in the novels of Sinclair Lewis.

Whereas *SPLENDOR IN THE GRASS* looked nostalgically at youth, *THE EXPLOSIVE GENERATION* in some ways anticipated the widespread youth activism of today. A sociology teacher introduces sex education into his classroom and is fired at the insistence of some irate parents. The high school students in his class strike to defend their teacher's freedom of speech. However, unlike today's destruction of school property and boycott of classes, these

A Man for All Seasons with
Paul Scofield (Columbia)

The Miracle Worker with Anne
Bancroft and Patty Duke
(United Artists)

young people fight back with the ultimate means of nonviolent disobedience, their total silence.

The slums of megalopolis as a seedbed of crime even in an affluent society were seen in the juvenile delinquency dramas *LET NO MAN WRITE MY EPITAPH* (1960), *THE YOUNG SAVAGES* (1961), and *STRANGERS IN THE CITY* (1962). In *LET NO MAN WRITE MY EPITAPH* amid the Chicago slum environment of alcoholics, "junkies," and hoods, a boy struggles to stay free from the criminality which virtually envelops him. *THE YOUNG SAVAGES* showed the efforts of a young assistant district attorney to deal understandingly with the Puerto Rican and Italian gangs who terrorize East Harlem. Even when he himself is beaten half to death by the young hoodlums and his wife also is terrorized, he defends the boys against the charge of gang murder. Burt Lancaster was the young lawyer who had come from these very slums and would have preferred to forget his impoverished background. One of the first films to examine the degrading conditions of El Barrio, the ghetto of Spanish Harlem in New York City, was *STRANGERS IN THE CITY*. The problems of the Alvarez family, newly arrived from Puerto Rico, their desperate poverty, their exploitation, and their inevitable despair, are shown candidly. Although the young Puerto Rican boy tries to stand apart from the crime in the streets, his sister is not so fortunate and becomes a tragic prostitute.

Society's obligation toward the mental retardate was a new theme for Hollywood in the Sixties, and two films of the decade treated this difficult subject with compassion and insight. In *A CHILD IS WAITING* (1936) Judy Garland was an employee at a home for backward children who makes the mistake of confusing pity with therapeutic understanding. After causing an emotional crisis for a retarded boy and his parents she begins to realize the chief doctor's wisdom in encouraging self-reliance in the children. Similarly modest in its intentions was *ANDY* (1965), whose central character was a forty-year-old mental retardate, the son of elderly foreign-born parents living in a slum. Unable to cope with his pitiful childishness they finally decide to commit him to an institution. The need for extraordinary patience and dedication in helping the handicapped, whether mentally retarded or suffering other physical afflictions, was also stressed in *THE MIRACLE WORKER* (1962) and

VIII

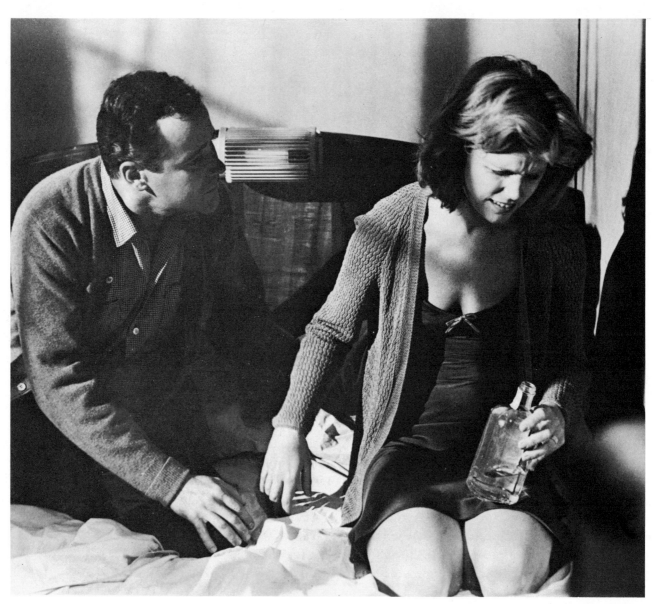

Jack Lemmon and Lee Remick in
Days of Wine and Roses
(Warner Brothers)

DAVID AND LISA (1963). *THE MIRACLE WORKER,* directed by Arthur Penn, was a stunning transfer to the screen of William Gibson's play about the childhood of Helen Keller and the determined efforts of her teacher, Annie Sullivan, to enable Helen to communicate with the world she can neither see nor hear. *DAVID AND LISA* showed how love and tenderness toward a schizoid girl by a fellow patient, a pyschoneurotic boy, enables her to leave her autistic shell and begin to accept the outside world.

The ever-present problem of alcoholism was treated in an extremely perceptive film of 1962, *DAYS OF WINE AND ROSES.* Although Jack Lemmon was as addicted to alcohol as Ray Milland was in *THE LOST WEEKEND,* the rapid growth of Alcoholics Anonymous between the Forties and Sixties made possible sympathetic, outside help to enable him to recover. Ironically, while the young husband is slowly curing himself, his wife (Lee Remick), whom he

Don Murray in *The Hoodlum
Priest* (United Artists)

had led into social drinking, slips deeper into dipsomania.

The therapeutic value of people in a small group attempting to overcome a common problem was also seen in *SYNANON* (1965), which dealt with drug addiction. "No pills and no lying to yourself" is the philosophy of the seminars organized by Charles Dederich, the real-life founder of this California haven for both narcotics and alcohol addicts. Edmund O'Brien as Dederich encourages the "patients" to talk out their problems as a beginning step of the healing process. The film was actually shot at Synanon House — neither a hospital nor a jail — on the beach at Santa Monica.

Another film of the Sixties based on the work of a dedicated individual trying to cope with a social malignancy, this time criminal recidivism, was *THE HOODLUM PRIEST* (1961). Don Murray was coproducer-writer and played the leading role in this biography of Reverend Charles Dismas Clark,

VIII

211

the Jesuit priest known for his work in rehabilitating ex-convicts in his St. Louis parish. Just as Synanon was a "halfway house" for the drug afflicted, Father Clark's Dismas House becomes a refuge for the perplexed ex-inmates who must readjust to a distrustful society.

Paul Newman and George Kennedy in *Cool Hand Luke* (Warner Brothers)

The struggle of the individual against a repressive prison system was the theme of both *BIRDMAN OF ALCATRAZ* (1962) and *COOL HAND LUKE* (1967). Unlike any prison picture that preceded it, *BIRDMAN OF ALCATRAZ* showed the determination of Robert Stroud, despite his 43 years in solitary confinement, to be a person and not a mere number. Defying the authorities that would totally crush his personality, Stroud becomes a world expert on bird diseases by authoring the definitive textbook in the field. Despite the fame which he achieved, Stroud was never released from prison. That the Bureau of Prisons was not sympathetic toward anyone making a film on Stroud's life is apparent. Director John Frankenheimer recalls that when the story was originally scheduled for television, officials of the Bureau of Prisons went to the CBS network and said, "If you do this show about this man you will never get any cooperation from us again on anything you do."[8]

Birdman of Alcatraz with Burt Lancaster (United Artists)

The difference between Mervyn LeRoy's *I AM A FUGITIVE FROM A CHAIN GANG* in 1932 and Stuart Rosenberg's *COOL HAND LUKE* some 35 years later is more than just a matter of time. Although both films take place

213

in a Southern chain-gang prison camp and both show the sadistic regimen imposed on the inmates, the essential change lies in the main characters portrayed by Paul Muni and Paul Newman. Whereas Muni acted a man victimized by social circumstances beyond his control and wants to become a respectable, contributing member of society, Luke is a loner and a cynical outcast through his own choice. Luke would rather die in the prison sweatbox than let the system crush his cockeyed independence. If his defiance has masochistic overtones, Luke also has a spiritual kinship with the *Till Eulenspiegels* of the world who even at the gallows can thumb their noses at those who would grind them down.

The belated treatment of the American Indian as something more than a savage, which had its turning point in *BROKEN ARROW* in 1950, also marked such films of the early Sixties as *THE UNFORGIVEN* (1960), *FLAMING STAR* (1960), *THE OUTSIDER* (1961), and *CHEYENNE AUTUMN* (1964). *THE OUTSIDER* was Ira Hayes, a Pima Indian from Arizona, who achieved military fame as one of the six men who raised the American flag in Iwo Jima. His subsequent turning to the alcoholism which ultimately killed him is seen as the result of the trauma suffered when his best friend and Marine sidekick dies in a battle. In *FLAMING STAR* the leading character, Pacer (Elvis Presley), is a half-breed torn between loyalty to the white settlement and to his Indian mother's tribe. Audrey Hepburn in *THE UNFORGIVEN* was a girl raised by a white family; she becomes the victim of prejudice in the community when her true racial origin as an Indian is discovered. Although there were many similar pictures which expressed pro-Indian viewpoints, the consummate statement of the Sixties on the shameful treatment of the Indians was *CHEYENNE AUTUMN* (1964).

Many events in the sad history of the white man's perfidy toward the Indians are mere footnotes in this saga of shame. John Ford took one such incident as the subject of his *CHEYENNE AUTUMN*, which was based on a book by Mari Sandoz, a noted historian of Indian culture. Putting their trust in the white man's promises, a small tribe of northern Cheyennes agree to leave their Yellowstone River country and be resettled in the Southwest. When their new home is found to be arid, barren, unproductive land, and the long-awaited assistance from the Federal government never arrives, the sick and starving Cheyenne begin their 1500-mile exodus back to their former land. Pursued by the U.S. Cavalry, plagued by wintry gales and disease, only a few survive the trek. Despite the treachery done to the Indians by their white oppressors, *CHEYENNE AUTUMN* also showed that some whites could take up the Indians' cause. An Army officer tries to convince the Washington bigwigs of the Cheyennes' plight, and a Quaker schoolteacher accompanies them throughout their pitiful journey homeward.

John Ford, who laughingly admits that he has killed more Indians in his films than Custer, Beecher, and Chivington put together, had wanted to make *CHEYENNE AUTUMN* for a long time, in order to show the Indians' side of the story. "Let's face it," he said, "we've treated them very badly — it's a blot on

Elvis Presley and Dolores Del Rio
in *Flaming Star*
(Twentieth Century-Fox)

The Unforgiven with Lillian Gish
and Audrey Hepburn
(United Artists)

our shield; we've cheated and robbed, killed, murdered, massacred and everything else, but they kill one white man, and God, out come the troops."[9]

Another John Ford Western that broke away from the stereotyped depiction of minorities was *SERGEANT RUTLEDGE* (1960). In the lost, strayed, or stolen history of the black man in the United States there is a little-known chapter about a group of brave Negro soldiers, including former slaves, who fought during the Indian wars. One of them was the atypical hero of *SERGEANT RUTLEDGE*. Woody Strode played Rutledge, the black cavalryman who is on trial for a double murder and the rape of a white girl. The innocent Rutledge is defended by a white officer friend. Fearful of the prejudice surrounding his trial, the black sergeant deserts his unit but returns when he learns his comrades are in danger. "The Ninth Cavalry is my home," says Rutledge, "my self-respect and my real freedom, and the way I was deserting it, I weren't nothing but a swamp running nigger. And I ain't that. I am a man!"

The Negro as a fighter in this country's wars was also seen in another 1960 film, *ALL THE YOUNG MEN*. Sidney Poitier was a Marine sergeant in the Korean War. The film had the expected character types found in combat movies: a Southern bigot who heckles the black sergeant, an American Indian who also feels the brunt of minority status, the wisecracking guy from the city streets, and so forth. In films like this the message becomes so obvious as to be painfully patronizing. For example, when Alan Ladd, the bitter ex-topkick whom Poitier had replaced, lies severely wounded and requires a blood transfusion, naturally it's Poitier's blood that saves him.

PRESSURE POINT (1962) presented an unusually frank encounter between a white man and a Negro. The period of the film is 1942; and the setting is a Federal prison where a black psychiatrist (Sidney Poitier) is treating a psychopathic convict, a foul-mouthed German Bundist and a hater of Negroes and Jews. The doctor finds himself on the defensive as the bigot constantly badgers him about his color and his subservient status in America. "They've got you singing *My Country, 'Tis of Thee* and they're walkin' all over ya!" scoffs the convict. For the cool, seemingly unshakable psychiatrist the case is a challenge to his ability to remain unprejudiced toward his racist patient.

Of the many films of the Sixties which probed black prejudice as a lingering malaise of American society, one of the finest was Robert Mulligan's *TO KILL A MOCKINGBIRD* (1962). Although the story of a white smalltown Southern lawyer defending a black man accused of rape was not a particularly novel situation, the strength of the film is the contrast between the warped adult world of ingrained prejudice and the innocence of the lawyer's two children who have not yet learned how to hate.

The implementation of the Supreme Court's historic school desegregation decision took on momentum in the early Sixties under the Kennedy administration. Attorney General Robert Kennedy ordered U.S. marshals, the regular Army, and the federalized National Guard to quell reprisals against both Negro and white "freedom riders" in Montgomery, Alabama, in 1961. One of the few films which tried to show the struggles of blacks for equal rights in the con-

Phillip Alford and Mary Badham in *To Kill a Mockingbird* (Universal-International)

Sergeant Rutledge with Jeffrey Hunter, Woody Strode, and Carleton Young (Warner Brothers)

temporary South was Roger Corman's daring *THE INTRUDER* (1962). Although independently produced and with a limited distribution, this film at least confronted an explosive subject which major studios did not touch. The story concerns a rabble-rousing, opportunistic white Northerner who goes to a small Southern town to block school integration. Despite many of the conventions of racism-in-the-South films — cross burnings, trumped-up charges of rape against an innocent Negro youth, and the snarling lynch mobs — *THE INTRUDER* added the new element of opposition to the Supreme Court's decision on schooling. A scene in which the courageous white newspaper editor leads a group of black high schoolers past the sullen faces of the community on their first day at an all-white school might well have come out of a television news report.

NOTHING BUT A MAN (1964) dealt with the efforts of a young Negro laborer in Alabama to get a decent job and live with a modicum of dignity. Like many blacks, Duff and the Baptist minister's daughter he marries are less concerned with becoming involved in civil rights' demonstrations than in trying to build a compatible life together. But Duff learns that jobs and opportunities will not come to him if he does not play the expected Negro role of subservience in Alabama.

BLACK LIKE ME (1964) was based on the true experiences of John Howard Griffin, a white man who temporarily changed the color of his skin to black in order to learn at firsthand the anatomy of racial prejudice. Hitchhiking throughout several states in the South he finds himself the target of bully-type busdrivers and learns painfully about discrimination in getting work.

As one looks at the historical development of the Hollywood message film it is difficult to imagine what scriptwriters would have done without the racially repressive, reactionary Southern town. In *THE CHASE* (1966) virtually every social ill that scenarist Lillian Hellman could muster — bigotry, apathy, racial prejudice, adultery, religious fanaticism, the self-indulging rich, and the shiftless poor — are the warp and woof of a small Texas community. In the simplistic sociology of *THE CHASE* it is the town per se which casts its evil shadow on all of its people. While acknowledging their shortcomings, Southerners might well ask of Hollywood: Does Satansville, U.S.A., *always* have to be south of the Mason-Dixon line?

Although *IN THE HEAT OF THE NIGHT* (1967) shifts its locale from an ugly Texas town to an equally loathsome Mississippi town, the Southern Community as Villain is still the dominant aspect of the film. An easy target for the town's ingrained racial hatred is a Northern Negro who is arrested by the surly, rednecked police chief for the murder of a prominent industrialist. The Negro, it turns out, is a crack homicide detective from Philadelphia who had been visiting in the town. To clear himself of suspicion he cooperates with the contemptuous police chief to solve the crime.

The melodramatic plot was merely a device for the larger comment in this Norman Jewison film: even in the locale of a totally corrupt Southern town a

Negro and a white man can grudgingly come to a mutual respect for each other's professional skills. Jewison has stated that black-white relations is an
aspect of America that must be dealt with in films and that his own interest in
the subject goes back to the end of World War II when he toured Alabama,
Arkansas, and Mississippi while still serving in the Canadian navy.[10]

There were a number of films during the Sixties in which the black man's
plight could not be blamed solely on the bigoted mores of a redneck Southern
town. Many of them, for that matter, took place in locales like Chicago, Paines-
ville, Ohio, or New York City's Harlem. Although the stigma of racial prejudice
is always present in these films, they examined such diverse matters as in-
adequate housing, the crime vortex of Harlem, or something as fundamental
as merely earning a livelihood. *A RAISIN IN THE SUN* (1961) told of a black
family's aspirations to buy a house in a decent neighborhood away from the
tenements of Chicago's South Side. Even after they overcome the pressures
from their future white neighbors to buy their "dream home," the insurance
money left by his father to purchase it is squandered by an impatient son in a
get-rich-quick scheme. *THE COOL WORLD* (1963) revealed the sordidness of
life in Harlem that draws young people into the world of drugs and violence.
Harlem as a sociological reality, a problem that refuses to fade away despite
whatever advances are being made in civil rights legislation or even on the
conscience of white Americans, is as much the villain in *THE COOL WORLD*
as any dusty town in Mississippi.

Whereas *PINKY* in 1949 dodged the issue of racial intermarriage by having
the light-skinned Negro girl give up her Northern white doctor lover, by 1964
the American film was not so timid. In *ONE POTATO, TWO POTATO* a white
divorcee with a child marries a Negro, despite the caveats given by their
friends and the husband's parents. Their happiness is virtually destroyed
when her first husband returns to obtain custody of the child. Despite the fact
that the real father is depicted as being unworthy of his daughter he is awarded

VIII

219

Sidney Poitier, Katharine
Houghton, Katharine Hepburn,
and Spencer Tracy in *Guess Who's
Coming to Dinner* (Columbia)

the child by the court, even though the child prefers her Negro foster father.

During the Sixties one of Hollywood's biggest box-office names was Sidney Poiter. An attractive, gifted actor, his career, starting with *NO WAY OUT* in 1950, parallels the development of the motion-picture industry's increasing interest in treating race relations on the screen. In fact, Poitier has had leading roles in the great majority of such films. Once he had achieved stardom, however (the audience went to see Sidney Poitier himself rather than a movie *with* Sidney Poitier), he was no longer cast solely as the black protagonist in racial confrontation films (*vide EDGE OF THE CITY, SOMETHING OF VALUE, THE DEFIANT ONES, PRESSURE POINT*). Indeed, as Poitier gained box-office "respectability" the range of his roles expanded to musicals such as *PARIS BLUES* (1961); sentimental drama as in *LILIES OF THE FIELD* (1963), *A PATCH OF BLUE* (1965), and *THE SLENDER THREAD* (1965), the Cold War adventure *THE BEDFORD INCIDENT* (1965), and romantic comedy such as *FOR LOVE OF IVY* (1968).

Among the Poitier films whose main concern was the dimensions of racial prejudice none raised such sharply divided opinions from diverse quarters as *GUESS WHO'S COMING TO DINNER* (1967). For white racists such as the National States Rights Party the interracial romance between Poitier and Katharine Houghton was a Jewish plot to mongrelize the white race with Negro blood. For black-militant film critics such as Maxine Hall Elliston of the Organization of Black American Culture, Poitier as the brilliant young scientist, potential Nobel laureate, was his "usual saccharine role of the good 'nigger,' an easy role that he has developed over the years with the help of the Fat White Cats in Hollywood."[11] Nor were young, liberal college audiences any less querulous about the film. Producer-director Stanley Kramer put himself in the lion's den when he traveled to nine college campuses showing his film to student audiences and rapping with them afterward. Objecting to Poitier's characterization, they said, "It's pretty old-fashioned to make the character of the Negro so pure and simple. You made him such an ideal fellow, we knew from the beginning that she would marry him." Kramer's retort was that *everybody* in the film was deliberately idealized, not just the Negro scientist. Thus, the only conceivable objection to the marriage could be the pigmentation of Poitier's skin.

Whether interpreted as a benchmark in the changing screen image of the black American, or as a hoked-up, Technicolor homily capitalizing on a sure-fire combo of Poitier, Katharine Hepburn, and Spencer Tracy, *GUESS WHO'S COMING TO DINNER* went far beyond the timorous interracial probings of what had seemed daring in the late Forties with *LOST BOUNDARIES* or *PINKY*. But within a few years, with the emergence of black directors such as Gordon Parks and Melvin Van Peebles, even *GUESS WHO'S COMING TO DINNER* would appear naïvely tame.

VIII

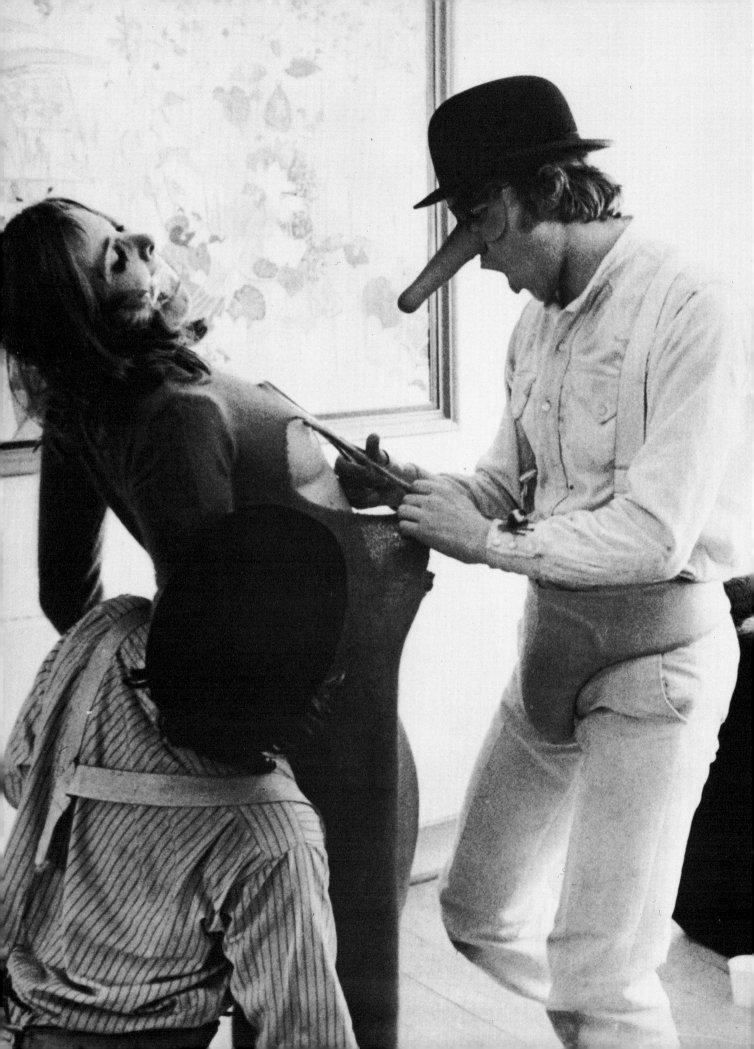

IX

The Great Motion Picture Rating Game

Message Films and the Youth Audience

Campus Upheaval

"Zabriskie Point"

Exploring — and Exploiting — the Generation Gap

The "Pot Scene"

"Medium Cool," Politics, and Vietnam

Antiwar Themes

The Negro Film Market

Black Militancy and "Sweet Sweetback"

A Shameful Chapter in the Winning of the West

Futurism: Dire Forebodings

The Urban Crisis

A Marathon Dance Contest

"Bless the Beasts & Children"

"What I consider the *big* problem, which is not
strictly a Hollywood problem, rather it's a
communication problem (it happens in films, in TV),
is that we are ignoring the world as it is.
Occasionally they salute the superficial changes
that take place in the world, or allusions to war or
to racial issues, but only as a way of stating that
they know it exists. It is characteristic of our
whole society that we live one life as it is, and we
create our dream world in our films and in TV,
not even as we think it should be but in another
way."

Haskell Wexler[1]

Malcolm McDowell (right) in
A Clockwork Orange
(Warner Brothers)

In 1966 Hollywood was economically pressured — for better or for worse — into crossing its Rubicon. As against the 1946 record, when moviegoing accounted for 20 percent of the nation's recreational spending, by the end of the Sixties this figure had diminished to a mere 3 percent. Relatedly, in 1946, 82 percent of all spectator amusement expenditures went to the movies; by 1970 this percentage had slipped to 47 percent despite the astronomical increase in admission prices. With a movie ticket, even for the neighborhood Strand, costing six to eight times what it did in the Thirties, it became obvious that films, more than ever, had to be "tailored" to meet the needs and interests of those who were willing to pay.

Just as the Production Code was liberalized during the Fifties to permit the treatment of once-taboo subjects as a spur to the box office, in 1966 an even less restrictive code was the hoped-for economic booster. While in 1955 *THE MAN WITH THE GOLDEN ARM* merely shook up the code, *WHO'S AFRAID OF VIRGINIA WOOLF?* in 1966 virtually decimated it. The success of *VIRGINIA WOOLF*, with its bitter spewing of four-letter words, was the beginning of the new screen permissiveness which Hollywood hoped would bring about a return to prosperity.

While Jack Valenti, the newly appointed Moses of the Motion Picture Association, was looking for a suitable Ten Commandments for filmmakers (one with more palatable Thou Shalt Nots) the errant Children of Movieland were merrily dancing around the Golden Calf of sex and violence. The new code established under Valenti's aegis was unfortunately a semantic conundrum which satisfied no one and lasted less than two years. The extent of its self-regulating caveats was the ambiguous disclaimer the Code Administration applied to hitherto "unacceptable" films, *Suggested for Mature Audiences.* Since profit-starved theater owners weren't about to engage a clinical psychologist as a ticket taker, the interpretation of "maturity" was anybody's prerogative.

The 1966 Code, which proved so elastic as to be ineffective, also brought on the threat of censorship by various local and state agencies. Taking a leaf from the method of film classification in Great Britain, the industry turned to a rating system. The Great Motion Picture Rating Game provided four categories to alert moviegoers as to a film's suitability for various audiences. With its "R" and "X" categories the system was designed to bar children under 17 from seeing movies that the industry's code people considered too vulgar, violent, or prurient. By the same reasoning that allows eighteen-year-olds to vote for the President of the United States, or fight in Vietnam, the industry decided that once youngsters had reached that ripe age not even Russ Meyer's *BEYOND THE VALLEY OF THE DOLLS* (1970) could corrupt them.

By mid-1971, however, such groups as the National Catholic Film Office were decrying the ratings as "misleading and worse than useless." The National Association of Theater Owners, an exhibitors' organization, expressed its skepticism of the leniency in handing out the ratings, particularly the "GP" (all ages admitted; parental guidance suggested). Many theater owners objected to the trend toward gartuitous nudity, offensive language, and excessive violence which the rating system inadvertently encouraged. They worried, not without reason, that the ratings were even further fragmenting the moviegoing audience, thus worsening their economic crisis. If, as has been estimated, 70 percent of all films produced today are financial failures, the need is to broaden the audience or to sharply reduce production budgets.

Producers, distributors, and exhibitors alike were truly in a dilemma in the Seventies. The nationwide research study which the Motion Picture Association engaged Daniel J. Yankelovich, Inc., to undertake in 1967 reaffirmed the industry's hunch about the audience. Only a small percentage of people over 40 were attending movies. Of the under-40s who were buying tickets, the great majority of them were between the ages of 16 and 24. The movies, which for decades had drawn its audiences from the entire age spectrum, now had to rely for economic sustenance primarily on people under 30, the so-called youth audience. These young moviegoers saw an average of 39 films a year, while their mothers and fathers were probably at home watching the TV screen. Understandably, then, the $64 million question in Hollywood became, "What do the kids want?"

Clearly the young people were not interested in super-musicals like *SWEET CHARITY* (1968), *PAINT YOUR WAGON* (1969), or *THE STAR* (1968); or big-budget epics like *TORA! TORA! TORA!* (1970), by which Darryl F. Zanuck had hoped to repeat the success of his 1962 *THE LONGEST DAY*. No longer could a picture be sold merely on the strength of established big names like Elizabeth Taylor or Marlon Brando. Dustin Hoffman, Jane Fonda and brother Peter, Kirk Douglas's son Michael, Jon Voight, and Jack Nicholson, all of whom seemed to represent the life style of the "youth culture," became the new screen idols. At a time when the password of young moviegoers was "relevance" one might have expected the result to be a veritable renaissance in the film of social comment.

Apart from the youth films that had such perennial subjects as motorbiking, beach parties, and rock festivals (and such counterculture films as *ALICE'S RESTAURANT* of 1969), there were a number of films which dealt with youth involvement in social issues. The phenomenal success of *THE GRADUATE* (1967) made it obvious that young people wanted to see movies that reflected their own milieu and experiences. One such area, of course, was the growing disenchantment of college students with the values of their parents as well as with the educational Establishment itself.

THE ACTIVIST, GETTING STRAIGHT, THE STRAWBERRY STATE-MENT, and *RPM,* all released in 1970, had the campus as the locus of agitation against America's role in Vietnam, outmoded pedagogy, and a political system from which young people felt themselves alienated. In *THE ACTIVIST,* on what could easily have been the Berkeley campus, a student leader spearheads an antiwar demonstration in front of an induction center. Echoing the headline stories about Mario Savio and the Free Speech Movement, the bloody demonstration in *THE ACTIVIST* runs into police brutality and is completely

IX

Elliot Gould (center) in *Getting Straight* (Columbia)

routed. The badge of honor in such student-protest films is a cracked skull from a policeman's club, and the visual pyrotechnics of a student-police melee became *de rigueur* in the "confrontation" film.

If after the turbulent events at Columbia University and the tragic death of four students at Kent State there was any expectation that the youth film might be the vehicle for serious examination of student unrest, *GETTING STRAIGHT* clearly wasn't it. Wavering between a kind of Bruce Jay Friedman type of black humor and purported serious comments about college crises, the film exploited all the contemporary typologies: a hero who was formerly a Freedom Rider, a Women's Lib heroine, a pompous, closed-mind Prexy, and the ever-present, sadistic campus cops to quell the climactic demonstration. Typical of the film's humor was the M.A. oral examination of protagonist Elliot Gould which becomes a travesty when a super-zealous professor uses the session to promulgate his pet theory that F. Scott Fitzgerald was a homosexual. Whether such caricatured figures of Academe shed any true light on the current discontent of many students is questionable.

If *GETTING STRAIGHT* was a mixed bag of contemporary youth-cult jelly beans, *THE STRAWBERRY STATEMENT* was an even worse exploitation of issues keenly felt by college students. Eyeing the success of James Simon Kunen's book about the 1968 Columbia University riots, the economically

faltering MGM evidently decided that student revolution was a highly salable commodity. When Bo Polk, who was at the time head of MGM, bought the film rights to Kunen's book, he ventured the opinion that there was profit to be made from movies about "current crises" such as "youth and the Establishment."[2]

In *THE STRAWBERRY STATEMENT* the student sit-in occupation of administration offices is triggered by the university's plan to construct an ROTC building on land which neighborhood black children used as a playground. Unfortunately, the rhetoric of the strikers in the film is hardly more than a chanting parody of campus slogan makers: "Strike because you hate cops . . . Strike because you hate war . . . Strike because there is poverty . . . Strike because there's no poetry in your lectures . . . Strike because classes are a drag."[3] Nor did it neglect the SDS-type of *agit-prop* iconography of posters of Che Guevara intermixed with pop-revolutionary graffiti. The hero's political "maturing" is symbolized by his replacing a poster of Robert Kennedy in his room with one of Che. As Brian De Palma astutely observed, the reason why a picture like *THE STRAWBERRY STATEMENT* failed was "you can't *stage* that stuff; we've seen it all on television."

To paraphrase Mark Twain, *THE STRAWBERRY STATEMENT* knew all the words but didn't know the tune. The youth audience for which the film was calculatedly fashioned didn't buy it, Period. If MGM had put its hopes in at-

The Strawberry Statement with Bruce Davison
(Metro-Goldwyn-Mayer)

IX

tracting the "youth market" and recouping the millions it had been losing for several years, pictures like *THE STRAWBERRY STATEMENT* or the equally disastrous *ZABRISKIE POINT*, released a few months before, were not the answer.

Few films in recent movie history were given the publicity build-up of *ZABRISKIE POINT* (1970). After the tremendous international success of his *BLOW-UP* (1966) it was to be the first American film for the famous Italian director, Michelangelo Antonioni. Newspaper columnists hung on every detail of the casting, the location shooting in Death Valley, and the director's scouting for background material for his script at demonstrations and SDS meetings on scattered campuses. That Antonioni was *simpatico* with the aims of radical students dominated the teatime chatter of New Left film critics.

The opening sequences of *ZABRISKIE POINT* suggested that here, indeed, might be the "authentic" story of student disaffection. A California university has been closed because black students have occupied a campus building. After a political rap session (with Eldridge Cleaver's wife in attendance), a student, Mark, goes out to buy a gun. At a confrontation later in the day between the blacks and the police a policeman is killed. Fearful that he will be blamed because he has a gun, Mark steals a small private plane and escapes to the desert.

From there on, campus issues are forgotten and the film meanders into a series of Antonioni's private visions of alienation, materialism, sexuality — the familiar bugaboos of what critic Andrew Sarris has called "Antoniennui." Clearly, MGM's expectations for a relevant *and* salable film about campus troubles weren't actualized. Whether Antonioni, despite his disclaimers, came as a latter-day De Tocqueville to scrutinize American society is not made clear in the film. It may well be that Antonioni's psychological red deserts are independent of the geography of either mod London or the arid Death Valley.

In an effort to make *RPM* a true-to-life picture of students' dissatisfaction with their college experience, producer-director Stanley Kramer engaged a working professor, Erich Segal, to write the script. A takeover of the administration building is yet again the culmination of the students' protest, but this time their "winter of discontent" concerns their lack of autonomy in curriculum planning, the hiring and firing of faculty, and setting criteria for the awarding of degrees. Like *GETTING STRAIGHT* and *THE STRAWBERRY STATEMENT*, *RPM* had only the veneer of the contemporary college scene. If the students were opposed to the curriculum at their university they offered no hint of what they would propose as an alternative, or what their standards would be for tenure of professors. These are, indeed, thorny questions in real-life Academe and perhaps to expect a film to solve them may be mere carping. Yet in a film that purports to be a serious look at the upheaval on America's campuses, such shortcomings diminish the film's validity.

For many of the youths of the Seventies, adherence to the new counterculture *ipso facto* placed their parents in the "enemy camp." Since most parents were over 30 there was little hope on the part of their children that

they could rap together. Films like *HAIL, HERO!* (1969), *ADAM AT 6 A.M.* (1970), *HOMER* (1971), and *SUMMERTREE* (1971) all emphasized the tension and disagreement within families over such matters as military service, taste in music, and — that touchy subject — to smoke or not to smoke pot.

In *HAIL, HERO!* a young man quits college and returns to the ranch of his Establishment family. The dropout and his parents become embroiled over his

Don Scardino in *Homer*
(National General)

long hair and his peacenik ideas. The central theme of *HOMER* is the conflict between a father and his son over the Vietnam War. As an act of defiance of his father, but also a gesture of protest against the war, Homer chains himself to the door of the local Veterans of Foreign Wars meetinghall. Unable to reach any kind of common ground between his father's values and his own, Homer takes to the road, flanked by his guitar. The protagonist of *ADAM AT 6 A.M.*, not unlike Jack Nicholson in *FIVE EASY PIECES* (1970), is in revolt against aesthetic intellectualism. Although he is a young instructor at a California college, he uses his summer vacation to get back to "God's own mud" as a laborer on a land-clearing crew. To his disillusionment he learns that even the earthy people of Missouri have been seduced by the materialism of the American Dream. *SUMMERTREE* looked at another confused young man, torn by conflict with his parents over the Draft. Michael Douglas was the prototype of thousands of young people today who seem to be wandering aimlessly between childhood and adulthood. After going to college to avoid military service, he drops out to study guitar at a music conservatory. But when even the music

Adam at 6 A.M. with Michael
Douglas and Joe Don Baker
(National General)

school turns him down and he is drafted, he plans to escape to Canada. During
a farewell visit to his parents, his father prevents him from leaving the country
by tampering with his automobile. The ironic ending is a television news shot
of a dead soldier in Vietnam.

If the youth audience turned thumbs down on the big studio youth films,
vide THE STRAWBERRY STATEMENT or *RPM,* they seemed more willing to
respond to low-budget efforts produced by independent filmmakers. *GREET-
INGS* (1968) and *HI, MOM!* (1969), both directed by under-30 Brian De Palma,
typified the irreverence for the Sacred Cows of Squaresville, USA, that the kids
liked to think they were rebelling against. *GREETINGS* took topical potshots
at the Draft, at Lyndon B. Johnson (by using a clip from a television speech:
"I'm not saying that you never had it so good — but that's a fact, isn't it?") and
even the Warren Commission's findings on the death of John F. Kennedy. *HI,
MOM!* was a broadside criticism of black militants, white liberals, and *cinéma
vérité* affectations among would-be moviemakers. But Hollywood in its ancient
wisdom got in the last word. To twist the old adage, "If you can't lick them,

Easy Rider with Dennis Hopper, Peter Fonda, and Jack Nicholson (Columbia)

Taking Off (Universal)

have them join you," Warner Brothers held out the big-budget carrot to Mr. De Palma and hired him to direct *GET TO KNOW YOUR RABBIT* (1972) with a cast including Orson Welles, Katharine Ross, and Tom Smothers.

Underground independent directors such as De Palma or Robert Downey, however, had not monopolized the satiric side of the contemporary youth scene. Milos Forman, the noted Czech director of such films as *LOVES OF A BLONDE* (1965) and *THE FIREMAN'S BALL* (1968), used the theme of runaway youths for a humorous dissection of suburban American values. Forman's mischievous *TAKING OFF* (1971) carried the audience to a monthly meeting of the fictitious Society for Parents of Fugitive Children. Perhaps he loaded his argument too much on the side of young people, for one look at the inane goings-on at the SPFC meeting left no doubt about why the children left home. In its intention to make us see the comic as well as the serious side of the parent-youth communications gap, Forman's film was a more insightful commentary on American society than Antonioni's dourly pretentious *ZABRISKIE POINT*.

The kids take off in *JOE* (1970) too, but here circumstances are tragic. After his daughter suffers an overdose of drugs, a vengeful advertising executive kills her dope-peddling boyfriend. The girl subsequently runs away from home. During the search for her, the father and his hippie-hating "hard-hat" ally, Joe, virtually massacre a group of young people living together in a commune. One of the victims is the daughter. In the lurid history of "exploitation movies" — exploitative in the sense of taking advantage of every angle of social discord, and also in the "trade" sense of marketing violence and sensationalism — *JOE* must surely rank at the top of the heap.

If the rebellious young people in the films of the Jazz Age Twenties rode in rumble seats with a flask of bootlegged hooch in hand, their movie descendants in the Seventies replaced a fifth of whiskey with a joint or two of pot. Whether at their pastoral rock festivals, Consciousness III communes at Haight-Ashbury, or New York's East Village, or their Ivy League campuses, the "pot culture" became so prevalent and even grudgingly acknowledged by 1971 that several state legislatures began to consider the possibility of legalizing marijuana.

This permissiveness on the part of a large segment of the American public toward narcotization, especially via the "soft stuff," was mirrored in many of the films about drugs. Indeed, whereas *THE MAN WITH THE GOLDEN ARM* and *A HATFUL OF RAIN* a decade of so earlier had delineated the deleterious consequences of drug usage, films like *EASY RIDER* (1969) showed drugs as a necessary accouterment of their hip protagonists. As critic Diana Trilling observed, *EASY RIDER*, perhaps the most successful youth film of the decade, casually accepted the fact of trafficking in drugs. Bike boys Peter Fonda and Dennis Hopper had financed their American odyssey by selling hard drugs to a higher-up parasite in a Rolls Royce. Further, there is no subterfuge that their respites from barreling down the highways were not stopovers for a Coke but rather for a joint of cannabis. One of the film's highlights is their indoctrination of a picaresque lawyer (Jack Nicholson) into the "joys" of marijuana.

Expectedly, the producers of exploitation pictures such as American International had a field day with the entire counterculture drug scene. Turning from their usual fare of *BEACH BLANKET BINGO* (1965), *I WAS A TEEN-AGE WEREWOLF* (1957), and their numerous bastardizations of the works of Edgar Allan Poe, American International released films like *THE TRIP* (1967) and *PSYCH-OUT* (1968). In both there is a spurious guru who guides young voyagers on a psychedelic mind-blowing marijuana/LSD/STP expedition. Peter Fonda regains his sexual prowess by going on an LSD excursion in *THE TRIP*. *PSYCH-OUT* takes a little bit of everything from the counterculture mystique. Susan Strasberg played a deaf runaway to Haight-Ashbury who is nearly seduced by a guru-buddy of her hippie lover while she is freaked out on STP. (Annette Funicello, where are you when we really need you!)

Not all drug films of the Sixties and early Seventies were of the exploitative variety. *THE CONNECTION* (1960), Shirley Clarke's film version of Jack Gelber's play, was neither sensational nor sentimental in its look at eight drug addicts in a Manhattan loft apartment waiting for a delivery of heroin. *CHAPPAQUA* (1967), directed by actor-poet Conrad Rooks, was a visually stunning film about a drug addict's struggle toward recovery. It is not so much willpower but rather sheer terror of his nightmarish hallucinations that impels him toward his cure. Along with Rooks himself as the addict and Jean-Louis Barrault, the cast included such idols of the "Beat Generation" as Allen Ginsberg and William S. Burroughs.

THE PEOPLE NEXT DOOR (1970) recognized that the problem of drug addiction was not confined to the Haight-Ashburys or Spanish Harlems; indeed, middle-class families were not immune to it. Originally a television play, this film was yet another story of the generation gap between teenagers and their bewildered parents, this time quarreling over drugs. With the frightening statistics of suburban teenagers dying every day from drug overdose, the grimness of *THE PEOPLE NEXT DOOR* belied the cynical and superficial advertising campaign by which the producers hoped to sell the film to the public. A typical advertisement read: "a trip in the suburbs . . . among all those trees and all that grass."

The plot of *THE PANIC IN NEEDLE PARK* (1971) could have been drawn from statistics compiled by New York City's Medical Examiner's office. During the first six months of 1971, according to the report, no fewer than 106 teenage drug addicts had died in New York mainly because of acute reactions to heroin. Almost clinical in its approach to the subject, *THE PANIC IN NEEDLE PARK* tells of two young lovers who meet in the junkie haven of Broadway and 72nd Street, dubbed Needle Park. The boy is a drug pusher and the girl, who has drifted to New York from Indiana, acquires the habit from him. Later she becomes a prostitute to raise enough money to sustain their addiction. The film was based on a *Life* magazine series and was unsparing in its tragic representation of the dropped-out derelicts whose vision of the future ends with the thrust of a needle into their veins. Although the film offered no solu-

The Panic in Needle Park
(Twentieth Century-Fox)

Conrad Rooks in Chappaqua
(Regional)

IX

235

Peter Bonerz (center) and Robert Forster (right) in *Medium Cool* (Paramount)

tion to the plight of Helen and Bobby, its revelations about the destructive life style of young addicts seemed authentic.

The release of *THE PANIC IN NEEDLE PARK* was another occasion for criticism of the rating system of the Motion Picture Association. Convinced that his film's message is so *anti*-drug that young people should be allowed to see it, director Jerry Schatzberg protested the "R" classification it received. At a time when a growing number of junior high school and even grammar school students are being hooked on heroin, Schatzberg felt that his film should not be cut off from this age group since they, too, could profit from the film's inherent warning. In Boston, exhibitor Ben Sack advertised that his theater showing *THE PANIC IN NEEDLE PARK* would disregard the "R" rating and admit anyone over ten years of age. His ad stated: "We feel that our youth, their parents, and the community at large will all benefit."

With *THE PANIC IN NEEDLE PARK* the cycle of films about youthful drug addiction was in full swing. *DUSTY AND SWEETS McGEE* (1971), Stuart Hagmann's *BELIEVE IN ME* (1971), *JENNIFER ON MY MIND* (1971), *BORN TO WIN* (1971) — all of them followed the pattern of combining an antidrug message with counterculture Romeos and Juliets. Like Schatzberg, the makers of these films felt a sense of personal mission. Floyd Mutrux, who directed

DUSTY AND SWEETS McGEE, avers that the final scene of his film in which the boy and girl commit suicide together is not intended to be "romantic." Rather he wanted it to be "so ugly it has got to turn the kids around."

It would be a canard to suggest that the only thing on the minds of today's youth is drugs, rock, and sex. One should not confuse open discussion of these matters with total preoccupation. While their parents were flipping a coin in the 1968 presidential election between Nixon and Humphrey, young people, in general, were turned off by both of these candidates. Their hopes for a reformed political order first had centered on Senator Eugene McCarthy because he was the first candidate to challenge Lyndon B. Johnson's Vietnam War policies. Another political hero of the hoped-for "new politics" was Robert F. Kennedy, who was on his way to creating a formidable coalition of the restless, idealistic young, the poor, the dispossessed, and various minority groups before a crazed assassin killed him. By the time the Democrats held their nominating convention in Chicago McCarthy had faded, Bobby Kennedy was dead and Hubert Humphrey, the heir-designate of LBJ, was in no position to overturn the established policies of his mentor. As if they knew that the Vietnam War would drag on interminably, thousands of politically activist young people went to Chicago in a kind of desperate, last-ditch effort to make themselves heard.

Director Haskell Wexler went there too. Four months before the convention even began he had completed his script for *MEDIUM COOL* (1969). Sensing that there would be altercations between the Chicago police and the antiwar demonstrators, he took his cast to Chicago during that turbulent week to incorporate his story into the real events that were taking place. What emerged from director Wexler's hybrid blend of fiction and actuality was one of the most personal political films ever to come from Hollywood. Whether consciously or not, *MEDIUM COOL* bore a close resemblance to the philosophy of such film revolutionaries as Jean-Luc Godard in France, Marco Bellocchio in Italy, and Glauber Rocha in Brazil. Wexler might well have been echoing the manifesto of Godard and his Dziga Vertov Film Group: "It is necessary to stop making movies on politics, to stop making political movies, and to begin making political movies politically."

It is interesting that Wexler, himself a noted cinematographer, should make the protagonist of *MEDIUM COOL* a TV news cameraman. At first, the cameraman is essentially apolitical, but as he becomes personally involved with the demonstrators in the Chicago streets he loses his cynical detachment and comes to a sharp political awakening. When he protests against handing over footage of the demonstrations to the FBI and CIA, he is fired from his job.

In its depiction of America as a violent society torn apart by racism, disparity between the rich and the very poor, and the angry voices of the young activists crying for peace against the deaf ears of the government, *MEDIUM COOL* indicates the latitude of political freedom on the American screen. That the film was released by a major company, Paramount, reveals the distance between the way Hollywood can deal with the most volatile subjects today in

IX

Paul Newman in *WUSA*
(Paramount)

Jon Voight (right) in *The
Revolutionary* (United Artists)

contrast to the timid Fifties, when the slightest frown from the House Un-American Activities Committee made studio heads tremble.

WUSA (1970) was a heavy-handed attempt to stress the danger of an extreme right-wing takeover of the United States by manipulation of the mass media. The theme was not a new one, for such villainy was also the subject of *MEET JOHN DOE* and *KEEPER OF THE FLAME* nearly 30 years before. Produced by and starring Paul Newman, whose liberal political activism is well known, *WUSA* is about an opportunistic drifter who is hired as a diskjockey by a reactionary, rabble-rousing radio station in New Orleans. At first, as politically apathetic as the cameraman in *MEDIUM COOL*, Newman goes along with station WUSA's hate propaganda. His realization of the consequences of broadcasting trumped-up editorials about crime and welfare chiseling finally leads him to denounce the bigots who employ him, and at a giant Americanism rally he tries to fight back. *WUSA* is an example of a message film in which the bad guys and the good guys are too deftly stacked against each other on opposite sides of the political spectrum. Consequently its naïve polemics become hardly more than a political cartoon.

If *WUSA* was too shrill in expounding its message, *THE REVOLUTIONARY* (1970) was too muted. The locale, for example, is never identified, although one infers that it is the United States from the uniforms of the policemen and the militancy of the blacks and the university campus. By the same token, Jon Voight, as the college expellee who is attracted to communism, is never quite sure of his ideological grounds. Despite a smattering of yippie anarchists, striking workers, and the National Guard marching against black militants, the film is a melange of ambiguity and equivocation. In the cop-out technique

Wild in the Streets
(American International)

reminiscent of *The Lady or the Tiger?*, the audience is asked to decide whether or not in the final sequence the young revolutionary will throw a bomb at a judge marked for assassination.

A number of recent politically oriented films, *WILD IN THE STREETS* (1968), *ICE* (1970), and *PUNISHMENT PARK* (1971), comment on current social issues by projecting their effects into the near future. The plot of *WILD IN THE STREETS* seemed as though it were created by a zonked-out coalition of writers from *Mad* magazine and *Rolling Stone*, with the ghost of George Orwell as continuity adviser. A 19-year-old pop singer is elected President of the United States after Congress is forced to lower the voting age to 14. That this is accomplished by putting LSD in the water supply is only one of the unorthodox techniques of persuasion used by the politicized youngsters. The new administration demands that adults retire at 30. At 35, moreover, the Senior Citizens are escorted by blue-jeaned security guards to rehabilitation camps where they are given compulsory soma. In its final satiric comment on Youth Power, *WILD IN THE STREETS* poses the ultimate generation-gap joke: the 3-year-olds threaten to revolt against the 15-year-olds!

Not surprisingly, some of today's boldest political films are being made by filmmakers who are not a part of the Hollywood Establishment. Seen mainly in museum programs, campuses, or specialized theaters, their films are not widely distributed. One of the most articulate filmmakers of the so-called New American Cinema is Robert Kramer, whose political films include *THE EDGE* (1968) as well as *ICE*. Whereas *THE EDGE* deals with the recent past — a would-be assassination of the President to atone for the killing in Vietnam — *ICE* speculates on urban guerrilla warfare against a neofascist authoritarian

IX

government of the near future. The film poses the situation of the United States committing aggression against Mexico, and concerns a group of guerrillas plotting sabotage and other revolutionary activities. The similarity of this network of young extreme leftists and the actual Weatherman faction of the SDS is more than fortuitous. Even more than Haskell Wexler's *hommage* to Godard in *MEDIUM COOL*, *ICE* is clearly influenced by the cinemarxism of the French director. It is noteworthy that in its work of encouraging new filmmakers The American Film Institute assisted in the financing of *ICE* by awarding Robert Kramer a grant.

A repressive U.S. government in the near future is also the political background of *PUNISHMENT PARK*, the first American film of British director Peter Watkins, acclaimed for his pacifist documentary, *THE WAR GAME* (1966). *PUNISHMENT PARK* tells of the massive arrests and detention of young political dissidents who are protesting the even further expansion of the war in Indochina. Because the prisons are so overflowing, the youthful rebels are given a choice of serving lengthy sentences or submitting to a three-day endurance test in Punishment Park, a desert area in Southern California. This life-or-death "game" has its own bizarre rules. The young prisoners of the "Corrective Groups" are given three days to reach, on foot, an American flag 57 miles away. Spotted a handicap of a two- or three-hour start, they are pursued by the National Guard. If they manage to reach the flag in the allotted time they are set free; if they are caught by the pursuing soldiers they are shot dead. They are given no food but are informed that there will be water at the halfway mark. The regression to the days of the gladiators of Nero's Rome in this political horror film is Watkins' terrifying comment on what could happen in American society.

No issue has contributed more to social discord in contemporary American life than our involvement in Vietnam. Because the war was deplored by a majority of Americans, especially the young people, Hollywood was reluctant to make any film about the conflict in Indochina. Stanley Kramer, who had planned a film on the Vietnam War but later shelved the project, remarked that the truth about the war had been so much obscured that he found it impossible to find a valid point of view. There were economic reasons, too, for Hollywood's avoiding a war that literally divided its potential audience. As director Mel Shavelson pointed out, "Hollywood can't take sides, because if it does it can't sell tickets to the other."

John Wayne disagreed; in fact, his credo being that filmmakers *had* to take a side, he produced, directed, and starred in *THE GREEN BERETS* (1968), the first and only major studio movie about the Vietnam War. The film is stacked with all of Wayne's righteous, rightist wrath against all dissenters to U.S. Vietnam policy. A key character in *THE GREEN BERETS* is a left-wing, dovish reporter who is at first skeptical of the war's purpose. In his own political awakening, he gradually changes from a "pinko creep" completely subservient to his liberal, East Coast publication ("If I write what I want to say I may not have a job," he tells Wayne) and becomes an all-out believer in the Pentagon

cause. *THE GREEN BERETS*, like the earlier *THE UGLY AMERICAN* (1963), used the events in Southeast Asia more as a background for adventuresome heroics than for elucidation of the complex nature of the war.

John Wayne in *The Green Berets* (Warner Brothers)

The antimilitarist sentiment, which had found growing expression in such films of the early Sixties as *DR. STRANGELOVE, SEVEN DAYS IN MAY,* and *THE VICTORS* as well as in the youth films that began to appear as the decade ended, continued into the Seventies. *M*A*S*H, CATCH 22,* and to some extent *PATTON,* all released in 1970, examined military leadership with something less than adulation. *M*A*S*H,* although in the tradition of the service comedy such as *MR. ROBERTS* (1955), *OPERATION MAD BALL* (1957), and *WAKE ME WHEN IT'S OVER* (1960), went beyond mere high jinks in its *reductio ad absurdum* of the military mystique. If the behavior of the two surgeons, played in grand comic style by Elliot Gould and Donald Sutherland, was

IX

241

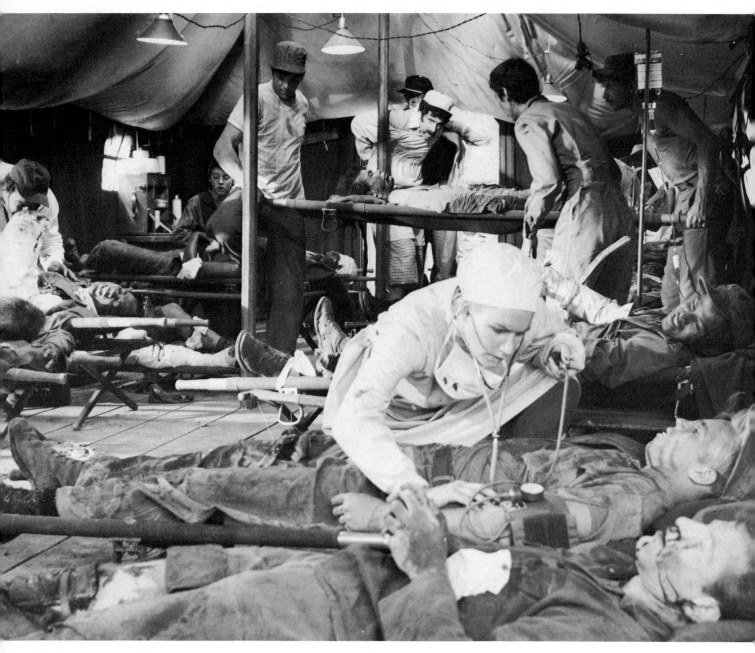

M*A*S*H (Twentieth Century-Fox)

irreverent toward the horror of mangled soldiers coming to a gory Mobile Army Service Hospital during the Korean War, it is because war itself is a gigantic slaughterhouse. Perhaps only by playing the lunatic game can they preserve their sanity, as psychiatrist R. D. Laing might agree.

While the lunacy of *M*A*S*H* has at least an anchor in reality, *CATCH 22* delineates the madness of war in a nightmarish interposing of realism and surrealism. Director Mike Nichols makes a vivid indictment of war's human consequences in the sequence when Yossarian wanders through the streets of Rome: we see a grotesque tableau of human corruption which reaches its evil pinnacle in time of war. Like the surgeons in *M*A*S*H*, Lieutenant Milo

Arthur Garfunkel and Alan Arkin
in *Catch 22* (Paramount)

Minderbender, the king of the black marketeers, has his own self-preserving code of cynical irrationality. But for Yossarian the price of abandoning all humanistic values in the carnage of war is too great; and as the film ends we see him paddling wildly in a tiny yellow canoe, still trying to find a way "out." In its caricature of military brass as willing collaborators in Minderbender's syndicate of wartime profiteering (*vide* Orson Welles's bloated General Dreedle) *CATCH 22* makes its most specific censure of the military apparatus.

By showing both the noble aspects of General Patton's character, as well as his haughty, spit-and-polish authoritarianism-*cum*-megalomania, actor George C. Scott and director Franklin J. Schaffner created a unique screen

IX

243

biography in *PATTON*. Although Patton was portrayed as a great military strategist, his arrogance, contempt for human shortcomings, and inability to cope sympathetically with the problems of peace, lead to his being relieved from a postwar occupation command. In an unusual pre-title overture to the film we see Patton in all his regalia, ivory-handled pistols and all, standing before an enormous American flag. As though addressing his Third Army — but also as a downstage monologue delivered to the audience — he expounds his pungent military credo, to wit: "No bastard ever won a war by dying for his country; he won it by making the other poor dumb bastard die for *his* country." The dualism of Patton's character in the film thus becomes immediately evident — allowing both hawks and doves to find support for their different viewpoints.

Perhaps because antiwar sentiment had intensified to new heights during the Vietnam War, the producers of *JOHNNY GOT HIS GUN* (1971) speculated that audiences would respond to this shocking story of a basket-case victim of World War I. Directed by Dalton Trumbo and based on his pacifist novel written in the Thirties, the film is about a soldier who idealistically goes to war and loses both arms, both legs, and most of his face in a shelling. Although the doctors believe he has suffered brain damage and can feel nothing, the living human trunk is, in fact, aware of his condition. His futile attempts to communicate with a compassionate nurse culminate when he taps out a message in Morse code by hitting his head against the bed. *Kill me*, he begs. But the military higher-ups refuse to allow this mangled hulk to be seen, or even to notify his family. He is locked in a darkened room and left to die. Even when the nurse tries to mercifully kill him the generals prevent this. Although previous films such as *THE BEST YEARS OF OUR LIVES* and *THE MEN* had been concerned with mutilated survivors of war, no film ever went so far in excoriating war's human toll. *JOHNNY GOT HIS GUN* is an example of Dalton Trumbo's conviction that art is a weapon for the betterment of mankind rather than a vain adornment of aesthetes and poseurs.

The equally unusual antiwar film *NO DRUMS, NO BUGLES* (1971) also looked back to another conflict. Set during the period of the American Civil War, the film's central character — and virtually only character — is a pacifist who "drops out" from the fighting and chooses a life of simplicity in the mountains of West Virginia. After the war is over he rejoices in the knowledge that he did not take part in the killing.

Just as the changing age composition of movie audiences was accountable for the plethora of youth films that began in the late Sixties, the changing racial composition resulted in an unprecedented number of films dealing with, starring, and directed by Negroes. By 1970 it was estimated that Negroes comprised nearly one-third of the moviegoers in the U.S. film market. Like the whiskey companies and car and tire manufacturers before them, the movie industry, over the past 15 or 20 years, has come to recognize the substantial purchasing power of the black population — nearly $40 billion a year. The Negro market for films has proliferated to the point where it is no longer limited

Jane Alexander and James Earl
Jones in *The Great White Hope*
(Twentieth Century-Fox)

to films about racial prejudice only but to pictures as diverse in subject as
PUTNEY SWOPE (1969), *COTTON COMES TO HARLEM* (1970), and *SHAFT*
(1971).

This is not to suggest that American society has solved its interracial
problems or that the N.A.A.C.P. has outlived its usefulness. In *SLAVES* (1969),
THE LIBERATION OF L. B. JONES (1970), and *THE GREAT WHITE HOPE*
(1970) racism is still a central issue. William Wyler's *THE LIBERATION OF
L. B. JONES*, despite its transplant of Peyton Place to the Deep South and its
hokey melodrama, took a position hitherto avoided by Hollywood — the violent revenge of a black against his white oppressor is treated sympathetically.
When a black man becomes the world's heavyweight boxing champion in *THE
GREAT WHITE HOPE*, and especially after he acquires a white mistress, racial

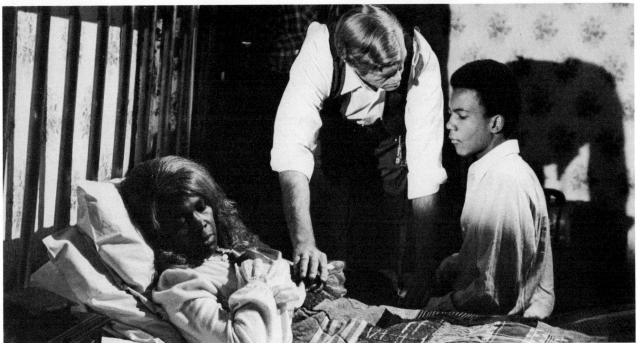

bigots are incensed and pursue him relentlessly until his career is finished. Herbert J. Biberman's *SLAVES* was an unsubtle tract about the antebellum South, complete with white masters ravishing their comely black female servants.

Emulating the box-office success of *IN THE HEAT OF THE NIGHT*, M-G-M cast Jim Brown as the first black sheriff of a small Southern town in *TICK . . . TICK . . . TICK* (1970). By working together with the white ex-sheriff, Brown averts a violent racial confrontation in the community by being equally firm with white supremacists as well as black militants.

Gordon Parks's autobiographical account of life in a Southern town in the Twenties was the source of his first directorial effort, *THE LEARNING TREE* (1969). The happiness of a black family is marred by the usual racial discrimi-

Jim Brown (center) in *Tick . . . Tick . . . Tick* (Metro-Goldwyn-Mayer)

The Learning Tree with Estelle Evans, Kevin Hagen, and Kyle Johnson (Warner Brothers)

Melvin Van Peebles in *Sweet Sweetback's Baadasssss Song* (Cinemation)

nation of a caste society. Perhaps in rebuttal to the charge that his film was too nostalgic, too sentimental, Parks said, "Reporters are constantly trying to make me out as non-militant and I'm beginning to resent it. I'm extremely militant, with my camera, with my pen. . . . I've been stoned and beaten and called 'nigger' like every other black man. How could I ever forget what I am?"[4]

Black militancy, which had been seen as early as 1950 in the climactic racial confrontation in *NO WAY OUT*, emerged even more strongly in *UP TIGHT* (1968), *THE LOST MAN* (1969), and *SWEET SWEETBACK'S BAAD-ASSSSS SONG* (1971). With the frustration caused by the slow implementation of well-intentioned, idealistic civil rights legislation into the fabric of everyday life, and the murder of Martin Luther King, nonviolence became an unworkable philosophy for many blacks. "Nonviolence is dead — it was killed in Memphis," says one of the black militants in *UP TIGHT*. It took a problem as socially explosive as this to bring director Jules Dassin back to American filmmaking after leaving Hollywood during the time of the HUAC investigations. Why Dassin had to regress to Liam O'Flaherty's novel, *The Informer*, and transpose the Irish Revolution to a 1968 Cleveland is difficult to understand. What seemed a plausible situation for Victor McLaglen in John Ford's masterful version of the novel was contrived and unconvincing in Dassin's film. The struggle of the black man for his rights in American society has too many ramifications to be treated in simplistic message terms which might have been acceptable in the films of the Thirties.

THE LOST MAN was another equally unsatisfying "black power" remake of a film that dealt with the Irish Revolution. In this rehash of the 1947 British film *ODD MAN OUT*, transferred to a contemporary American setting, the shift from James Mason as an Irish rebel sought by the police after a daring robbery to Sidney Poitier as a black militant leader was painfully patronizing toward the Negro cause. It was as if Poitier's career mentors decided it was time for him to become more "socially committed." If this film had any intention of clarifying a topical problem, it should have avoided its cliché-ridden dialogue that would have made a real black militant wince. Perhaps it was the poor response to *THE LOST MAN* on the part of both audiences and critics which sent the gifted Poitier back to such roles as *BROTHER JOHN* (1971), a "bigger than life" characterization reminiscent of *LILIES OF THE FIELD* and *A PATCH OF BLUE*.

"You bled my Momma, you bled my Poppa . . . but you won't bleed me!" screams the protagonist of *SWEET SWEETBACK'S BAADASSSSS SONG*, a film which would seem to indicate that race relations on the American screen have come full turn from the time of *THE BIRTH OF A NATION*. The depiction of every white man as a vicious racist predator in the Melvin Van Peebles film is as fallaciously stereotyped as the rapacious blacks in Griffith's silent epic.

Perhaps chagrined after his *WATERMELON MAN* (1970), in which he used satiric irony to express how it feels to be a black man in a white-dominated society, made little impact, the militant Van Peebles pulled out all emotional stops in the hysterical inverse racism of *SWEET SWEETBACK*. The protagonist is an outlaw from the Los Angeles ghetto who declares his own private revolution against white policemen as he leaves a trail of brutal killings in his escape to Mexico. "Of all the ways we've been exploited by the Man," Van Peebles has commented, "the most damaging is the way he destroyed our self-image. The message of SWEETBACK is that if you can get it together and stand up to the Man, you can win."[5]

Whether so patently racially polarizing and incendiary a film has any social value for the Negro audience to whom it is clearly vectored is uncertain. What is undeniable, however, is Van Peebles' right to make and exhibit his antiwhite film in a country that has never hesitated to examine its failures via the public media. Indeed, when D. W. Griffith wrote *The Rise and Fall of Free Speech in America* in 1916 as a rebuttal to those who would censor the movies, he was envisioning the day when a Van Peebles would be able to express himself on the screen with such freedom.

By the early Seventies the many films being written, directed, and produced by black artists indicated that a viable "black cinema" could become a reality. Al Freeman, Jr., the promising young actor, was also the director and star of *A FABLE* (1971), which was based on LeRoi Jones's play *Slave*, an acrimonious comment on race relations which indicted even so-called white liberals. Set in the near future during a chaotic racial war in the United States, *A FABLE* was yet another of the increasingly militant black films.

Produced in the Watts section of Los Angeles with the cooperation of city officials, *THE BUS IS COMING* (1971) also deals with hostilities between whites and blacks. Avoiding the kind of wholesale condemnation of every white, as in *SWEET SWEETBACK*, *THE BUS IS COMING* has the militant Black Fists trying to make a martyr of a nonviolent Negro who was killed by a racist white policeman. The brother of the murdered man must decide whether to join the militants and take up guns, or to keep faith that the corrupt cop will be punished through due process of law. The film was directed by Wendell Franklin, the first black admitted to the Screen Directors Guild.

One way in which a "black cinema" may be financed is indicated by the release of *BLACK CHARIOT* (1971). A film also concerning black militancy, its production cost was entirely underwritten by the black population of California. In addition to the investment of 24 limited partners in the company, personal loans were made to the producing firm through solicitation in black communities throughout the state.

Ossie Davis, a well-established black actor and director, was clearly not content to make inconsequential programmers like *COTTON COMES TO HARLEM*, even though it partially fulfilled his aim to create employment for black actors and technicians. Because of his interest in creating a thriving Third World cinema, Davis went to Nigeria to direct *KONGI'S HARVEST* (1971), a co-production with the embryonic Nigerian film industry.

Perhaps reflecting the passionate quest of many young people today to redress the neglect and social injustice inflicted on America's minority groups, the stereotyped representation of the American Indian on the screen was also

IX

Soldier Blue (Avco Embassy)

dramatically reversed in several recent films. *SOLDIER BLUE* (1970) described a terrible chilling aspect of the "winning of the West" — which except for such films as *THE VANISHING AMERICAN* in the Twenties and *CHEYENNE AUTUMN* in the Sixties was rarely given attention. With an obvious symbolic allusion to the My Lai massacre in Vietnam, whose consequences are still disturbing the equanimity of American Army leaders, director Ralph Nelson looked back in history at the equally, if not more, nauseating carnage against Indian warriors, women, and children at the 1864 Sand Creek massacre in Colorado. Although the Cheyenne were flying a flag of peace and wanted to surrender to Colonel Chivington and his Colorado Volunteers, they were attacked and butchered by the American cavalry troops. In sparing none of the details of rape and mutilation of Indian women and murder of children, Nelson was accused of excessive violence. Defending *SOLDIER BLUE* as a "moral lesson" and an accurate historical account, he traveled to numerous countries to argue against censorship. As he said about his research for the film, "The more I read, the more of a sense of rage I developed as to exactly what had happened, and I thought that this was part of the guilt of the American conscience and we should face it, be aware of it, and do something for the Indian's existence as it is today."[6]

Arthur Penn's *LITTLE BIG MAN* (1970), although essentially a picaresque comedy about the American frontier, nevertheless had as scathing an indictment of the treatment of Indians by the U.S. Army as *SOLDIER BLUE*. Equally shameful as the events at Sand Creek was the massacre of the Indians at Washita in 1868 as seen in *LITTLE BIG MAN*. General Custer, in Penn's film,

is so clearly identified as the cold, power-mad, psychopathic militarist responsible for the slaughter that audiences loudly rooted for the Indians when Custer and his Seventh Cavalry are ambushed at Little Big Horn. Like Nelson, director Penn sees parallels between Custer's inhuman butchery and recent events in Vietnam. In his own research for *LITTLE BIG MAN*, Penn became aware that most American Westerns had merely perpetuated the *legend* of the West rather than its *reality*. Of such films he said, "If it were necessary, they changed the nature of the character who lost — they changed him from a good man to an evil man in order to prove that the good must always win. That's what used to happen to the Indian. He was converted in films from his pacific and sublime nature to a man who was a bloodthirsty savage."[7]

Dustin Hoffman and Amy Eccles
in *Little Big Man*
(National General)

251

Flap with Anthony Quinn
(Warner Brothers)

That the American Indian is today still the object of exploitation and discrimination is emphasized in *FLAP* (1970), *JOURNEY THROUGH ROSEBUD* (1972), and *BILLY JACK* (1971). *FLAP* is a contemporary tragicomedy about an attempted revolution by a group of Indians resentful of the squalid conditions on their reservation. Anthony Quinn as Flapping Eagle was a combination of tribal revolutionary and con-man in this unusual film for British director Carol Reed. *JOURNEY THROUGH ROSEBUD* was a more realistic depiction of the struggles of Indians on reservations to maintain their dignity.

The plight of the American Indian was also treated realistically in *BILLY JACK*, the story of a halfbreed Indian who returns from Vietnam to his home on a government reservation. Disenchanted with war and violence, the ex-Green Beret uses his training to stop the wholesale killing of wild mustangs for dog food. Acting as a Big Brother for a local Freedom School he encourages cooperation among blacks, whites, Indians, and Chicanos. Another of the film's multi-messages is the school's promotion of its antidrug program with music, street drama, and other creative arts as a surrogate for freaking out.

With the disappearance of the Production Code and the implementation of the rating system, the genre of prison films was inevitably affected. Although such prison films as *THE BIG HOUSE, 20,000 YEARS IN SING SING,* and *CAGED* were critical of the treatment of inmates, none of them had dared, under the old Production Code, to even allude to the matter of homosexuality behind bars. *FORTUNE AND MEN'S EYES* (1971), in dealing explicitly with

Wendell Burton in *Fortune and
Men's Eyes*
(Metro-Goldwyn-Mayer)

the rape of a young prisoner by callous homosexuals, is a prime example of
the new freedom of the screen to pursue social problems which hitherto could
be treated so frankly only on the stage or in the print media. Even as an off-
Broadway play, John Herbert's sordid exploration of how young inmates are
degraded was considered daring; yet a year or so later the screen, too, could
confront this subject.

The Greeks of Homer's age used to divine the future by "reading" the en-
trails of a sacrificed bull. If, indeed, movies are, as Marshall McLuhan has
suggested, a DEW Line helping us to foresee the shape of things to come, recent
futuristic films offer a foreboding tomorrow. Whether the calamitous future is
in the area of political repression as in *PUNISHMENT PARK* and *ICE*, or the
angst of a global nuclear holocaust or ecological breakdown, all these and
similar dire themes dominate the vision of contemporary filmmakers utilizing
the futuristic metaphor for social comment. Indeed, except for *2001: A SPACE
ODYSSEY* (1968), which despite its enigmatic message seems to suggest that
man will not only survive but will follow the mystic obelisk to the farthest
reaches of outer space, futuristic films are extremely pessimistic.

THE SHOES OF THE FISHERMAN (1968) projects the situation of a widespread famine in China as triggering a threatened global war. Cornel Wilde's
NO BLADE OF GRASS (1970) graphically describes starvation caused by environmental pollution. With the world's food supply in danger of complete
erasure, an English family migrates from London to the Lake district. In their

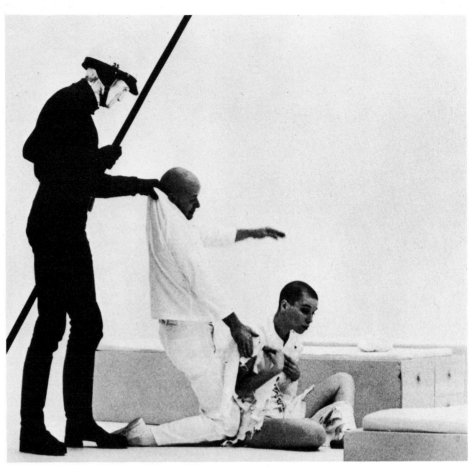

struggle for survival against the very breakdown of civilization, they encounter the New Barbarians — a horde of leather-jacketed Huns on motorcycles.

The specter of technology running wild and overriding man's humanistic values, a repeated theme of mass culture since Jules Verne's prognostications more than a century ago, persisted in *THE FORBIN PROJECT* (1970), *THX 1138* (1971), *A CLOCKWORK ORANGE* (1971), *THE ANDROMEDA STRAIN* (1971), and *THE OMEGA MAN* (1971). *THE FORBIN PROJECT* speculates on what could happen if two gigantic interlocked computers were to decide that man's ratiocinative powers are too limited to rule the world. *THX 1138* stresses the complete enslavement and dehumanization in a regimented, computer-programmed future technocracy. Even uglier than Huxley's *Brave New World*, the populace in this film is required to take daily doses of drug sedation. The unforgivable crime in this de-emotionalized, asexual world is to feel the reactionary urge for human copulation. When technician THX and his female roommate LUH purposely evade taking drugs and engage in intercourse, they are apprehended via the omnipresent television eye that deprives all the inhabitants of privacy.

After his *DR. STRANGELOVE* and *2001: A SPACE ODYSSEY* director Stanley Kubrick offered another enigmatic view of the future in *A CLOCK-WORK ORANGE*. Continuing Kubrick's apparent concern with the human

Charlton Heston in *The Omega
Man* (Warner Brothers)

consequences of science and technology, *A CLOCKWORK ORANGE* poses the
possibility of controlling violent, antisocial behavior by a combination of drugs
and conditioned-reflex therapy. By means of "The Ludovico Technique" Alex,
the droog rapist, is deprived of his free will and reduced to a robot-like "model
citizen." Part psychological fairy tale and part satire on totalitarian governments, *A CLOCKWORK ORANGE* would be less chilling were the scientific
methods of brain control not already available.

   THE ANDROMEDA STRAIN raised the frightening possibility of a deadly
extraterrestrial virus brought to earth by the contaminated shell of a U.S. space-
probing missile. A frenzied team of scientists works to avert global plague. In
THE OMEGA MAN Charlton Heston (having escaped from the planet of the
apes) finds himself in an even more precarious situation. It is 1975, and a
bacteriological war between Russia and China unleashes a contaminated ICBM
which virtually decimates the West Coast. Heston acts the leader of a band of
survivors who must keep civilization alive against the hideous human mutants
prowling Los Angeles.

   The apocalyptic vision, which permeates so many of these futuristic films,
is experienced through the eyes of a young couple in *GLEN AND RANDA*
(1971). Born in the ruined world of a post-thermonuclear holocaust, Glen and
Randa are scavengers in search of a legendary distant city called Metropolis.

255

Shirley MacLaine in
Desperate Characters (Paramount)

During their odyssey toward this mystical Eldorado they traverse the wreckage of a broken civilization and a whole world lost. Near what remains of a Howard Johnson's they meet a magician who tells them: "I was fifteen when the whole thing was totaled."

The shame of the American cities in the Seventies is no less in need of solution than in the first decade of this century when the muckrakers were engaged in social crusades. Indeed, a latter-day Ida Tarbell or Lincoln Steffens would find, in addition to venal political practices and slum housing, the accentuated problems of drug addiction, street crime, pollution by noise, dirt, and smut — indeed all the accumulated woes of America's profit-at-any-cost, industrial society. If Griffith and his contemporaries even in the silent era of

THE
CELLULOID
WEAPON

256

the movies were commenting on these squalid conditions in urban America, filmmakers of today are also aware that much of the corruption and malaise in American society is at its worst in the large cities. The alienation felt by the individual submerged in the mass society of a Chicago or Los Angeles is not much different from that of his fellow *homo urbanus* in Detroit or St. Louis or New York. As early as 1928 King Vidor had tried to express this encroaching anomie in his *THE CROWD.*

Violence and the anxiety it engenders, so much a part of day-to-day living in New York City, was orchestrated in such films as *THE INCIDENT* (1967), *LITTLE MURDERS* (1971), and *DESPERATE CHARACTERS* (1971). The plot of *THE INCIDENT* could have been an extension of many news stories in the

257

Michael Sarrazin and Jane Fonda
in *They Shoot Horses, Don't They?*
(Cinerama)

They Shoot Horses, Don't They?
(Cinerama)

New York press in the late Sixties. A group of people riding in a subway car
are terrorized by two drunken, murderous punks until one passenger is finally
moved to the point of action. *LITTLE MURDERS* is writer Jules Feiffer's thren-
ody to the Decline and Fall of Manhattan. Amidst a barrage of brown-outs,
black-outs, obscene phone calls, apartment looting, and unsolved sniper
killings, the kooky Newquist family tries to muddle through the larger insanity
that pervades the City. Feiffer's asphalt jungle wouldn't have appeared so sick,
sick, sick if his dark humor weren't anchored in the realities of life in Gotham.
While eschewing the hyperbole and caricature of *LITTLE MURDERS*, *DES-
PERATE CHARACTERS* catches the same feeling of individual helplessness
in a community too large for people to communicate with each other. During
two consecutive days in the life of a childless Manhattan couple we see the
psychological toll of the city's senseless vandalism, inefficient services (doctors
can only be reached via impersonal answer-phones), and the bitterness which
causes one fed-up urbanite to say, "It's like being alive at your own funeral."

Of the many recent films that have captured what Henry James called "the
imagination of disaster," none is so despondent as *THEY SHOOT HORSES,
DON'T THEY?* (1969). Although the film depicts a marathon dance contest
during the Depression of the Thirties, the cruel, insatiable, voyeuristic crowd
could just as well have been watching bearbaiting in Elizabethan England. All
the poor and despised have-nots throughout history, straining their bodies
beyond endurance to catch the brass ring of a prize, are symbolized by the
weary, almost mechanical, dancers. Even the slick impresario who holds out

the carrot of Winning feels the ennui of the game that can end only when all but two of the contestants have dropped. In the tradition of screen morality plays like GREED, THE TREASURE OF THE SIERRA MADRE, and ACE IN THE HOLE, Sydney Pollack's THEY SHOOT HORSES, DON'T THEY? is a condemnation of all insensitive people who have exploited the weaker for the amusement of the stronger.

The various themes of "relevance" which numerous recent films have strived to express were drawn together in Stanley Kramer's BLESS THE BEASTS & CHILDREN (1971). The children are six "misfit" boys, each with his own psychological hang-up, at a camp in Arizona; and the beasts are captive buffalo marked for another sportsmen's shootout. These rejected boys, reviled and humiliated by their fellow campers, feel an empathy toward the entrapped animals and determine to execute a dawn raid to let them escape. By freeing the buffalo from the ugly society of men who would destroy them, the boys intuit that they will be setting themselves free too. In addition to making critical comments on ecological unbalance, the gun cult and the generation gap, the encompassing messages of BLESS THE BEASTS & CHILDREN is that man must recognize the kinship among all living things.

That the children, despite the death of their leader in the daring and outlandish raid, are finally successful in freeing both the animals and, symbolically, themselves is an appropriate message for an American society permeated by the fashionable despair of the Seventies.

IX

259

Rewind

"The cinema camera is the agent of Democracy," wrote D. W. Griffith in 1917. "It levels barriers between races and classes." What Griffith perceived, as have all makers of message films in the silent and sound eras, is the potential of the film medium for social education as well as diversion. Recognizing the necessity to first stir men's hearts in order to change their attitudes, Hollywood message-filmmakers have utilized the entertainment *story* film as a vehicle for expressing a social viewpoint. By couching their social comment within an emotion-involving dramatic story, these filmmakers have been instinctively aware that to "teach" and persuade mass audiences, a movie must first engage and hold their attention.

Persuaders armed with the celluloid weapon have dealt with the entire spectrum of problems and issues endemic to American society. For almost seventy years the American message film has explored such social problems as racial and ethnic prejudice, drug addiction, alcoholism, labor inequities, penal inhumanity, crime and juvenile delinquency, corruption in politics and government, and that most cancerous of all social ills, war. Certainly all of these problems have existed throughout most of America's history, but in the twentieth century they seem more demanding of public attention and solution. Indeed, as these problems have become more acute and aggravated at certain crucial moments of the twentieth century, the message film has reflected the anxiety surrounding them. Because message films deal with social issues when they are most nagging and topical, and because the viewpoints they espouse are dependent on acceptance by large "paying" audiences, they have represented an important index to social thought in America since the turn of the century.

The opinions expressed in message films are, of course, as different and often as contradictory as the social values of filmmakers themselves; they are certainly as various as there are viewpoints concerning a particular social issue. For example, just as the development of the American cinema reveals a politically pro-Left *BLOCKADE*, there was also a pro-Right *MY SON JOHN*; and just as there was a *THE BATTLE CRY OF PEACE* so, too, was there a *PATHS OF GLORY*. When they plead their causes in message films, filmmakers are not *ipso facto* immune to partisanship. Indeed some of them, while aiming the celluloid weapon at vast audiences, intentionally overload their argument and are extremely biased in their zeal to influence and persuade.

Such deliberate overloading of propagandistic message films raises perennial questions regarding their effects on audiences. Can a message film actually convince moviegoers to accept a particular viewpoint as their own and thereby alter their social behavior? Throughout this book we have scrupulously avoided suggesting any causal relationship between the content of a message film and social behavior — simply because no one knows enough about the complex variables that come between a moviegoer and what he sees on the screen. As many filmmakers mentioned in this book have indicated, message films can be a means of *prodding* audiences toward social action, but it is doubtful whether any message film ever decisively changes anyone's mind. For example, for nearly three decades we have had numerous films dealing with black prejudice, but still the problem plagues our country.

Whatever may be the ultimate effects, positive or negative, of message films, it is essential that the American cinema be free of censorship to examine all areas of our society. As outspoken as many message films have been, they are built-in compromises with economic demands of the box office and the desire of audiences to be entertained. Such pressures on freedom of expression as the HUAC hearings, for example, only serve to discourage filmmakers from treating delicate and controversial social themes. The strength of the American cinema has been its eagerness to allow diversity of thought, putting its confidence in audiences as the final arbiters of a film's content. Moreover, in exporting its films overseas, Hollywood has not merely shown the idealistic aspects of American society. Films like IN THE HEAT OF THE NIGHT and BLACKBOARD JUNGLE have, in effect, been an airing of America's dirty linen before the scrutiny of our world neighbors. Only a society as sure of its identity as ours can afford such openness.

The decline in moviegoing in the Seventies and the narrowing of audiences to primarily people under 30 offer two alternative possibilities for the future of the message film. Deprived of the necessary financial wherewithal to underwrite "risky" problem films, economically beleaguered studios may be forced to concentrate their resources on purely "escapist" films. On the other hand, the under-30 moviegoers may challenge the industry to become more socially *engagé* than ever before. With the encouraging response of the under-30 audience a new talent pool of socially committed young filmmakers may be generated — and we may well see a "new" D. W. Griffith, Lewis Milestone, Walter Wanger, Nedrick Young, Frank Capra, or Stanley Kramer. Hopefully, the young producers, directors, and screenwriters of the future will add their own social visions to the bold tradition of the American message film.

IX

Notes

1. Anthony Slide, *Early American Cinema* (New York: A. S. Barnes & Co., 1970), 120.
2. Lewis Jacobs, *The Rise of the American Film* (New York: Teachers College Press, Columbia University, 1969), 72.
3. Richard J. Meyer, "The Films of David Wark Griffith: The Development of Themes and Techniques in Forty-two of His Films," *Focus on D. W. Griffith*, edited by Harry M. Geduld (Englewood Cliffs, New Jersey: Prentice-Hall, Inc., 1971), 113.
4. Slide, *op. cit.*, 18-19.
5. Terry Ramsaye, *A Million and One Nights* (New York: Simon and Schuster, Inc., 1964), 618.
6. Robert M. Henderson, *D. W. Griffith: The Years at Biograph* (New York: Farrar, Straus and Giroux, 1970), 171.
7. Edward Wagenknecht, *The Movies in the Age of Innocence* (Norman, Oklahoma: University of Oklahoma Press, 1962), 100.
8. Norman Kagan, "Black American Cinema," *Cinema*, Fall 1970, 2.
9. Lillian Gish (with Ann Pinchot), *The Movies, Mr. Griffith and Me* (Englewood Cliffs, New Jersey: Prentice-Hall, Inc., 1969), 163.
10. Paul O'Dell, *Griffith and the Rise of Hollywood* (New York: A. S. Barnes & Co., 1970), 84.
11. Kevin Brownlow, *The Parade's Gone By . . .* (New York: Alfred A. Knopf, Inc., 1968), 300-302.

chapter 2 . . .

1. V. F. Perkins and Mark Shivas, "Interview with King Vidor," *Movie*, July/August 1963, 10.
2. David Robinson, *Hollywood in the Twenties* (New York: A. S. Barnes & Co., 1968), 10-11.
3. Edward Wagenknecht, *The Movies in the Age of Innocence* (Norman, Oklahoma: University of Oklahoma Press, 1962), 129-130.
4. Kevin Brownlow, *The Parade's Gone By . . .* (New York: Alfred A. Knopf, Inc., 1968), 299.
5. Charles Higham and Joel Greenberg, *The Celluloid Muse: Hollywood Directors Speak* (London: Angus and Robertson, 1969), 228.
6. Bob Thomas, *Thalberg: Life and Legend* (Garden City, New York: Doubleday & Company, Inc., 1969), 83-84, 86.
7. Eileen Bowser (ed.), *Film Notes* (New York: The Museum of Modern Art, 1969), 62.

chapter 3 . . .

1. Frank Capra, *The Name Above the Title: An Autobiography* (New York: The Macmillan Company, 1971), 240.
2. *Ibid.*, 137.
3. King Vidor, *A Tree Is a Tree* (New York: Harcourt, Brace and Company, 1953), 222-223.
4. Charles Higham and Joel Greenberg, *The Celluloid Muse: Hollywood Directors Speak* (London: Angus and Robertson, 1960), 154.
5. Martin Quigley, Jr., and Richard Gertner, *Films in America 1929-1969* (New York: Golden Press, 1970), 24-25.
6. Bernard Rosenberg and Harry Silverstein, *The Real Tinsel* (New York: The Macmillan Company, 1970), 90.
7. Lindsay Anderson, "John Ford," *Cinema*, Spring 1971, 36.
8. Rosenberg and Silverstein, *op. cit.*, 342.
9. Peter Noble, *The Negro in Films* (London: Skelton-Robinson, 1947), 64-67.
10. Charles Chaplin, *My Autobiography* (New York: Simon and Schuster, 1964), 383.
11. Frank Capra, "Do I Make You Laugh?" *Films and Filming*, September 1962, 14.

12. Jeffrey Richards, "Frank Capra and the Cinema of Populism," *Cinema* (England), February 1970, 22-28.
13. Frank Capra, *The Name Above the Title*, 190.

chapter 4 . . .

1. Peter Bogdanovich, *Fritz Lang in America* (New York: Frederick A. Praeger, Inc., 1967), 16.
2. Mel Gussow, *Don't Say Yes Until I Finish Talking* (Garden City, New York: Doubleday & Company, Inc., 1971), 92.
3. Bernard Rosenberg and Harry Silverstein, *The Real Tinsel* (New York: The Macmillan Company, 1970), 85.
4. Charles Chaplin, *My Autobiography* (New York: Simon and Schuster, 1964), 392.
5. Frank Capra, *The Name Above the Title* (New York: The Macmillan Company, 1971), 288, 292.
6. Donald Ogden Stewart, "Writing for the Movies," *Focus on Film*, Winter 1970, 54.
7. Sinclair Lewis and Dore Schary, *Storm in the West* (New York: Stein and Day, Inc., 1963), 15-17.

chapter 5 . . .

1. Darryl F. Zanuck, "How To Be Self-Critical While World-Popular," *Show*, April 1964, 77.
2. Bernard R. Kantor, Irwin R. Blacker, and Anné Kramer (eds.), *Directors at Work* (New York: Funk & Wagnalls, 1970), 437.
3. Mel Gussow, *Don't Say Yes Until I Finish Talking* (Garden City, New York: Doubleday & Company, Inc., 1971), 150.
4. Richard Winnington, "Here Today . . ." *Sight and Sound*, March 1950, 29.
5. Gussow, *op. cit.*, 154.
6. Billy Wilder, "Broadcast to Kuala Lumpur," *Action*, November-December 1970, 18.
7. Bernard Rosenberg and Harry Silverstein, *The Real Tinsel* (New York: The Macmillan Company, 1970), 142.
8. Charles Chaplin, *My Autobiography* (New York: Simon and Schuster, 1964), 455.
9. Terry Hickey, "Accusations Against Charles Chaplin for Political and Moral Offenses," *Film Comment*, Winter 1969, 53.
10. Tom Milne (ed.), *Losey on Losey* (Garden City, New York: Doubleday & Company, Inc., 1968), 76.

chapter 6 . . .

1. Joseph Losey, "Speak, Think, Stand Up," *Film Culture*, Summer-Fall 1970, 58.
2. Herbert Biberman, *Salt of the Earth: The Story of a Film* (Boston: Beacon Press, 1965), 154.
3. Gordon Hitchens, "The Defiance in *The Defiant Ones*," *Film Culture*, Summer-Fall 1970, 64.
4. Ian Cameron, Mark Shivas, Paul Mayersberg, and V. F. Perkins, "Interviews with Richard Brooks," *Movie*, Spring 1965, 6.
5. Nicholas Ray, "Story into Script," *Sight and Sound*, Autumn 1956, 73.

chapter vii . . .

1. Robert Hughes (ed.), *Film: Book 2 — Films of Peace and War* (New York: Grove Press, Inc., 1962), 171.
2. Joseph McBride and Michael Wilmington, "The Private Life of Billy Wilder," *Film Quarterly*, Summer 1970, 7.
3. Charles Higham and Joel Greenberg, *The Celluloid Muse: Hollywood Directors Speak* (London: Angus and Robertson, 1969), 251.
4. Robert Warshow, *The Immediate Experience* (Garden City, New York: Doubleday & Company, Inc., 1962), 148-149.

5. Pauline Kael, *Kiss Kiss Bang Bang* (New York: Bantam Books, Inc., 1969), 349.
6. Andrew Sarris, *Confessions of a Cultist: On the Cinema, 1955/1969* (New York: Simon and Schuster, 1971), 387.
7. "Playboy Interview: John Wayne," *Playboy*, May 1971, 90.
8. Higham and Greenberg, *op. cit.*, 31.

chapter 8 . . .

1. Bernard R. Kantor, Irwin R. Blacker, and Anne Kramer (eds.), *Directors at Work* (New York: Funk & Wagnalls, 1970), 418.
2. Gerald Pratley, *The Cinema of John Frankenheimer* (New York: A. S. Barnes & Co., 1969), 100-101.
3. *Ibid.*, 9-10.
4. Joseph Gelmis, *The Film Director as Superstar* (Garden City, New York: Doubleday & Company, Inc., 1970), 309.
5. Richard Whitehall, "One . . . Two . . . Three?" *Films and Filming*, August 1964, 9.
6. John Coen, "Producer/Director Cornel Wilde," *Film Comment*, Spring 1970, 56.
7. Andrew Sarris, "Film Fantasies, Left and Right," *Film Culture*, Fall 1964, 34.
8. Pratley, *op. cit.*, 64.
9. Peter Bogdanovich, *John Ford* (Berkeley: University of California Press, 1968), 104.
10. Gordon Gow, "Confrontations — Norman Jewison Interviewed," *Films and Filming*, January 1971, 22-23.
11. Maxine Hall Elliston, "Two Sidney Poitier Films," *Film Comment*, Winter 1969, 28.

chapter 9 . . .

1. Ernest Callenbach and Albert Johnson, "The Danger Is Seduction: An Interview with Haskell Wexler," *Film Quarterly*, Spring 1968, 13.
2. Gary Crowdus, "The Strawberry Statement," *Film Society Review*, April 1970, 31.
3. Stephen Farber, "Movies from Behind the Barricades," *Film Quarterly*, Winter 1970-71, 26.
4. Verina Glaessner, "The Negro in the Contemporary Cinema," *Film*, Spring 1971, 15.
5. *Time*, August 16, 1971, 47.
6. Ralph Nelson, "Massacre at Sand Creek," *Films and Filming*, March 1970, 26.
7. Gordon Gow, "Metaphor: Arthur Penn in an Interview," *Films and Filming*, July 1971, 21.

Additional Bibliographic Sources

The American Film Institute Catalogue: Feature Films 1921-1930. New York: R. R. Bowker Company, 1971.
Baxter, John. *The Gangster Film*. New York: A. S. Barnes & Co., 1970.
_____. *Hollywood in the Thirties*. New York: A. S. Barnes & Co., 1968.
Bergman, Andrew. *We're in the Money: Depression America and Its Films*. New York: New York University Press, 1971.
Bessie, Alvah. *Inquisition in Eden*. New York: The Macmillan Company, 1965.

Blum, Daniel. *A Pictorial History of the Silent Screen*. New York: Grosset & Dunlap, 1953.
_____ and John Kobal. *A New Pictorial History of the Talkies*. New York: Grosset & Dunlap, 1970.
Carey, Gary. *Lost Films*. New York: The Museum of Modern Art, 1970.
Cutts, John, and Penelope Houston, "Blacklisted," *Sight and Sound* (Summer 1957), 15-19, 53.
Dimmitt, Richard Bertrand. *A Title Guide to the Talkies*. 2 vols. New York: The Scarecrow Press, Inc., 1965.
Everson, William K. *The Bad Guys*. New York: The Citadel Press, 1964.
Film Comment, "The Hollywood Screenwriter" issue (Winter 1970-71).
Film Culture, "Hollywood Blacklisting" issue (Summer-Fall 1970).
The Film Index: A Bibliography (Volume I: The Film as Art). New York: The Museum of Modern Art Film Library and the H. W. Wilson Company, 1941.
Furhammar, Leif, and Folke Isaksson. *Politics and Film*. New York: Praeger Publishers, 1971.
Gow, Gordon. *Hollywood in the Fifties*. New York: A. S. Barnes & Co., 1971.
Griffith, Richard, and Arthur Mayer. *The Movies*. New York: Simon and Schuster, Inc., 1957.
Hampton, Benjamin B. *A History of the Movies*. New York: Arno Press & The New York Times, 1970.
Higham, Charles, and Joel Greenberg. *Hollywood in the Forties*. New York: A. S. Barnes & Co., 1968.
"HUAC-adoo," *Take One* (March-April 1969), 7-13; (May-June 1969), 6-14.
Jacobs, Lewis. "World War II and the American Film," *Film Culture* (Summer 1969), 28-42.
Jarvie, I. C. *Movies and Society*. New York, Basic Books, Inc., 1970.
Johnson, Albert. "The Negro in American Films: Some Recent Works," *Film Quarterly* (Summer 1965), 14-30.
Knight, Arthur. *The Liveliest Art*. New York: Mentor Books, 1959.
Larkins, Robert. "Hollywood and the Indian," *Focus on Film* (March-April 1971), 44-53.
MacCann, Richard Dyer. *Hollywood in Transition*. Boston: Houghton Mifflin Company, 1962.
_____. "The Problem Film in America," *Film and Society* (edited by Richard Dyer MacCann). New York: Charles Scribner's Sons, 1964, 51-59.
Macgowan, Kenneth. *Behind the Screen*. New York: Delacorte Press, 1965.
Maltin, Leonard (ed.). *TV Movies*. Signet Books, 1969.
Michael, Paul (editor-in-chief). *The American Movies Reference Book: The Sound Era*. Englewood Cliffs, New Jersey: Prentice-Hall, Inc., 1969.
Movie Lot to Beachhead by the Editors of *Look* Magazine. Garden City, New York: Doubleday, Doran and Company, Inc., 1945.
The New York Times Film Reviews 1913-1968. New York: Arno Press & The New York Times, 1970.
The New York Times Film Reviews 1969-1970. New York: Arno Press & The New York Times, 1971.
Rotha, Paul, and Richard Griffith. *The Film Till Now*. London: Spring Books, 1967.
Sarris, Andrew. *The American Cinema*. New York: E. P. Dutton & Co., Inc., 1968.
Scheuer, Steven H. *TV Movie Almanac & Ratings: 1958-1959*. New York: Bantam Books, 1958.
Schlesinger, Arthur, Jr. "When the Movies Really Counted," *Show* (April 1963), 77-78,125.
Spears, Jack. *Hollywood: The Golden Years*. New York: A. S. Barnes & Co., 1971.
Thompson, Howard (ed.). *The New York Times Guide to Movies on TV*. Chicago: Quadrangle Books, 1970.
Variety (various issues).

Index of Film Titles

Index of Names

This book was set in Melior, a typeface designed by Herman Zapf, composed by Mono Typesetting Company of Hartford, Connecticut. The press work is by the Halliday Lithograph Corporation of Hanover, Massachusetts, using Tosca, a paper made by the Mohawk Paper Mills, Inc., of Cohoes, New York, supplied by Carter Rice Storrs & Bement of Boston, Massachusetts. The binding is by the Van Rees Press of New York City, using silver Sturdetan covering material made by The Holliston Mills, Inc., of Norwood, Massachusetts.

The photo research was done by Richard Averson. This book was designed by Richard C. Bartlett, with the assistance of Leo Durling and Pamela Osborn.